Lab Manual to Accompany Essentials of Health Information Management: Principles & Practices
Fourth Edition

Mary Jo Bowie, MS, BS, AAS, RHIA, RHIT
Consultant and Owner
Health Information Professional Services
Binghamton, New York
Associate Professor in Health Information Management
Program Director
Mount Wachusett Community College
Gardner, Massachusetts

CENGAGE

Australia • Brazil • Mexico • Singapore • United Kingdom • United States

Lab Manual to accompany Essentials of Health Information Management: Principles & Practices, Fourth Edition
Mary Jo Bowie

SVP, GM Skills & Global Product Management: Jonathan Lau

Product Director: Matthew Seeley

Product Team Manager: Stephen Smith

Associate Product Manager: Lauren Whalen

Product Assistant: Jessica Molesky

Executive Director, Content Design: Marah Bellegarde

Director, Learning Design: Juliet Steiner

Learning Designer: Deborah Bordeaux

Vice President, Strategic Marketing Services: Jennifer Ann Baker

Marketing Director: Sean Chamberland

Marketing Manager: Jon Sheehan

Senior Director, Content Delivery: Wendy A. Troeger

Senior Content Manager: Karen Caldwell

Senior Content Manager: Kara A. DiCaterino

Digital Delivery Lead: Lisa Christopher

Senior Designer: Angela Sheehan

Cover & Interior Design image(s):
kentoh/Shutterstock.com
sumkinn/Shutterstock.com

For product information and technology assistance, contact us at **Cengage Customer & Sales Support, 1-800-354-9706 or support.cengage.com.**

For permission to use material from this text or product, submit all requests online at **www.cengage.com/permissions.**

Lab Manual ISBN: 978-1-337-55369-8
Core Text ISBN: 978-1-337-55367-4

Cengage
20 Channel Center Street
Boston, MA 02210
USA

Cengage is a leading provider of customized learning solutions with employees residing in nearly 40 different countries and sales in more than 125 countries around the world. Find your local representative at **www.cengage.com.**

Cengage products are represented in Canada by Nelson Education, Ltd.

To learn more about Cengage platforms and services, visit **www.cengage.com**

To register or access your online learning solution or purchase materials for your course, visit **www.cengagebrain.com.**

Notice to the Reader
Publisher does not warrant or guarantee any of the products described herein or perform any independent analysis in connection with any of the product information contained herein. Publisher does not assume, and expressly disclaims, any obligation to obtain and include information other than that provided to it by the manufacturer. The reader is expressly warned to consider and adopt all safety precautions that might be indicated by the activities described herein and to avoid all potential hazards. By following the instructions contained herein, the reader willingly assumes all risks in connection with such instructions. The publisher makes no representations or warranties of any kind, including but not limited to, the warranties of fitness for particular purpose or merchantability, nor are any such representations implied with respect to the material set forth herein, and the publisher takes no responsibility with respect to such material. The publisher shall not be liable for any special, consequential, or exemplary damages resulting, in whole or part, from the readers' use of, or reliance upon, this material.

Printed at CLDPC, USA, 03-19

Contents

Preface

Welcome to *Lab Manual to Accompany Essentials of Health Information Management*, 4th Edition. This student lab manual contains application-based assignments organized according to textbook chapters. These assignments will reinforce learning and encourage skill building. The lab assignments allow students to apply concepts learned from reading and studying corresponding textbook chapters. Completing each assignment will prepare the student for related health information tasks assigned during professional practice experiences (internships). Because the lab assignments simulate on-the-job experiences in a health information department or physician's office, the student can also feel confident applying for the following entry-level positions:

- Abstractor
- Assembly clerk
- Analysis clerk
- File clerk
- Receptionist
- Release of information processing clerk

These positions allow the student to earn income while attending school, and perhaps more important, when a technical position becomes available in the health information department or physician's office, the student (or graduate) is considered an internal candidate.

OBJECTIVES

The objectives of this lab manual are to allow students to:

1. Apply health information management concepts common to allied health professionals.
2. Visit a health care facility and interview a professional to explore career opportunities.
3. Analyze actual patient records for documentation deficiencies.
4. Sequence patient record numbers in straight numeric and terminal-digit order.
5. Redesign an outdated patient record form.
6. Calculate patient record storage based on case scenarios.
7. Abstract patient cases for health data collection.
8. Process requests for release of information.
9. Complete a hospital financial report using DRG base rates to calculate total reimbursement rates.
10. Update a clinic encounter form by verifying/editing codes.
11. Discuss the implementation of ICD-10-CM and ICD-10-PCS.

This lab manual is designed to be used by college and vocational school programs to train allied health professionals (e.g., cancer registrars, coders, health information administrators and technicians, medical assistants, medical office administrators, medical transcriptionists). It can also be used as an in-service training tool for new health care facility personnel and independent billing services, or individually by health information specialists.

FEATURES OF THE LAB MANUAL

- Introduction at the beginning of each chapter provides an overview of content.
- Lab assignments provide students with an opportunity to apply textbook chapter concepts.
- Objectives for each lab assignment clearly indicate purpose of application-based activity.
- Step-by-step instructions for each lab assignment communicate exactly how each is to be completed.
- The accompanying Student Companion website at www.Cengage.com includes practice records and more.

- New! Appendix II includes additional lab activities using EHR Go™, the all-new version of Neehr Perfect®. A subscription is required for using EHR Go™. Please visit www.ehrgo.com/Cengage and contact your instructor for more information.

SUPPLEMENTS

The following supplements accompany this lab manual.

INSTRUCTOR'S MANUAL

The instructor's manual consists of two parts, one for the text and one for the student lab manual. Lesson plans, answers to chapter exercises and reviews, chapter quizzes, and answers to student lab manual assignments are included. The Instructor's Manual is located on the Instructor Companion website.

STUDENT COMPANION WEBSITE

Additional resources can be found online at www.Cengage.com. Search by author name, ISBN, or title to locate the Student Companion website for *Essentials of Health Information Management*, 4th Edition. Resources include downloadable files to support the student lab manual and textbook, product updates, related links, and more. The student resources include Adobe pdf files for select assignments that can be completed as forms and sent as an e-mail attachment to instructors for evaluation. (Go to www.adobe.com to download the latest version of Adobe Reader to fill in forms.) Save completed forms as electronic files using the naming convention required by your instructor.

FOR CUSTOMER SERVICE:

For technical issues with accessing or using EHR Go (already using product):
EHR Go Help Desk (24/7):
support@ehrgo.com, 877-907-2186

For questions about an activity in the Lab Manual:
Contact your Cengage Learning sales representative.

For general information about EHR Go:
EHR Go Sales and Customer Service (8am-5pm Central):
contact@ehrgo.com, 877-742-3926

Chapter 1

Health Care Delivery Systems

🍄 INTRODUCTION

This chapter focuses on the historical development of medicine and health care delivery from prehistoric/ ancient medicine to modern times, familiarizing the student with the Hippocratic Oath, seventeenth-, eighteenth-, and nineteenth-century medical discoveries, hospital ownership, organizational structure and accrediting organizations, and committee composition and minutes.

LAB ASSIGNMENT 1-1   Organizational Charts

OBJECTIVES

At the end of this assignment, the student should be able to:

- Prepare an organizational chart
- Interpret the organizational relationship among health care facility departments

Overview

An organizational chart (Figure 1-1) illustrates formal relationships among departments. It also depicts lines of authority within a department or between a department manager and facility administration. This assignment will familiarize the student with the creation of an organizational chart.

Instructions

1. Review the following case scenario, which depicts the organizational structure of a health information department.

   The health information manager is head of the department. An assistant manager reports directly to the health information manager. A coding supervisor and a document imaging supervisor report to the assistant manager. The department secretary reports directly to the health information manager. The following employees report to the coding supervisor: the inpatient coder, the outpatient coder, the ED coder, and the abstractor. Two document imaging clerks and an analysis clerk report to the document imaging supervisor.

2. Create an organizational chart that accurately illustrates the lines of authority depicted in the case scenario.

   NOTE: Organizational charts can be drawn by hand or with software such as OrgPlus (www.orgplus.com), an automated organizational chart creation program. The site contains an OrgPlus free trial.

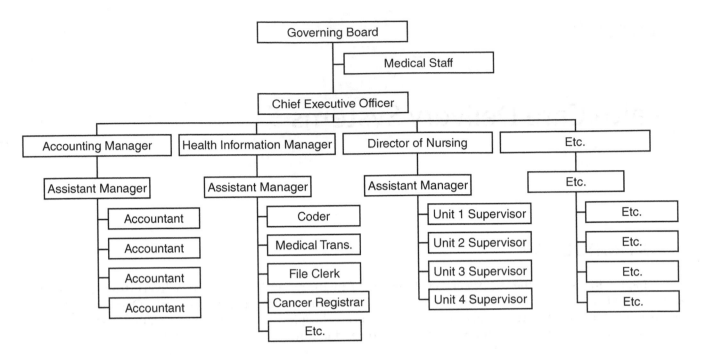

Figure 1-1 Portion of Facilitywide Organizational Chart

LAB ASSIGNMENT 1-2   Information Literacy

OBJECTIVES

At the end of this assignment, the student should be able to:

- Develop and increase information literacy skills
- Select, search, and evaluate information resources
- Prepare an annotated bibliography

Overview

Information literacy expands upon essential technical skills (knowing how to use computers and access information) to include critical thinking about the nature of information and its cultural, philosophical, and social context and impact. The purpose of this assignment is to assist you with developing and increasing your information literacy skills, which will, in turn, allow you to select, search, and evaluate information resources. You will prepare an annotated bibliography (Figure 1-2), which contains a brief description for each citation that summarizes the accuracy, quality, and relevance of the reference source, followed by the citation. (An annotation is *not* an abstract, which is a descriptive summary of a citation.) The annotated bibliography is descriptive *and* critical because it reveals the author's point of view.

Instructions

Prepare an annotated bibliography that contains two citations.
a. Select a bibliography topic that interests you (e.g., HIPAA privacy, Medicare Access and CHIP Reauthorization Act of 2015 (MACRA), Merit-based Incentive Payment System (MIPS)).
b. Locate two citations (e.g., journal articles) about your topic.
c. Review the citations to determine whether they contain useful information and ideas about your topic. Select two citations and read them thoroughly.
d. Prepare the annotated bibliography.
   - Cite each article using American Psychological Association (APA) style.

   NOTE: The APA established a style used in all of its published books and journals. Many authorities in the social and behavioral sciences adopted this style as their standard. The Modern Language Association (MLA) recommends its MLA style for the preparation of scholarly manuscripts and student research papers.

e. Summarize the article, incorporating at least four of the items below:
   - Description of article's content and/or focus
   - Consideration of whether the article's content is useful
   - Article's limitations (e.g., outdated)
   - Audience for which the article is intended
   - Evaluation of research methods used in the article
   - Author's background
   - Conclusions the author(s) make about the topic
   - Your reaction to the article

This informative, practical article by the project director of the Payment Error Prevention Support Peer Review Organization (PEPSPRO) in Texas discusses the issue of diagnosis-related group (DRG) billing as a major contributor to inaccurate Medicare payments and describes the negative consequences of undercoding and upcoding for the hospital. Recommendations are made and tools provided for completing a comprehensive assessment of records, staff qualifications, training, and use of coding resources, coding policies, and safeguards against upcoding. The author also discusses the various aspects of following up on a completed assessment, including implementing new policies, providing appropriate training, and monitoring compliance.

Fletcher, Robin. The importance of addressing inaccurate diagnosis related group assignment as a risk area. (2002). *Journal of Health Care Compliance, 45,* 40–46.

The author reports on the trend of hospitals using Internet-based automated compliance checking in place of more traditional billing methods in order to fulfill the requirements of the Medicare Correct Coding Initiative (CCI). Using Holy Cross Hospital in Ft. Lauderdale, Florida, as a case example, the author fully details the many benefits of using the automated system, including the reduction of billing errors, ease of use, evaluation of coding risk areas, and preventing noncompliance and the resulting penalty fees.

Moynihan, James J. Automated compliance checker helps ensure billing accuracy. (2000). *Healthcare Financial Management, 54,* 78.

Figure 1-2   Sample Annotated Bibliography Containing Two Citations

LAB ASSIGNMENT 1-3   Committee Minutes

OBJECTIVES

At the end of this assignment, the student should be able to:

- Observe the functioning of a committee meeting
- Take notes during the committee meeting
- Prepare minutes of the committee meeting and an agenda for the next meeting

Overview

Minutes document actions and discussions that occur during a committee meeting and should be recorded at each meeting. This assignment will familiarize the student with following a committee agenda, taking notes during meetings, preparing committee minutes, and creating an agenda for the next meeting.

Instructions

1. Select a committee meeting to attend. Upon arrival, be sure to request a copy of the committee agenda (Figure 1-3).

    NOTE: Committee meetings are routinely held at health care facilities (e.g., health information committee). Contact the health information department manager at a local facility to request permission to sit in on a meeting to take notes and prepare the minutes for a class assignment. If you are unable to attend a meeting at a health care facility, attend a meeting of your local American Red Cross office, school board, or the like.

2. Attend the meeting and take notes of topics discussed and actions taken (Figure 1-4). Be sure to include elements 3a–i below in your handwritten notes.

3. Prepare minutes of the meeting (Figure 1-5) based on notes recorded. Be sure to include the following elements:
    a. Date, place, and time of the meeting
    b. Members present
    c. Members absent
    d. Guests present
    e. Items discussed
    f. Actions taken
    g. Time meeting adjourned
    h. Location, time, and date of next meeting
    i. Closing

4. Prepare an agenda to be used at the next scheduled committee meeting.

Agenda

Health Information Committee

Chairperson:	David Lynn, M.D.	**Timekeeper:**	Thomas Kincaid
Facilitator:	Mary Jo Bowie, RHIA	**Note taker:**	Sally Brumley

Date/Time/Location: Wednesday, October 15th, Noon, Crandall Room

----- Agenda Topics -----

1. Ongoing record review
2. Revision of ICU/CCU nurses' notes
3. Transcription turnaround time
4. Conversion to electronic health record (EHR)
5. Health Information Technology Week

Figure 1-3   Sample Health Information Committee Agenda

Health Information Committee Meeting

Chairperson:	David Lynn, M.D.	**Timekeeper:**	Thomas Kincaid
Facilitator:	Mary Jo Bowie, RHIA	**Note taker:**	Sally Brumley

Date/Time/Location: Wednesday, October 15th, Noon, Crandall Room

Time Meeting Adjourned:

Date/Time/Location of Next Meeting:

Members Present:

Members Absent:

Guests Present:

----- **Agenda Topics** -----

1. Ongoing record review

    Discussion:

    Conclusions:

Action items:	Person responsible:	Deadline:

2. Revision of ICU/CCU nurses' notes

    Discussion:

    Conclusions:

Action items:	Person responsible:	Deadline:

Figure 1-4   Portion of Form Used to Record Minutes During a Committee Meeting

[NAME OF COMMITTEE]

Meeting Minutes

The meeting of the NAME OF COMMITTEE was called to order at [time] on [date] in [location] by [name of chairperson].

Present: [names and titles of members in attendance]
Absent: [names and titles of members not in attendance]
Guests Present: [names and titles of other individuals in attendance]

Approval of Minutes
The minutes of the previous meeting were unanimously approved as distributed.

Open Business
[Use paragraph format to summarize discussion, conclusions, and actions for each agenda item. Include the name of the person responsible for following through on any action and the deadline.]

New Business
[Use paragraph format to summarize discussion, conclusions, and actions for any new issues addressed during this meeting that were not included on the agenda. Include the name of the person responsible for following through on any action and the deadline.]

Agenda for Next Meeting
[List items to be discussed at the next meeting. These items serve as the basis for preparing the next meeting's agenda.]

Adjournment
The meeting was adjourned at [time] by [name of person]. The next meeting will be held at [time] on [date] in [location].

Respectfully submitted,   Approved,

[Name of recording secretary]   [Name of chairperson]
Recording Secretary   Chairperson

Figure 1-5   Format Used When Preparing Committee Minutes

Chapter 2

Health Information Management Professionals

🍎 INTRODUCTION

This chapter familiarizes students with locating professional association websites, interviewing a professional, creating a résumé and cover letter, interpreting professional codes of ethics, networking with other professionals via professional discussion forums, and interpreting (and understanding) information from professional journal articles.

LAB ASSIGNMENT 2-1   Interview of a Professional

OBJECTIVES

At the end of this assignment, the student should be able to:

* Delineate the responsibilities of a professional employed in the student's field of study
* Explain why the professional's position is one that the student would (or would not) be interested in obtaining

Overview

Health information management professionals often have similar educational backgrounds, but their job responsibilities and roles within organizations vary greatly. This assignment will familiarize students with the specific job responsibilities of a professional employed in their field of study.

Instructions

1. Prepare 10 questions that you would like to ask a professional employed in your field of study.

   NOTE: Your instructor might devote classroom time to brainstorming such questions (or use a discussion forum if you are an Internet-based student). This will allow you to share questions with other students in your course and to obtain additional questions to ask the professional.

2. Identify a credentialed professional in your field of study. Medical assistant students should interview a CMA or an RMA; coding students should interview a CCS or CPC; health information students should interview an RHIT or RHIA; and so on. Contact the professional to schedule an on-site interview. Conduct yourself in a professional manner and explain that you are a student completing a required assignment.

   NOTE: If it is not possible to schedule an on-site interview, check with your instructor to determine whether a telephone or email interview would be acceptable.

3. Prepare for the interview by reviewing and organizing the questions you will ask the professional.

4. Dress appropriately (as for a job interview), and arrive 10 minutes early for the interview.

5. Adopt a professional and respectful manner when asking interview questions, and be prepared to answer questions asked of you. Be sure to take notes as the professional responds to the interview questions. If you choose to record the interview, ask the professional for permission to do so.

6. After the interview, thank the professional for his or her time. Be sure to follow up the interview by mailing a handwritten thank-you note within 10 days.

7. Prepare a three-page paper summarizing the interview, as follows:
   a. Identify the professional's name, position, and facility.
   b. Writing in the third person, summarize the professional's responses to interview questions. Organize the interview content in logical paragraphs. (A paragraph consists of at least three sentences.) *Do **not** prepare this paper in a question/answer format.* If you have questions about how to write this paper, ask your instructor for clarification.
   c. In the last paragraph of the paper, summarize your reaction to the interview and whether you would be interested in having this professional's position (along with why or why not). Also, describe your future by writing about where you will be in 10 years (in terms of employment, family, etc.).

LAB ASSIGNMENT 2-2   Cover Letters and Résumés

OBJECTIVES

At the end of this assignment, the student should be able to:

- List the elements of a résumé and cover letter
- Demonstrate an understanding of the purpose of creating a résumé and cover letter that contain no errors
- Prepare a résumé and cover letter that can be submitted to a prospective professional practice site or for future employment opportunities
- Use the Internet to locate prospective job opportunities

Overview

Some facilities require students to submit a cover letter and résumé for consideration by the clinical supervisor prior to placement for professional practice. This assignment will result in the student creating a professional résumé and cover letter.

Instructions

1. Prepare a résumé and cover letter based on the examples in Figures 2-1 and 2-2, substituting your specific information. (Microsoft Word users can access the Résumé Wizard by clicking on File, New, then opening the résumé template.)
2. Consider having a rough draft of each professionally proofread by your school's career services department or someone at your local or state unemployment office.

SALLY S. STUDENT

5 Main Street   Binghamton, NY 13901   (607) 555-1234

EDUCATION

Sunny Valley University, Binghamton, New York.
Candidate for Associate in Science, Health Information Technology, May YYYY

Honors & Awards: Dean's List, Fall YYYY, Spring YYYY, and Fall YYYY. Member, Phi Theta Kappa National Honor Society

CERTIFICATION

R.H.I.T. eligible, May YYYY

PROFESSIONAL ORGANIZATIONS

Student Member, American Health Information Management Association, New York Health Information Management Association, and Sunny Valley Regional Health Information Management Association.

Member, Health Information Management Club, Sunny Valley University.

PROFESSIONAL PRACTICE

Student Health Information Technician, Health Information Management Department, Sunny Valley Medical Center, Binghamton, New York. Summer YYYY. Assembled and analyzed discharged patient records, filed and retrieved records, answered the telephone, processed release of information requests, attended health information committee meetings, and coded inpatient, outpatient, and emergency department records according to ICD-9-CM, CPT, and HCPCS Level II.

Student Health Information Technician, Quality Management Department, Sunny Valley Medical Center, Binghamton, New York. Spring YYYY. Performed quality management studies under the direction of the facility's quality manager, and assisted with risk management, utilization management, and physician credentialing procedures.

Student Health Information Technician, Sunny Valley Nursing Facility, Hilltop, New York. Spring YYYY. Filed and retrieved records, answered the telephone, processed discharged patient records, and attended committee meetings.

Student Health Information Technician, Allright Health Insurance Company, Claims, New York. Spring YYYY. Verified the accuracy of ICD-10-CM, CPT, and HCPCS codes submitted on insurance claims, reviewed patient records to determine medical necessity of procedures reported, and attended meetings.

WORK EXPERIENCE

Cashier, Burger King, Treats, New York. Assisted customers, operated cash register, and opened/closed store. August YYYY-Present.

Resident Assistant, Sunny Valley University, Binghamton, New York. Responsible for supervising the housing of 250 student residents, planning student activities, enforcing disciplinary procedures, and scheduling student staff.

AVAILABILITY

June 1, YYYY

REFERENCES

Sally Supervisor, Sunny Valley Medical Center, Binghamton, NY (607) 555-5626

Bob Boss, Burger King, Treats, NY (607) 555-8956

Patty Professor, Sunny Valley University, Binghamton, NY (607) 555-5434

Figure 2-1   Sample Résumé

5 Main Street
Binghamton, NY 13901
April 15, YYYY

Edward Employer
Human Resources
Sunny Valley Medical Center
100 Main St.
Sunny Valley, NY14802

Dear Mr. Employer:

Please accept this letter of application for the position of Health Information Technician as advertised in the April 10, YYYY, edition of *The Buffalo News.*

I will be graduating from the Sunny Valley University of New York, College of Technology at Alfred in May YYYY with an Associate degree in Applied Science in Health Information Technology. In addition to taking formal course work, I also completed professional practices, which allowed me to apply the skills that I learned in the classroom. Please refer to the attached résumé for a detailed listing of my responsibilities at each practice site.

In June YYYY, I will be eligible to take the RHIT credentialing examination offered by the American Health Information Management Association. I am interested in interviewing for the above position and would appreciate your contacting me at (607) 555-0234 to schedule an interview.

Thank you for your consideration. I look forward to hearing from you soon.

Sincerely,

Sally S. Student

Enclosure

Figure 2-2 Sample Cover Letter

LAB ASSIGNMENT 2-3   Professional Discussion Forums (Listserv)

OBJECTIVES

At the end of this assignment, the student should be able to:

- Explain the value of joining professional discussion forums
- Join a professional discussion forum
- Review discussion forum contents to identify topics relevant to a particular field of study
- Demonstrate participation in a professional discussion forum

Overview

Networking, or sharing information among professionals, is a valuable professional activity. The Internet has made it much easier to network with other professionals by using web-based professional forums. This assignment will familiarize the student with the value of Internet professional discussion forums.

Instructions

1. Select a professional discussion forum from Table 2-1 and follow its instructions to access forums.
2. Access archived forum discussions and observe current discussions for the period designated by your instructor (e.g., 1–3 weeks), noting topics that are relevant to your field of study.
3. Post a discussion comment or question on the forum and observe responses from subscribers.
4. At the end of the period of observation and participation, determine whether the forum would be helpful to you on the job.

Table 2-1   Discussion Forums and Internet Sites for Professionals

Professional	Name of Forum	Internet Site
AHIMA Members	Communities of Practice	http://www.ahima.org In order to access the Communities of Practice Forum you must be a member of AHIMA.
Coders/Medical Transcriptionists	Forums, Blogs	http://health-infomation.advanceweb.com Click on COMMUNITY, Forums or click on COMMUNITY, Blogs
Other Professionals	Names of NIH forums vary. Medicaid Program Updates	https://list.nih.gov Next to the heading Browse, click on List of Lists. This will display a listing of all NIH LISTSERV titles. Discuss with your instructor those that apply to your field of study.

LAB ASSIGNMENT 2-4   Professional Code of Ethics

OBJECTIVES

At the end of this assignment, the student should be able to:

- State the reason a profession develops a code of ethics
- Discuss the importance of adhering to a professional code of ethics
- Identify situations in which a professional code of ethics has been breached
- Suggest ways to address situations in which a code of ethics is breached

Overview

A professional code of ethics provides guidelines for professional actions. This assignment will familiarize students with the code of ethics unique to their professional field of study and allow students to respond to case scenarios that require application of the code of ethics.

Instructions

1. Refer to the code of ethics for your field of study supplied to you by your instructor. At the time of publication the AHIMA Code of Ethics is found at http://bok.ahima.org/doc?oid=105098#.WcpsHsZrzIV
2. Carefully review each case scenario below and identify which code was breached.
3. Summarize how the breach could have been avoided, and explain how each situation should be handled once a breach occurs.

Case Scenarios

1. Her neighbor asks Chris Professional whether she should consult Dr. Smith. Chris Professional replies, "Heavens, no! He doesn't have many cases at the hospital and his patients have a lot of complications after surgery. Go to Dr. Jones; he's wonderful!"

2. The hospital planned to buy new transcription equipment and evaluated the products of several companies. Chris Professional believed that one product was the most suitable for the needs of the department and so informed her administrator when her opinion was sought. After the equipment had been purchased and installed, Chris Professional received an expensive-looking day planner from the salesperson, given in gratitude for her help in influencing the hospital's choice. Since she really thinks that the filing equipment is the best, Chris Professional accepts this unexpected gift.

3. Chris Professional is in charge of the professional practice for students placed by a local college. She instructs students in a variety of duties, and one day shows two students some new equipment. The subject of the health of another student in the program comes up. Chris Professional says, "Oh, just a minute, her emergency department record came into the department today; let's see what it says." She finds the record and shares its contents with the two students.

4. A record was subpoenaed for production in court. Chris Professional had not yet been placed on the stand and had the record in her possession when the noon recess was called. The attorney who had subpoenaed the record, and who had been unable to secure the patient's permission to review it, invites Chris Professional to lunch. During lunch, he asks her to let him see the record, explaining that he will get the information anyhow once she is placed on the witness stand. He says that it will save time and expedite justice if she will let him have this quick "preview." Chris Professional agrees and passes the record to him.

5. An inexperienced woman has been employed to manage patient records in a small, neighborhood home health agency. She asks Chris Professional for advice about what she should do. Chris Professional, believing that she has more than enough to do attending to her own work, tells her she cannot help.

6. Chris Professional agrees to supply a natural baby food service with the names and addresses of all mothers delivered of living infants in the hospital. For this service she will receive $5.00 per name.

7. When applying for a fellowship in the American College of Surgeons, Dr. Monroe uses, as examples of his own surgical work, the cases of several patients who were actually cared for by a senior surgeon on the staff. When his list of cases is sent to the hospital for verification, Chris Professional, knowing that the young surgeon is eager to obtain the qualification and not wanting to make trouble, verifies by her signature the statements that these were Dr. Monroe's patients.

8. Since doctors rarely use the disease index, and because she hopes to be married and gone by the time of the next visit from the Joint Commission surveyor, Chris Professional does not bother to make any entries in this index, believing that her other duties are more important.

9. Returning from a meeting of the Tissue Committee, where she took notes, Chris Professional excitedly informs the assistant department director, "You know Dr. Tardy, the one who's always so ugly about completing his records? Well, they said today that the big operation he did last month on Mary Jones wasn't necessary at all, and they're recommending that his surgical privileges be suspended!"

10. Chris Professional was sent to an educational institute by her hospital but decided to spend two of the four afternoons of the institute week shopping and sightseeing instead of attending the sessions.

11. Chris Professional notices a laboratory report that documents the patient as having a positive venereal disease research laboratory slide test, which screens for syphilis, so she adds the diagnosis of "syphilis" to the face sheet of the patient's record.

12. Chris Professional notices that the patient record of another hospital employee is to be reviewed as part of her job. As she reviews the documentation, she notices that it references human immunodeficiency virus (HIV, which causes AIDS). She shows the document to the employee sitting at the next desk and asks if he is aware of this information. Chris Professional then returns to her other tasks.

13. Chris Professional, a HIM professional at Sunny View Nursing Facility, is asked by her neighbor for the diagnoses of his mother's roommate. Chris replies by giving the neighbor the list of diagnoses.

14. Chris Professional was conducting an audit at a nursing facility on medication administration. She notices that her neighbor's father was late dosed three times the previous month. She shares this with her neighbor.

15. Chris Professional completed the coding on her ex-sister-in-law's record, which states alcohol addiction. She shares this information with the ex spouse, who is seeking custody of their two children.

LAB ASSIGNMENT 2-5   Journal Abstract

OBJECTIVES

At the end of this assignment, the student should be able to:

* Identify the journal of the professional association in the student's field of study
* Write a journal abstract of an article

Overview

Professional association journals communicate information about health care advancements, new technology, changing regulations, and so on. This assignment will familiarize students with the contents of their professional journal and require students to prepare a journal abstract (summary) of a selected article.

Instructions

1. Select your professional association's journal from Table 2-2.
2. Select an article from your professional association's journal. Locate a journal by:
   a. Going to its website (many journals are posted online)
   b. Borrowing a journal through interlibrary loan (e.g., college library, local library)
   c. Borrowing a journal from a professional in your field of study or your instructor

NOTE: Borrowing a journal from a professional in your field of study is an excellent way to start the networking process that will lead to employment. However, if you borrow a journal, return it promptly and include a thank-you note.

NOTE: Student members of professional associations receive professional journals. However, it usually takes eight weeks to receive your first journal.

3. Read an article published in a recent edition of your professional association's journal.
4. Prepare a one-page, double-spaced summary of the journal article, which includes the following information:
   a. Name of article
   b. Name of author
   c. Name of journal
   d. Date of journal
   e. Journal article summary (paragraph format, double-spaced), which summarizes the article's content. Do *not* include your opinion about content of the article.

Table 2-2 Professional Journals

Profession	Professional Journal	Professional Association
Cancer Registrar	*Journal of Registry Management*	National Cancer Registrars Association
Coding & Reimbursement Specialist	*Healthcare Business Monthly*	American Academy of Professional Coders
Health Information Technician or Administrator	*Journal of the American Health Information Management Association*	American Health Information Management Association
Medical Assistant	*CMA Today*	American Association of Medical Assistants
	AMT Events Magazine	American Medical Technologists
Medical Staff Coordinator	*Synergy*	National Association of Medical Staff Services
Medical Transcriptionist	*Plexus*	Association for Healthcare Documentation Integrity (formerly the American Association of Medical Transcription)

Chapter 3

Health Care Settings

🌱 INTRODUCTION

This chapter focuses on familiarizing the student with a variety of health care settings, including acute care, ambulatory and outpatient care, behavioral health care facilities, home care and hospice, long-term care, managed care, and federal, state, and municipal health care.

LAB ASSIGNMENT 3-1   Health Care Facility Tour

OBJECTIVES

At the end of this assignment, the student should be able to:

- Discuss the health care services offered by a given facility
- Determine whether the facility would employ a professional in the student's field of study

Overview

A wide variety of health care facilities provide patients with appropriate levels of care based on patient medical needs. This assignment will familiarize the student with such facilities located in the community, along with professional positions available.

Instructions

1. Identify a health care facility in your community that you would like to tour.

   NOTE: If your instructor arranges for you to visit a facility with your class as a field trip, you won't need to complete this assignment.

2. Contact a professional in your field of study who is employed at the facility to arrange a tour.

   NOTE: Contact the facility and ask to be connected to the department that houses your field of study (e.g., health information department). Ask to speak with the department manager. Explain that as a student you are required to tour a facility to learn about your field of study. Schedule a specific date and time to tour the facility and the department.

3. Prepare for the tour by identifying questions you will ask to determine health care services offered by the hospital, types of patients treated, average length of stay, and so on.

4. Dress appropriately for the tour (as for a job interview), and arrive 10 minutes early.

5. Conduct yourself in a professional manner during the tour, and be sure to take notes of the responses you receive to questions you ask. During the tour, inquire about professional positions available in your field of study.

6. At the conclusion of the tour, thank the individual who conducted the tour. Follow up the tour with a hand-written thank-you note (no later than 10 days after the tour).

7. Prepare a brief summary of the tour, as follows:
   a. Identify the name and location (city, state) of the facility and department toured.
   b. Summarize information provided in response to questions asked during the tour.
   c. Comment on whether you would be interested in working for the facility.

LAB ASSIGNMENT 3-2   The Joint Commission

OBJECTIVES

At the end of this assignment, the student should be able to:

- Discuss the types of organizations accredited by The Joint Commission
- Identify the resources available on The Joint Commission website

Overview

The Joint Commission accredits numerous types of health care facilities. This assignment will familiarize the student with the types of facilities that are accredited by The Joint Commission.

Instructions

1. Log on The Joint Commission website at www.jointcommission.org.
2. Click on accreditation programs and review the types of facilities that are accredited. Select one of the types of facilities, that is, ambulatory care, behavioral health care, critical access hospitals, and so on and review the information that is available on the site.
3. Prepare a two-page typewritten paper that includes:
   a. The types of health care facilities accredited by The Joint Commission
   b. A summary of the information that is found relevant to the type of facility that you selected to review

Reference
1) Author. } website
2) Year.
3) Accreditation
4) the Joint Commission (I)
⑤ URL Retrieved September 10, 2019 from (website)
   *must be in alphabetical order
   * second line in reference needs to be indented

Citation (Author year)
[Author Abreviation]
can be used in future with in paper.

Mary Jo Bowie (2019). Health care facilities.
Essentials of Health management (pp. 64-68)

LAB ASSIGNMENT 3-3   Health Care Facilities

OBJECTIVES

At the end of this assignment, the student should be able to:

* Recognize various types of health care facilities that treat specific patient populations

Overview

Patients are treated at various types of health care facilities based on the patients' specific health care needs. This assignment will familiarize the student with the various types of health care facilities.

Instructions

1. Review the following cases and identify one type of health care facility/service from the following list that would provide health care services to the patient described in the case.
   * Acute care hospital
   * Ambulatory surgery center
   * Chemical dependency inpatient program
   * Facility for the developmentally disabled
   * Home care services
   * Hospice care services
   * Pain management clinic
   * Respite care facility

2. Explain your rationale for choosing this type of health care facility.

Case 1

Asmer Natali is a 59-year-old male patient who has been diagnosed with an opioid addiction. He has been treated on an outpatient basis but currently has relapsed and needs to undergo detox and requires medically directed care management. His primary care outpatient addiction counselor feels he needs to have a more intensive level of service than outpatient care. *Chemical dependency inpatient program*

Case 2

Mr. Lamb, a 45-year-old patient, was diagnosed with severe kidney disease. He has been on dialysis for the last five years and has not been placed on a transplant list due to his many other health problems. At this time he has decided that he would like to receive palliative care rather than curative care services.

Case 3

Eileen Penna is a 27-year-old woman who suffered a cervical spine injury due to a motor vehicle accident three years ago. She has undergone surgery and is still experiencing pain that prevents her from performing daily activities. Eileen's primary care provider feels that her case should be evaluated through a multidisciplinary approach to attempt to provide her relief.

Case 4

Thomas is the primary caregiver for his 93-year-old father, Keith. Thomas and Keith live in the same house. Keith needs assistance with all of his activities of daily living and mealtime preparation due to his diagnosis of dementia. Thomas needs to go out of town for one week and does not feel that his father is able to stay at their residence alone.

Case 5

Mike James, an 84-year-old man, had open heart surgery three months ago. Following the surgery he was placed in a skilled nursing facility for intensive cardiac rehabilitation. He wants to be discharged but still needs assistance with daily living activities and the management of his illness.

Case 6

Tim, a 5-year-old boy, has a diagnosis of profound intellectual disability and also has numerous medical issues. His parents have kept him at home, but they are finding it more difficult to manage his care. They feel that he needs to be placed in a facility that can address his developmental and physical health concerns.

Case 7

Lisa, a 74-year-old woman, fell at home and was taken to the emergency department (ED). The ED physician called an orthopedic surgeon to review the case. It was determined that she has a fracture of the left hip and needs surgery.

Case 8

Kayla is a 7-year-old girl who has had an ongoing sore throat and enlarged tonsils for the last six months. Her physician feels that she needs to have her tonsils removed. Kayla has no other health concerns that present a risk to her having a tonsillectomy.

LAB ASSIGNMENT 3-4   U.S. Department of Health and Human Services Career Opportunities

OBJECTIVES

At the end of this assignment, the student should be able to:

- Recognize various agencies, divisions, and programs that are part of the U.S. Department of Health and Human Services and the health information professional career opportunities that exist within the agencies, divisions, and programs.

Overview

There are various agencies, divisions, and programs that are overseen by the U.S. Department of Health and Human Services which employ health information professionals as part of their health care teams. This assignment will familiarize the student with the various component agencies, divisions, and programs and the role of the health information professional within the U.S. Department of Health and Human Services.

Instructions

1. Log on to the U.S. Department of Health and Human Services website at www.hhs.gov.
2. At the bottom of the page click on Careers. This will take you to the following page: www.hhs.gov/about /careers/index.html.
3. On this page click on Job Openings. This will display a comprehensive list of jobs available for the entire family of HHS agencies.
4. Select one of the operating or staff divisions listed and search on an open job opportunity in the health information management field.
5. Prepare a two-page summary of the job and the agency in which there is an opening. Also discuss if you would apply for the position.

Chapter 4

Introduction to the Patient Record

❦ INTRODUCTION

This chapter focuses on familiarizing the student with patient record content, formats, development and completion, and provider documentation requirements.

LAB ASSIGNMENT 4-1   Administrative and Clinical Data

OBJECTIVES

At the end of this assignment, the student should be able to:

- Differentiate between administrative and clinical data
- Critique a physician's office patient record form

Overview

Administrative and clinical data is captured from the time the patient initiates contact for medical care to the time of discharge. This assignment will familiarize the student with both administrative and clinical data that is collected on a registration form.

Instructions

1. Refer to Table 4-1 in Chapter 4 of your textbook to review examples of administrative and clinical data.
2. Review the registration form (Figure 4-1) used in a physician's office for the following information:
   a. Demographic
   b. Socioeconomic
   c. Financial
   d. Clinical
3. Create a table, as seen on the next page, and list all administrative and clinical items in column one, and enter the type of element in column two. (To get you started, the first four entries are included in the table.) The list of items should include:

Patient name	Admission date and time	Medication allergies/reactions
Patient address, city, state, and zip code	Primary insurance plan	Current medications
Telephone	Primary insurance plan ID#	BP, P, R, T, WT (vital signs)
Gender	Secondary insurance plan	Chief compliant (CC)
Date of birth	Secondary insurance plan ID#	Past medical history (PMH)
Patient number	Occupation	Note
	Name of employer	

Student Name _____

Administrative and Clinical Data Item	Type of Element
Patient name	Demographic
Address	Demographic
Primary insurance plan	Financial
Current medications	Clinical

Sunny Valley Medical Center
100 Main St, Binghamton NY 13901
(607) 555-1234

PHYSICIAN OFFICE RECORD

EIN: 12-345678

PATIENT INFORMATION:

NAME:	DOE, John	PATIENT NUMBER:	123456
ADDRESS:	100 South Ave	ADMISSION DATE & TIME:	05-16-YYYY
CITY:	Alfred	PRIMARY INSURANCE PLAN:	BCBS of WNY
STATE:	NY	PRIMARY INSURANCE PLAN ID #:	12345678
ZIP CODE:	14802	SECONDARY INSURANCE PLAN:	N/A
TELEPHONE:	607-555-3264	SECONDARY INSURANCE PLAN ID #:	N/A
GENDER:	Male	OCCUPATION:	Accountant
DATE OF BIRTH:	07-07-1956	NAME OF EMPLOYER:	State College

NURSING DOCUMENTATION:

MEDICATIONS ALLERGIES/REACTIONS: None

CURRENT MEDICATIONS: Lithium 1,500 mg

BP: 130/80   P: 84   R: T: WT: 265

CC: Patient states he feels well today.

PMH: Bipolar disorder, manic type.

NOTES: Here for scheduled appointment. Voices no concerns.

SIGNATURE OF PRIMARY CARE NURSE: Jeanette Allen, R.N.

PHYSICIAN DOCUMENTATION:

Notes:

HISTORY: Patient seen today for regular appointment. He appears relaxed, cooperative, and coherent. No evidence of recurrent manic behavior. He is a 46-year-old, divorced twice, Navy veteran, who served from 1971 to 1975 as an accountant in non-combat situation. He has been suffering from bipolar disorder, manic type, and takes medication, Lithium 1,500 mg a day, which seems affective.

He has been employed at Alfred State College as an accountant for nine years, full time.

Mental Status Exam: He has been doing very well with the current medication. No evidence of memory loss or any psychotic behavior, He affect is appropriate, and mood is stable. Insight and judgment are good. He is not considered a danger to himself or others.

DIAGNOSIS: Bipolar disorder, manic type.

PLAN: Continue lithium 1,500 mg a day.

SIGNATURE OF PROVIDER: Raymond E. Massey, M.D.

Raymond E. Massey, M.D

Figure 4-1   Sample Physician Office Record

LAB ASSIGNMENT 4-2   Provider Documentation Guidelines

OBJECTIVES

At the end of this assignment, the student should be able to:

- Explain provider documentation responsibilities
- Interpret provider documentation guidelines

Overview

Health care organizations are responsible for ensuring that health care services rendered to patients are documented according to federal and state regulations as well as accreditation, professional practice, and legal standards. This assignment will familiarize the student with patient record documentation standards.

Instructions

1. Refer to the *Provider Responsibilities* section in Chapter 4 of your textbook:
    a. Authentication of patient record entries
    b. Abbreviations used in the patient record
    c. Legibility of patient record entries
    d. Timeliness of patient record entries
    e. Amending the patient record
2. Use the chart format on the following page to summarize key concepts associated with provider documentation responsibilities.

Student Name _____

Provider Documentation Guidelines	
Provider Documentation Responsibilities	**Summary of Key Concepts**
Authentication of patient record entries	
Abbreviations used in the patient record	
Legibility of patient record entries	
Timeliness of patient record entries	
Amending the patient record	

LAB ASSIGNMENT 4-3   Flow of Patient Information

OBJECTIVES

At the end of this assignment, the student should be able to:

- Illustrate the flow of patient information from admission to discharge
- Identify the health care provider who is responsible for documenting patient record information

Overview

The inpatient record contains documents that are completed by various hospital personnel and providers. This assignment will familiarize the student with the inpatient record and the individuals responsible for the completion of the documents.

Instructions

1. The chart on the following page contains the flow of information developed for the patient record from the time of admission to discharge.
2. Enter the hospital staff member (e.g., ER nurse) or physician (e.g., attending physician) responsible for completing documentation listed.

Student Name _____

Flow of Patient Information	
Flow of Documentation	**Responsible Staff Member or Physician**
Face Sheet	Nursing staff
Admission Consent	Nursing staff
Nursing Assessment	Nursing staff
Physician Orders	Attending Physician
Admission History and Physical	Attending Physician
Laboratory Test Results	
Operative Note	
Physical Therapy Exam and Treatment	
Discharge Instructions	
Discharge Summary	

LAB ASSIGNMENT 4-4   Medicare Conditions of Participation

OBJECTIVES

At the end of this assignment, the student should be able to:

- Locate the Code of Federal Regulations (CFR) for public health and Medicare conditions of participation
- Interpret the Medicare Hospital Conditions of Participation: Medical Record Services

Overview

The Medicare Conditions of Participation (COP) are federal regulations that health care organizations must comply with in order to receive federal funds for services provided to patients. The COP are contained in the Code of Federal Regulations (CFR), which is the codification of general and permanent rules published in the *Federal Register* by executive departments and agencies of the federal government. It consists of 50 titles that represent broad areas subject to federal regulation, which are updated once each calendar year. Each title is divided into chapters (according to name of the issuing agency) and parts (covering specific regulatory areas). Large parts may be further subdivided into subparts.

NOTE: The searchable CFR database is available at www.federalregister.gov, where you can search the database.

EXAMPLE 1: Go to www.federalregister.gov, enter "conditions of participation: clinical records" in the Search box, and click on SUBMIT. Several citations are displayed. To view the content, click on the description of the information displayed.

Instructions

1. Review the conditions of participation for hospital medical record services (Subpart 482.24) (Figure 4-2).
2. Interpret medical record services conditions by summarizing the intent of each.
3. Enter the interpretation of each condition using the table format that follows. Be sure to enter the condition from Figure 4-2 in column one and your interpretation in column two.

Code of Federal Regulations
Title 42
Part 482-Conditions of Participation For Hospitals
Subpart C-Basic Hospital Functions

TITLE 42-PUBLIC HEALTH
CHAPTER IV-HEALTH CARE
DEPARTMENT OF HEALTH AND HUMAN SERVICES

§482.24   CONDITION OF PARTICIPATION: MEDICAL RECORD SERVICES.

The hospital must have a medical record service that has administrative responsibility for medical records. A medical record must be maintained for every individual evaluated or treated in the hospital.

(a) *Standard: Organization and staffing.* The organization of the medical record service must be appropriate to the scope and complexity of the services performed. The hospital must employ adequate personnel to ensure prompt completion, filing, and retrieval of records.

(b) *Standard: Form and retention of record.* The hospital must maintain a medical record for each inpatient and outpatient. Medical records must be accurately written, promptly completed, properly filed and retained, and accessible. The hospital must use a system of author identification and record maintenance that ensures the integrity of the authentification and protects the security of all record entries.
  (1) Medical records must be retained in their original or legally reproduced form for a period of at least 5 years.
  (2) The hospital must have a system of coding and indexing medical records. The system must allow for timely retrieval by diagnosis and procedure, in order to support medical care evaluation studies.
  (3) The hospital must have a procedure for ensuring the confidentiality of patient records. Information from or copies of records may be released only to authorized individuals, and the hospital must ensure that unauthorized individuals cannot gain access to or alter patient records. Original medical records must be released by the hospital only in accordance with Federal or State laws, court orders, or subpoenas.

(c) *Standard: Content of record.* The medical record must contain information to justify admission and continued hospitalization, support the diagnosis, and describe the patient's progress and response to medications and services.
  (1) All patient medical record entries must be legible, complete, dated, timed, and authenticated in written or electronic form by the person responsible for providing or evaluating the service provided, consistent with hospital policies and procedures.
  (2) All orders, including verbal orders, must be dated, timed, and authenticated promptly by the ordering practitioner or by another practitioner who is responsible for the care of the patient only if such a practitioner is acting in accordance with State law, including scope-of-practice laws, hospital policies, and medical staff bylaws, rules, and regulations.
  (3) Hospitals may use pre-printed and electronic standing orders, order sets, and protocols for patient orders only if the hospital:
      (i) Establishes that such orders and protocols have been reviewed and approved by the medical staff and the hospital's nursing and pharmacy leadership;
      (ii) Demonstrates that such orders and protocols are consistent with nationally recognized and evidence-based guidelines;
      (iii) Ensures that the periodic and regular review of such orders and protocols is conducted by the medical staff and the hospital's nursing and pharmacy leadership to determine the continuing usefulness and safety of the orders and protocols; and
      (iv) Ensures that such orders and protocols are dated, timed, and authenticated promptly in the patient's medical record by the ordering practitioner or by another practitioner responsible for the care of the patient only if such a practitioner is acting in accordance with State law, including scope-of-practice laws, hospital policies, and medical staff bylaws, rules, and regulations.
  (4) All records must document the following, as appropriate:
      (i) Evidence of—
          (A) A medical history and physical examination completed and documented no more than 30 days before or 24 hours after admission or registration, but prior to surgery or a procedure requiring anesthesia services. The medical history and physical examination must be placed in the patient's medical record within 24 hours after admission or registration, but prior to surgery or a procedure requiring anesthesia services.
          (B) An updated examination of the patient, including any changes in the patient's condition, when the medical history and physical examination are completed within 30 days before admission or registration. Documentation of the updated examination must be placed in the patient's medical record within 24 hours after admission or registration, but prior to surgery or a procedure requiring anesthesia services.
      (ii) Admitting diagnosis.
      (iii) Results of all consultative evaluations of the patient and appropriate findings by clinical and other staff involved in the care of the patient.
      (iv) Documentation of complications, hospital acquired infections, and unfavorable reactions to drugs and anesthesia.
      (v) Properly executed informed consent forms for procedures and treatments specified by the medical staff, or by Federal or State law if applicable, to require written patient consent.
      (vi) All practitioners' orders, nursing notes, reports of treatment, medication records, radiology, and laboratory reports, and vital signs and other information necessary to monitor the patient's condition.
      (vii) Discharge summary with outcome of hospitalization, disposition of case, and provisions for follow-up care.
      (viii) Final diagnosis with completion of medical records within 30 days following discharge.

[51 FR 22042, June 17, 1986, as amended at 71 FR 68694, Nov. 27, 2006; 72 FR 66933, Nov. 27, 2007; 77 FR 29074, May 16, 2012]

Figure 4-2   Subpart 482.24-Hospital Medicare Conditions of Participation: Medical Record Services

Student Name _____

Condition of Participation: Medical Record Services (Hospital) (Subpart 482.24)	
Condition	**Interpretation**
(a) *Standard: Organization and staffing.* The organization of the medical record service must be appropriate to the scope and complexity of the services performed. The hospital must employ adequate personnel to ensure prompt completion, filing, and retrieval of records.	• Hospital must establish a medical record (or health information) department and provide appropriate physical space for it to perform its functions. • Hospital must hire enough qualified individuals to perform tasks necessary to maintain patient records for the facility.

LAB ASSIGNMENT 4-5   Amending the Patient Record

OBJECTIVES

At the end of this assignment, the student should be able to:

* Explain the procedure used to amend patient records
* Recognize appropriate and inappropriate amendments made to patient records

Overview

Laws, regulations, and standards that originally applied to the maintenance of paper-based records also apply to electronic (or computer-based) records that are properly created and maintained in the normal course of business. This assignment will require the student to recognize appropriate and inappropriate amendments made to patient records.

Instructions

1. Review the section entitled "Amending the Patient Record" found in Chapter 4 of your textbook. For added information also review the following AHIMA website. Go to www.ahima.org. At the bottom of the page click on HIM Body of Knowledge, then click on Practice Briefs. Locate the following two practice briefs.

   * 10/2/13—Patient Access and Amendment to Health Records
   * 9/15/99—Correcting and Amending Entries in a Computerized Patient Record

2. Review the patient record entries in Figure 4-3, determine whether each is appropriately or inappropriately amended, and provide a justification for each.

Student Name _____

Instructions:	Review the amended patient record entries located in Figure 4-3. If correctly documented, enter an × in the Yes box. If not, enter an × in the No box.
	Write a justification for your selection indicating why the amended patient record entry was appropriately or inappropriately documented.

Case No.	Correctly documented?		Justification statement:
1	o Yes	o No	
2	o Yes	o No	
3	o Yes	o No	
4	o Yes	o No	
5	o Yes	o No	
6	o Yes	o No	
7	o Yes	o No	
8	o Yes	o No	
9	o Yes	o No	
10	o Yes	o No	

CASE 1	Dr. Smith corrects the entry below by crossing out the 70 mg Lasix dosage and entering 80 mg. He then initialed and dated the new entry. Is this the proper way to amend the record? If not, indicate the correct method.

7/9/YYYY	*Mary Patient is seen today because of swelling of both lower*
	extremities. Her current medications include Prinivil for congestive
	cardiac failure and 40 mg of Lasix.
	Exam revealed the following findings.
	Heart: regular sinus rhythm.
	Lung: scattered basilar rales.
	Abdomen: soft. Liver/spleen: not palpable.
	Extremities: 2 to 3+ bilateral pedal edema.
	PLAN: Increase Lasix to 70 mg daily. 80 mg RS 7/9/YYYY
	Roger Smith MD

CASE 2	After documenting the 8/02/YYYY note, Dr. Smith realizes it was entered in the wrong patient's record. He obliterates the note from this patient's record and enters it in the correct patient's record. Is this the proper way to amend the record? If not, indicate the correct method.

8/02/YYYY	*Ralph is seen today because of a fever of 101. Exam reveals he has a*
	cough and is short of breath. He appeared to be in distress during the
	exam. Heart: regular sinus rhythm. Lung: bilateral congestion.
	Abdomen: soft. Liver/spleen: normal. The patient has acute bronchitis.
	Medications: Z pack as directed.
	Roger Smith. MD

CASE 3	Dr. Robert Jones dictated an operative report on 1/3/YYYY, which was transcribed and placed in the patient record on 1/4/YYYY. After review of the operative report, Dr. Jones redictated the report because "he did not like the way it read." The transcriptionist transcribed the new dictation, and instructed the file clerk to remove and destroy the original report and place the newly transcribed operative report in the patient's record. Is this the proper way to amend the record? If not, indicate the correct method.

Figure 4-3   Amended Patient Record Entries

(Continues)

CASE 4	Alice Grey, RN, charted the following nurses' notes, including the one timed as 1030 in advance of the 0900 and 0945 entries. She contacted the health information department to determine how to correct this entry. She was instructed to cross out the first entry and re-enter it at the appropriate time. Is this the proper way to amend the record? If not, indicate the correct method.
2/3/YYYY 0815	30-year-old gravida II para I admitted via ER in active labor. Called Dr. Patten's office. Has NKMA. EDC is 1/28/XX. Membranes are intact. Labor progressing as per noted on labor record and clinical observation sheets. Alice Grey RN
~~2/3/YYYY~~ ~~1030~~	~~Medications given as per physician orders. See medication administration record. Alice Grey RN~~
2/3/YYYY 0900	Patient sleeping on and off for most of shift Denies any discomfort Frequency of contractions decreased. Alice Grey RN
2/3/YYYY 0945	Contractions are becoming 8-10 minutes apart. See labor record. Alice Grey RN
2/3/YYYY 1030	Medications given as per physician orders. See medication administration record. Alice Grey RN
CASE 5	When entering the APGAR score for Reflex Irritability below, the nurse made an error and corrected the entry. Is this the proper way to amend the record? If not, indicate the correct method.

	Score 0	Score 1	Score 2	1st Score	2nd Score	
Heart Rate	Absent	Slow Below 100	Over 100	2	2	
Respiratory Effort	Absent	Slow, Irregular	Good, Crying	2	2	
Muscle Tone	Limp	Same of Extremity	Active Motion	2	2	
Reflex Irritability	No response	Grimace	Cough or Sneeze	2	~~1~~	2
Color	Blue, Pale	Body, Pink Extremities, Blue	Completely Pink	1	2	
			Total	9	10	

CASE 6	Polly Tops, a former patient, comes to the HIM department with a handwritten list of amendments that she wants made to her medical record. She previously obtained a copy of her record with her physician's approval. The HIM clerk accepts the amendments from Polly and files them at the back of the patient's record. Is this the proper way to amend the record? If not, indicate the correct method.

Figure 4-3   Amended Patient Record Entries (Continued)

(Continues)

CASE 7	The progress note below was documented by Jane Smith, MD. Upon analysis of the record, the clerk realized the note was unsigned and indicated on the deficiency slip that Dr. Fog should authenticate it. Dr. Fog signed the note and handed the completed record to the HIM clerk for processing. Upon re-analysis, the clerk discovers the signature error and marks the deficiency slip for Dr. Smith to sign the note and make a notation that Dr. Fog signed in error.
1/3/YYYY	*Mary has dementia, ischemic heart disease and she had an acute MI last month. According to nursing her vital signs have been stable. She is alert, conscious, and is able to speak to me. On exam her heart is in regular sinus rhythm. No additional cardiac findings at this time. Lungs are clear. Abdomen is soft. Continue orders as noted on 1/2/XX.*
	Thomas Fog, MD
CASE 8	Alfred State Medical Center transcribes progress notes onto adhesive-backed blank paper forms that are placed on blank progress note pages in the medical record. A progress note dated 3/3/YYYY was transcribed and appropriately placed in the record. Upon review, the responsible physician notices transcription errors (e.g., typographical errors) and instructs the transcriptionist to rekey the note onto an adhesive-backed form and adhere the new note on top of the original note. Is this the proper way to amend the record? If not, indicate the correct method.
CASE 9	Nurse Anne Brown discovered that she had forgotten to document a 9:15 a.m. (0915 in military time) nurses' note in a patient's record. There was no room to squeeze the entry between the 0900 and 1000 notes, so she documented the 0915 entry below the 1000 entry, marking the 0915 entry as a late entry. Is this the proper way to amend the record? If not, indicate the correct method.

DATE/TIME	PROGRESS NOTE
4/15/YYYY 0900	*55-year-old male admitted with chest pains by Dr. Jones. See initial nursing assessment. Bob Town, RN*
4/15/YYYY 1000	*Patient transferred to cardiac lab for testing. Bob Town, RN*
LATE ENTRY 4/15/YYYY 0915	*Physician orders received via phone, orders noted. Anne Brown RN*

CASE 10	Nurse Mary Brown expanded on her original 5/13/YYYY note by entering an addendum two entries after the original. Is this the proper way to amend the record? If not, indicate the correct method.
5/13/YYYY 0500	*Patient admitted via ambulance from possible domestic violence situation. See initial nursing intake report. Mary Brown, R.N.*
5/13/YYYY 0515	*Completed physical exam as noted on ER exam report Cynthia Lewis, R.N.*
5/13/YYYY 0530	*Addendum to note of 5/13/YYYY at 0500. Patient stated that police were called prior to ambulance coming to her home. She does not want to see her husband if he comes to the ER. Please call police. Mary Brown, R.N.*

Figure 4-3   Amended Patient Record Entries (*Continued*)

Chapter 5

Electronic Health Records

❦ INTRODUCTION

This chapter focuses on the development and use of electronic health care records.

LAB ASSIGNMENT 5-1   Electronic Health Record Systems

OBJECTIVES

At the end of this assignment, the student should be able to:

- Identify an electronic health record (EHR) system and identify the types of facilities that would use the selected system
- Summarize the features of the electronic record system

Overview

Numerous electronic health record systems are used in health care. This assignment will allow the student to identify various systems and require the student to summarize the features of a system.

Instructions

1. Using an Internet browser (e.g., Microsoft Internet Explorer, Google Chrome), search for the term "electronic health record system."
2. Select a system located via the search.
3. Prepare a two-page summary of the system.
   a. List the name of the system and the website.
   b. Summarize the features of the system.
   c. Discuss the types of facilities that would benefit from installation of the system.

Revenue cycle managemnt

EClinical works
www.eclinicalworks.com
Cloud Based
easy documentation
Access to patien data anytime, anywhere
PC/mac , web browser ; smart phone

patient engagement
create cycle of care
(EVa) virtual assistant
Telemedicine

LAB ASSIGNMENT 5-2   Topics Relevant to Health Information Technologies & Processes

OBJECTIVES

At the end of this assignment, the student should be able to:

- Identify the location of topics relevant to Health Information Technologies & Processes on the website of the American Health Information Management Association
- Summarize information relevant to a topic in Health Information Technologies & Processes

Overview

Electronic health records play an essential role in the documentation of patients' health experiences. This assignment will familiarize the student with Health Information Technologies & Processes. Numerous topics are under discussion by health care professionals as the use of Health Information Technologies & Processes becomes widespread.

Instructions

1. Using an Internet browser (e.g., Microsoft Internet Explorer, Google Chrome), go to www.ahima.org.
2. Click on HIM Body of Knowledge. Topic headings relevant to Health Information Technologies & Processes will appear. Select the topic heading Health Information Technologies & Processes. Select one of the articles written within the last two years.
3. Read through the article.
4. Prepare a one-page summary of the article, discussing how it is relevant to the health care industry today.

LAB ASSIGNMENT 5-3   AHIMA's myPHR

OBJECTIVES

At the end of this assignment, the student should be able to:

* Locate the AHIMA website, myPHR
* Discuss the benefits of patients developing personal health records

Overview

Personal health records benefit both patients and the health care community. This assignment will familiarize students with a website maintained by AHIMA that addresses the many benefits of personal health records. This website also discusses how to create a personal health record.

Instructions

1. Using an Internet browser (e.g., Microsoft Internet Explorer, Google Chrome), go to www.myphr.com.
2. Explore this site by reading some of the stories and viewing the videos.
3. Select a story or video and summarize the benefits of having a personal health record. Submit a one-page document to your instructor.

LAB ASSIGNMENT 5-4   Resistance to EHR

OBJECTIVES

At the end of this assignment, the student should be able to:

- Discuss how to address resistance to EHR
- Identify the benefits of EHR

Overview

Change is difficult for some individuals to accept. Many providers and staff members of health care facilities are resisting the implementation of electronic health record systems. This assignment will prepare students to address the resistance to EHR that can exist in health care.

Instructions

Assume that you are the HIM director at Sunny Valley Health Care. Sunny Valley Health Care is comprised of two acute care facilities, one long-term care facility, and 15 clinics that are within a 60-mile radius. It has been determined that the organization will be implementing an EHR system that will be used in all levels of care. Administration has determined that there is staff resistance to the implementation of the EHR system. You have been asked by the CEO to present a PowerPoint presentation on the benefits of implementing the system.

1. Research the benefits of EHR systems.
2. Prepare a 15-slide PowerPoint presentation on the benefits of EHR systems.

Chapter 6

Patient Record Documentation Guidelines: Inpatient, Outpatient, and Physician Office

❦ INTRODUCTION

This chapter will familiarize the student with aspects of inpatient, outpatient, and physician office records, including general documentation issues, administrative and clinical data, and forms control and design.

LAB ASSIGNMENT 6-1   Chart Assembly

OBJECTIVES

At the end of this assignment, the student should be able to:

- List the reports typically found in an acute care facility inpatient record
- Sequence acute care facility inpatient reports in a logical filing order

Overview

The acute care facility inpatient record contains numerous reports that are documented by various facility personnel and medical staff providers. Each facility establishes a filing order for inpatient and discharged patient reports to ensure that information can be easily located in the record. This assignment will familiarize the student with the content of an inpatient record and the typical order of reports filed in a discharged patient record.

NOTE: Some facilities adopt a *universal chart order*, which means the filing order of the inpatient and discharged patient record remains the same. This eliminates the task of assembling the discharged patient record.

Instructions

1. The chart on the next page contains a list of acute care discharged patient reports.
2. Reorder the reports (1–15) according to the way they would be filed in a discharged patient record. (To get you started, numbers 1 and 15 have been entered.)

Student Name _____

Sequence	Reports
	Advanced Directives
	Anesthesia Record
	Ancillary Testing Reports
	Consent To Admission
	Consultation Reports
	Discharge Summary
1	Face Sheet
	History and Physical Examination
	Nursing Section
	Operative Report
	Pathology Report
15	Patient Property Form
	Physician Orders
	Physician Progress Notes
	Recovery Room Record

LAB ASSIGNMENT 6-2   Quantitative and Qualitative Analysis of Patient Records

OBJECTIVES

At the end of this assignment, the student should be able to:

- Analyze patient records to identify quantitative and qualitative documentation deficiencies
- Complete deficiency forms, indicating quantitative and qualitative documentation deficiencies

Overview

Quantitative and qualitative analyses of discharged patient records identify provider documentation deficiencies (e.g., missing authentication, incomplete diagnoses on face sheet). This assignment will require the student to analyze records to determine whether or not documentation is complete, and to complete a deficiency form (Figure 6-1) for each case.

NOTE: Some health care facilities perform concurrent analysis, which means records are analyzed while patients are still in the facility receiving care. The advantage to this is that the record is conveniently located on the nursing unit where providers routinely care for patients. The disadvantage is that more than one provider needs to access records at the same time, often making them unavailable for analysis and completion.

Instructions

1. Go to the Student Companion website and print one deficiency form for each patient record to be analyzed (10 total).
2. Refer to Appendix I, where Case01 through Case10 are located.
3. Refer to the Instructions for Completing the Deficiency Form (Table 6-1), and review the Guide for Quantitative Analysis of Acute Care Hospital Discharged Inpatient Records (Figure 6-2).
4. Review the Quantitative Analysis: Walkthrough of Case01 (Figure 6-3), which will familiarize you with completing the deficiency form for quantitative and qualitative analysis of discharged patient records.
5. Analyze Case01, and go to the Student Companion website to compare your completed deficiency form to the answer key. (Refer to Figure 6-3 for clarification of the answer key.)

NOTE: When performing quantitative and qualitative analysis, refer to the Guide for Quantitative Analysis of Acute Care Hospital Discharged Inpatient Records (Figure 6-2), and ask the following questions as you review each record:

- Is patient identification included on each report in the record?
- Are all necessary reports present, completely documented, and authenticated?

    EXAMPLE: Provider documents order for consultation in physician order. Was a consultation report dictated, transcribed, and filed in the record?

    EXAMPLE: A chest x-ray is missing the impression: the radiologist is responsible for documenting it.

- Are all entries authenticated (signed)?

    EXAMPLE: A resident documents the patient's history and physical examination, and authenticates it.
Did the attending physician document additional information to support or dispute the resident's documentation? Did the attending physician also authenticate that entry?

- Are all diagnoses and procedures documented on the face sheet?

    EXAMPLE: Attending physician documents diabetes mellitus on the face sheet of discharged patient record. Does documentation in the patient record support adult-onset type and/or insulin dependency?

    EXAMPLE: Upon review of the discharged patient record, you notice that the responsible physician neglected to document several procedures that were performed during the stay.

    NOTE: On the job, follow your department's procedure for communicating questions to the responsible provider regarding incomplete or missing diagnoses and/or procedures.

6. Analyze Case02 through Case05, and go to the Student Companion website to compare your completed deficiency forms with the answer keys.

    NOTE: Reanalyze Case02 through Case05 for practice.

7. Analyze Case06 through Case10, and complete a deficiency form for each.

8. Submit completed deficiency forms to your instructor for evaluation.

Table 6-1 Instructions for Completing the Deficiency Form

1. Enter the patient name
2. Enter the case number (e.g., Case01 from the face sheet)
3. Enter the admission date from the face sheet. (This identifies the case analyzed in the event more than one record is stored in the same folder.)
4. Enter the attending doctor's name.
5. Enter the other doctor's name if a deficiency is present (e.g., emergency department physician).
6. Enter the other doctor's name if a deficiency is present (e.g., consultant, surgeon, anesthesiologist).
7–18. Review each report in the patient record, and compare to the Guide for Quantitative Analysis of Acute Care Hospital Discharged Inpatient Records (Figure 6-2):
    a. Circle **Authenticate** if the doctor needs to sign a report.
    b. Circle **Document** if the doctor needs to enter pertinent information to complete the report. On the line provided, enter specific information that needs to be documented (e.g., impression on physical examination).
    c. Circle **Dictate** if the doctor needs to dictate the entire report.
    d. Circle **Date** if the doctor needs to date a report, progress note, physician order, or other document.

NOTE: Shaded areas on the deficiency form are included to assist you in identifying the responsible doctor for each report.

EXAMPLE 1: When reviewing the inpatient face sheet, if the attending physician documented abbreviations, circle **No Abbreviations**. The physician would then write out the meanings of abbreviations.

EXAMPLE 2: When reviewing the record, if the discharge summary is missing, circle **Dictate** so that the physician is prompted to dictate the report. When the report is later transcribed and placed in the record, cross off **Dictate** and circle **Sign**. You won't be able to complete that aspect of analysis during this assignment.

EXAMPLE 3: If the patient had a consultation ordered, and the report is present on the record but not signed, enter the consulting doctor's name after **Other Dr:** in column 3, and circle **Sign** for the **Consultation Report** entry.

Deficiency Form

Patient Name: _____ Patient Number: _____ Admission Date: _____

NAME OF REPORT	Dr[1]: _____			Dr[2]: _____			Dr[2]: _____		
Inpatient Face Sheet	Sign No Abbreviations Complete _____								
Discharge Summary	Dictate	Sign							
History & Physical	Dictate	Sign							
Consultation Report				Dictate	Sign		Dictate	Sign	
Admission Progress Note	Document	Date	Sign						
Daily Progress Notes	Document	Date	Sign	Document	Date	Sign	Document	Date	Sign
Discharge Progress Note	Document	Date	Sign						
Physician Orders	Document	Date	Sign	Document	Date	Sign	Document	Date	Sign
Discharge Order	Document	Date	Sign						
Anesthesia Report				Document	Sign		Document	Sign	
Preanesthesia Evaluation				Document	Sign		Document	Sign	
Postanesthesia Evaluation				Document	Sign		Document	Sign	
Operative Report	Dictate	Sign		Dictate	Sign		Dictate	Sign	
Pathology Report				Dictate	Sign		Dictate	Sign	
Recovery Room Record				Document	Sign		Document	Sign	
Radiology Report				Document	Sign		Document	Sign	
Other: _____ _____	Document Date	Dictate Sign		Document Date	Dictate Sign		Document Date	Dictate Sign	

Figure 6-1 Deficiency Form (also located on the Student Companion website)

Name of Inpatient Record Report	Quantitative Analysis Guidelines
Patient Identification	Review each report for: • Patient name • Patient record number • Hospital room number • Date of admission • Attending physician
Face Sheet	Review for presence of admission date/time, discharge date/time, and admission diagnosis. If dates/times are missing, enter them based on documentation in progress notes and physician orders. If admission diagnosis is missing, contact the Admission Department for information to be entered. Review for attending physician documentation of: • Principal diagnosis • Secondary diagnoses (e.g., comorbidities, complications) • Principal procedure • Secondary procedures • Condition at discharge • Authentication by attending physician **Note:** Abbreviations are not allowed when documenting diagnoses and/or procedures. If abbreviations are noted, instruct attending physician to write out full diagnosis/procedure.
Informed Consents for Admission/ Treatment, Release of Information, Advance Directives, and Surgery	Completed upon admission of patient to facility. (If not properly completed, contact your supervisor so Admission Department staff can receive in-service education.)
Discharge Summary	Review for documentation of: • Chief complaint (or reason for admission) • History of present illness • Significant findings during inpatient care, including preadmission testing (PAT) • Procedures performed/treatment rendered, and patient's response • Condition at discharge • Discharge instructions (e.g., physical activity, medications, diet, follow-up care) • Final diagnoses (principal diagnosis, comorbidities, and complications) • Authentication by attending physician **Note:** A discharge progress note (containing elements above) may be substituted for a discharge summary *if* the patient's stay is less than 48 hours, or for normal newborn infants and uncomplicated obstetrical deliveries.
Emergency Department (ED) Record[1]	Review for documentation of: • Arrival date, time, mode (including responsible party, such as ambulance co.) • History of present illness/injury • Physical findings (including vital signs) • Emergency care provided prior to arrival in ED • Treatment rendered in ED and results • Diagnosis • Inpatient admission order, if applicable • Referrals to other care providers • Authentication by ED physician [1]An emergency department record is included in the record only if the patient was admitted through the emergency department.

Figure 6-2   Guide for Quantitative Analysis of Acute Care Hospital Discharged Inpatient Records

(Continues)

History	Review for documentation of:
	• Admission date
	• Chief complaint
	• History of present illness
	• Past, family, and social history (PFSH)
	• Review of systems (ROS)
	• Authentication by attending physician
	Note: The history must be dictated and filed in the record within 24 hours of admission.
Physical Examination	Review for documentation of:
	• Findings for each body structure (e.g., neck, chest, abdomen)
	• Impression (or provisional diagnosis, admission diagnosis, tentative diagnosis)
	• Results of PAT
	• Inpatient hospital plan
	• Authentication by attending physician
	Note: The physical examination must be dictated within 24 hours of admission.

Note: If a *complete* history and physical examination was documented in the physician's office within 30 days prior to inpatient admission, a legible copy may be placed in the inpatient record instead of requiring the attending physician to document a new history and physical examination.

Interval History and Physical Examination[2]	Review for documentation of:
	• Chief complaint
	• History of present illness
	• Changes in patient's condition since previous admission
	• Changes in physical examination findings since previous admission
	• Impression
	• Authentication of attending physician
	[2]An Interval history and physical examination is documented only if patient is readmitted to hospital within 30 days for the same condition *and* the hospital utilizes a unit medical record. The previous inpatient history and physical examination report must be made available (e.g., copy filed in the current admission record). If the patient is scheduled for surgery during current inpatient admission, a complete physical examination is documented.
Consultation	Review for documentation of:
	• Date of consultation
	• Statement that patient was examined and record was reviewed
	• Findings
	• Opinion
	• Recommendations
	• Authentication by consulting physician
	Note: Be sure to review physician orders for documentation of consultation order by attending physician.
Progress Notes	Review each progress note for documentation of:
	• Date
	• Frequency dependent on patient's condition (e.g., intensive care unit patient record contains multiple daily progress notes)
	• Authentication by documenting physician
	In addition, review for documentation of:
	• Admission note
	• Discharge note
	Note: A discharge progress note (containing discharge summary elements) may be substituted for a discharge summary *if* the patient's stay is less than 48 hours, or for normal newborn infants and uncomplicated obstetrical deliveries.

Figure 6-2 *(Continued)* **Guide for Quantitative Analysis of Acute Care Hospital Discharged Inpatient Records**

(Continues)

Physician's Orders	Review each physician order for documentation of:
	• Date
	• Authentication by responsible physician
	In addition, review for documentation of:
	• Discharge order (except in the case of patient expiration)
	Note: Verbal orders (e.g., telephone order or voice order) are documented by qualified personnel (nurse, pharmacist, and so on as determined by facility) and authenticated (countersigned) by responsible physician within 24 hours.
Anesthesia Record	Review for documentation of:
	• Anesthetic dosages and fluids
	• Techniques
	• Unusual events
	• Documentation of vital signs
	• Status of patient at conclusion of anesthesia
	• Date of surgery
	• Name of procedure/surgeon/anesthesiologist
	• Authentication of anesthesiologist
Preanesthesia Note	Review for documentation of:
	• Note prior to surgery
	• Patient's capacity to undergo anesthesia
	• Physician's review of objective diagnostic data
	• Interview with patient to discuss medications/anesthetics/drug history
	• Patient's physical status
	• Type of anesthesia to be administered
	• Procedure to be performed
	• Patient risks/complications
	• Authentication by anesthesiologist
Postanesthesia Note	Review for documentation of:
	• Note 3-24 hours after surgery
	• Postoperative abnormalities or complications (if any)
	• Vital signs and level of consciousness
	• Presence or absence of swallowing reflex and/or cyanosis
	• General condition of patient
	• IV fluids and drugs administered
	• Unusual events and postoperative complications (and management)
	• Authentication by anesthesiologist
Operative Report	Review for documentation of:
	• Dictation immediately following surgery (in progress notes)
	Note: If operative report cannot be dictated by surgeon immediately following surgery, surgeon should document complete handwritten report in progress notes.
	• Preoperative and postoperative diagnoses
	• Name of operation/procedure performed
	• Names of surgeon and assistants (if any)
	• Description of operative findings
	• Technical procedures utilized

Figure 6-2 (*Continued*) **Guide for Quantitative Analysis of Acute Care Hospital Discharged Inpatient Records**

(Continues)

	• Specimens removed	
	• Authentication by surgeon	
Recovery Room Record	Review for documentation of:	
	• Vital signs	
	• Level of consciousness upon transfer to and from recovery room	
	• Order for patient to return to room (physician orders)	
	• Authentication by nurse or anesthesiologist	
Pathology Report	Review for documentation of:	
	• Report within 24 hours of completion of tissue macroscopic/microscopic review	
	• Gross (macroscopic) exam of tissue	
	• Microscopic exam of tissue	
	• Pathological diagnosis	
	• Date of exam of tissue	
	• Authentication by pathologist	
Ancillary Service Reports	Review for documentation of:	
	• Physician's order for ancillary service (e.g., ECG, laboratory)	
	• Date	
	• Name of exam	
	• Results	
	• Authentication by responsible provider	
	Note: Laboratory reports are usually unauthenticated because they are computer-generated printouts. They may contain the printed name (or initials) of the laboratory technician.	
Radiology Reports	Review for documentation of:	
	• Physician's order for radiology service	
	• Date	
	• Name of exam	
	• Results	
	• Impression	
	• Authentication by radiologist	
Physical Rehabilitation	Review for documentation of:	
	• Reason for referral (attending physician's progress note and/or physician order)	
	• Date of physical rehabilitation progress note (e.g., physical therapy, occupational therapy, psychological services, recreational therapy, social work services, speech/language pathology, audiology services, vocational rehabilitative services)	
	• Summary of patient's clinical condition	
	• Goals of treatment	
	• Treatment plan	
	• Treatment and progress notes with ongoing assessments	
	• Authentication by therapist	
	Note: Responsible physician should document progress notes reflecting patient's response to therapy	
Autopsy Report	Review for documentation of:	
	• Provisional anatomic diagnosis (within 3 days after autopsy)	
	• Complete protocol (within 60 days after autopsy)	
	• Authentication by pathologist	

Figure 6-2 (*Continued*) **Guide for Quantitative Analysis of Acute Care Hospital Discharged Inpatient Records**

Retrieve Case01 and a blank deficiency slip, and review this quantitative analysis "walkthrough." *To get started, enter the following information at the top of the deficiency slip:*

- *Marsha Dennis* (patient name)
- *Case01* (patient number)
- *4-27-YYYY* (admission date)
- *Thompson* (Dr[1]:) (He is the attending physician and, therefore, responsible for the majority of documentation.)

NOTE: As you review the case for deficiencies, if you notice documentation that seems out of place, it is likely that it is incorrectly documented in that patient's record (e.g., progress note written in wrong patient's record). Be sure to mark the deficiency slip so that the responsible physician corrects the entry. (To correct this type of entry, the responsible physician draws one line through the entry, writes the words "error; entry documented in wrong patient record," and dates and authenticates the entry.)

INPATIENT FACE SHEET

- Review the entire record to determine whether any diagnoses are missing from the inpatient face sheet.
- For Case01, the physician did not document all of the diagnoses; review the pathology report to see what I mean. *To determine if procedures are missing from the face sheet, review the operative report(s). Circle **Complete** in column 1 of the deficiency slip, and enter "dx" so the doctor knows to enter the complete diagnostic statement and additional diagnoses. (For other cases, review the inpatient face sheet to determine if it is missing diagnoses or procedures when compared to documentation in the record.)*
- The abbreviation D&C is used on the face sheet. Circle the words "No abbreviations." The words "No abbreviations" means that no abbreviations can be used on the face sheet.
- The "discharge instructions" are not documented. *You already circled **Complete** on the deficiency slip because the diagnoses are incompletely documented, so enter "disch instr" to alert the doctor to complete this section of the form.*
- There is no physician authentication (signature) at the bottom of the form. *Circle **Sign** in column 1 of the deficiency slip. In a facility, you would also flag this page with a paperclip, post-it note, etc., so the doctor can easily refer to the form to complete it.*
- Verify that **Discharge Date**, **Time**, and **Days** have been entered. If information is incomplete, refer to physician orders for discharge date and progress notes for discharge time, and calculate days by counting the day of admission in the total but **not** the date of discharge. *For Case01, the discharge date is 4-29-YYYY, the discharge time is 1:35 p.m. (1335 in military time) on the physician discharge order, and days are calculated as 2 (because you count the day of admission but not the day of discharge).*

CONSENT TO ADMISSION

- This form is completed by patient registration staff upon admission of the patient to the hospital.
- If incomplete at discharge, bring to your supervisor's attention so patient registration staff can receive in-service education as to proper completion of the form.
- *Case01 Consent to Admission is properly completed.*

ADVANCE DIRECTIVE

- This form is also completed by patient registration staff upon admission of the

Figure 6-3   Quantitative Analysis: Walkthrough of Case01

(Continues)

> patient to the hospital. **Federal law requires completion of this type of form by each patient upon admission.**
>
> - If incomplete at discharge, bring to your supervisor's attention so patient registration staff can receive in-service education as to proper completion of the form.
> - *Case01 Advance Directive is properly completed.*
>
> ## DISCHARGE SUMMARY
>
> - The discharge summary must be placed on the record within 30 days after discharge. The attending physician usually dictates the discharge summary, and health information department medical transcriptionists transcribe the report and file it on the discharged inpatient record.
> - *Case01 does not contain discharge summary, so circle **Dictate** in column 1 of the deficiency slip.*
>
> ## HISTORY & PHYSICAL EXAM
>
> - The history & physical exam must be placed on the record within 24 hours of admission.
> - *Case01 contains no history & physical exam, so circle **Dictate** in column 1 of the deficiency slip.*
>
> ## CONSULTATION REPORT
>
> - Review the physician orders for an order for consultation.
> - *Because Case01 does not contain an order for consultation, no consultation report is required; so, leave this blank on the deficiency slip.*
>
> ## ADMISSION PROGRESS NOTE
>
> - Review the progress notes for documentation of an admission progress note. Be sure it is authenticated.
> - *Case01 does not contain an admission progress note, so circle **Document** in column 1 of the deficiency slip.*
>
> ## DAILY PROGRESS NOTES
>
> - Review the daily progress notes to be sure they are documented as warranted by the patient's condition. Usually there is at least one progress note document for each day the patient remains in the hospital. However, sometimes multiple progress notes are documented on a single day (e.g., critical patient). It would be unusual for a physician to not document a progress note for each day, but this occasionally happens. If the patient is stable, this might not be a deficiency that the physician would need to correct.
> - *Case01 contains daily progress notes, but the 4/27/YYYY note is not authenticated. So, circle **Sign** in column 2 on the deficiency slip. Because this note was documented by the anesthesiologist, enter Galloway at the top of that column. He is the anesthesiologist. In order to determine that this note was documented by the anesthesiologist, you must read and understand the content of progress notes.*
> - *The 4/28/YYYY and 4/29/YYYY progress notes documented by Dr. Thompson are unauthenticated. So, circle **Sign** in column 1 on the deficiency slip.*
>
> ## DISCHARGE PROGRESS NOTE
>
> - Review the final progress note to determine if it is the discharge progress note.
> - *Case01 contains an incomplete discharge progress note because it doesn't include documentation of the patient's hospital outcome, condition on discharge (disposition), provisions for follow-up care including instructions,*

Figure 6-3 *(Continued)* **Quantitative Analysis: Walkthrough of Case01**

(Continues)

*and final diagnoses. So, circle **Document** in column 1 of the deficiency slip.*

PHYSICIAN ORDERS

- Review physician orders to make sure that entries are dated and authenticated.
- *For Case01, Dr. Thompson did not authenticate the 4/27/YYYY order, so circle **Sign** in column 1 of the deficiency slip.*

NOTE: On 4/27/YYYY, Dr. Townsend called the nursing unit to dictate physician orders to the nurse; this is called a telephone order (T.O.). L. Mosher, RN, documented the order and the abbreviation "RAV," which means "read and verified" – this means the nurse followed the hospital policy that requires any order called in by the physician to be dictated back to the doctor for verification of accuracy. She also authenticated the order as "T.O. Dr. Townsend/L Mosher, RN." Dr. Townsend then cosigns the order within 24 hours.

DISCHARGE ORDER

- The attending physician is responsible for documenting a discharge order (except when a patient dies). It can be as simple as "Discharge." However, it is best if the physician documents the discharge destination (e.g., home, home health care, nursing facility).
- *Case01 discharge order is documented and authenticated, so leave this blank on the deficiency slip.*

CONSENT FOR OPERATION(S) AND/OR PROCEDURE(S) AND ANESTHESIA

- This form is completed by the operating physician after discussion of the procedure, potential risks, and complications with the patient.
- If incomplete at discharge, bring to your supervisor's attention so surgeons can receive in-service education as to proper completion of the form.
- *Case01 Consent for Operation(s) and/or Procedure(s) and Anesthesia is properly completed.*

ANESTHESIA RECORD

- The anesthesia record is documented and authenticated by the circulating and scrub nurses, and it is also authenticated by either the anesthesiologist or certified registered nurse anesthetist (CRNA), whoever provided anesthesia services during surgery.
- *Case01 anesthesia record is properly documented and authenticated, so leave this blank on the deficiency slip.*

PREANESTHESIA AND POSTANESTHESIA RECORD

- This preanesthesia report is documented by the anesthesiologist 24 hours or more prior to the patient's surgery. The postanesthesia evaluation is documented by the anesthesiologist about 3 hours after surgery. **NOTE:** Some anesthesiologists document their pre- and postanesthesia evaluations in the progress notes instead of on this record.
- *Case01 preanesthesia and postanesthesia record is properly documented and authenticated, so leave this blank on the deficiency slip.* **NOTE:** Dr. Galloway documented progress notes in addition to the pre- and postanesthesia record.

OPERATIVE REPORT

- The operative report is to be dictated by the surgeon immediately following surgery, transcribed, and placed on the patient's record. This is important in case the patient develops complications and physicians need to refer to the operative report documentation shortly following treatment. If there is a medical transcription delay, the surgeon must document comprehensive progress notes describing the surgery.

Figure 6-3 *(Continued)* **Quantitative Analysis: Walkthrough of Case01**

(Continues)

- *Case01 operative report is present and authenticated by the surgeon, so leave this blank on the deficiency slip.*

PATHOLOGY REPORT

- The pathologist reviews tissue (and other items removed from patients) during and after surgery and dictates a pathology report, which is placed on the patient's record.

- *Case01 pathology report is present and authenticated by the pathologist, so leave this blank on the deficiency slip.* If the pathology report was missing or the pathologist's authentication was required, indicate this deficiency in column 3 of the deficiency slip (because neither the attending physician nor anesthesiologist is responsible for the pathology report).

RECOVERY ROOM RECORD

- The recovery room record is documented and authenticated by the recovery room nurse. Neither the anesthesiologist nor the surgeon authenticates this report.

- *Case01 recovery room report is present and authenticated, so leave this blank on the deficiency slip.*

LAB REPORTS

- Review the physician orders to make sure that any lab work ordered by the physician is present in the record. Do not mark the deficiency slip for completion if absent. Instead, find the reports and file them in the record.

- EXAMPLE: If the physician ordered a urinalysis, look for the results of urinalysis in the lab data section of the record.

- *On the job, you would locate the reports and place them in the record.*

RADIOLOGY REPORT

- Review the physician orders to make sure that the results of any x-rays ordered by the physician are present in the record.

- EXAMPLE: If the physician ordered a chest x-ray, look for a transcribed radiology report that is authenticated by the radiologist.

- *Case01 radiology report is present and authenticated, so leave this blank on the deficiency slip.*

Figure 6-3 (*Continued*) **Quantitative Analysis: Walkthrough of Case01**

LAB ASSIGNMENT 6-3   Operative Report Documentation Elements

OBJECTIVES

At the end of this assignment, the student should be able to:

* Identify the documentation elements that are included in an operative report.

Overview

A paper-based record system requires that a single individual be responsible for the control and design of all forms adopted for use in the patient record. In an electronic health care record, the same documentation elements that were previously recorded on paper need to be documented in the electronic health record.

Instructions

1. In your textbook, go to the section of Chapter 6 that discusses documentation requirements for an operative report. Compare those requirements to the paper-based operative report (Figure 6-4) used by Sunny Valley Medical Center. You will find that this operative report is out-of-date.

2. Assume that you have been asked to design a format for a computer screen that will capture all the documentation elements that are needed for an electronic version of the operative report. Be sure to include all of the documentation elements as well as the following:
   a. Patient identification information such as name, patient record number, etc.
   b. Header for the name and address of the facility.

```
                                              OPERATIVE RECORD

Name                          Ward

Date                          Hist #

Service                       Surgeon

Preoperative Dx:

Postoperative Dx:

Surgery Performed:

Postion                       Duration

Anesthetist

Duration

DESCRIPTION (Incision, Findings, Technique, Sutures, Drainage Culture, Specimen,
Clean, Borderline, Septic)













Condition:
Medication:
Drains:
F 550
```

Figure 6-4   Operative Report Used by Sunny Valley Medical Center

Chapter 7

Numbering & Filing Systems and Record Storage & Circulation

❦ INTRODUCTION

This chapter will focus on familiarizing the student with numbering and filing systems, filing equipment, file folders, filing controls, circulation systems, and the security of health information.

LAB ASSIGNMENT 7-1   Straight Numeric and Terminal-Digit Filing

OBJECTIVES

At the end of this assignment, the student should be able to:

- Sequence patient record numbers in straight numeric filing order
- Sequence patient record numbers in terminal-digit filing order

Overview

In straight numeric filing, records are filed in strict chronologic order according to patient number, from the lowest to the highest number. Terminal-digit filing is used in health care facilities that assign six-digit patient numbers because the number can be easily subdivided into three parts: primary, secondary, and tertiary digits. This assignment will familiarize the student with organizing patient numbers according to the straight numeric and terminal-digit filing order.

Instructions

1. Refer to the straight numeric and terminal-digit filing sections of Chapter 7 in your textbook.
2. Resequence patient record numbers in straight numeric order in column 2 and in terminal-digit order in column 3.
3. Then assign the next straight numeric and terminal-digit number in the sequence.
4. To get you started, the first two rows of each are completed.

Student Name _____

Straight Numeric and Terminal-Digit Order of Patient Record Numbers

PART I: Resequence patient record numbers in straight numeric order (column 2) and terminal-digit order (column 3).

	Straight Numeric Order	Terminal-Digit Order
031950	031950	878912
101075	061946	884325
212153		
651473		
451450		
901895		
608946		
516582		
878912		
061946		
990855		
894851		
619546		
625497		
884325		
606339		
129456		
213526		

PART II: State the next straight numeric and terminal-digit number for the sequencing of records in the file.

	Straight Numeric Order	Terminal-Digit Order
651430	651431	661430
845626	845627	855626
489225		
231027		
689212		
948312		
980855		
894851		
619546		
625497		
884325		
606339		
129456		
213526		

LAB ASSIGNMENT 7-2   Calculating Record Storage Needs

OBJECTIVES

At the end of this assignment, the student should be able to:

- Calculate record storage needs
- Determine the number of shelving units needed to store patient records

Overview

When purchasing filing equipment, the number of filing units for purchase must be predetermined. This assignment will familiarize the student with calculating record storage needs and determining the number of filing units needed.

Instructions

1. Calculate the number of filing units to be purchased for each of the five cases on the following page.

    EXAMPLE: A 9-shelf unit contains 50 inches per shelf. There are 18,000 inches of current records to be housed, and it is projected that an additional 5,000 filing inches will be needed.

    Step 1:   Calculate the total filing inches available per shelf unit.

    $9 \times 50 = 450$ filing inches per unit

    Step 2:   Total the inches of current records and projected inches.

    $18,000 + 5,000 = 23,000$ inches to be housed

    Step 3:   Divide inches to be housed by filing inches per unit, which determines the number of shelving units to be purchased.

    $23,000 \div 450 = 51.1$ shelving units

    NOTE: Because ".1" (one-tenth) of a filing unit cannot be purchased, round to 52 filing units.

Student Name _____

Calculating Record Storage Needs

Case 1
10-shelf unit. 50 inches/shelf. 15,000 inches of
current records. 8,000 projected inches needed
for future.

Case 2
12-shelf unit. 150 inches/shelf. 21,000 inches of
current records. 6,000 projected inches needed
for future.

Case 3
20-shelf unit. 125 inches/shelf. 145,000 inches of
current records. 20,000 projected inches needed
for future.

Case 4
10-shelf unit. 135 inches/shelf. 27,000 inches of
current records. 2,400 projected inches needed
for future.

Case 5
15-shelf unit. 50 inches/shelf. 15,000 inches of
current records. 10,000 projected inches needed
for future.

LAB ASSIGNMENT 7-3   Guiding Terminal-Digit Files

OBJECTIVES

At the end of this assignment, the student should be able to:

- Calculate the number of file guides needed for a terminal-digit filing system
- Determine the number pattern for terminal-digit file guides

Overview

File guides are used to facilitate the filing and retrieval of patient records in a file system. This assignment will familiarize the student with identifying the number of file guides needed for file areas, as well as the pattern used to guide the files.

Instructions

1. Determine the number of file guides to be purchased as well as the pattern used to guide the terminal-digit files.

    EXAMPLE: The terminal-digit file area contains 125,000 records, and the standard rule of 50 records between file guides will be used. (Remember, there are 100 primary sections in a terminal-digit system, and there are 100 secondary sections in each primary section.)

    Step 1:   Calculate the number of file guides to be purchased.

    125,000 ÷ 50 = 2,500 file guides

    Step 2:   Determine the number of secondary guides for each primary section.

    2,500 ÷ 100 = 25 secondary guides for each primary section

    Step 3:   Determine the pattern to guide each primary section.

    100 ÷ 25 = 4

    Thus, for primary section 00, secondary guides will appear as:

    00 04 00
    00 08 00
    00 12 00
    00 16 00
    00 20 00
    etc.

Student Name _____

Guiding Terminal-Digit Files

1. Hospital XYZ has 60,000 records in its terminal-digit file area.

2. Hospital ABC has 80,000 records in its terminal-digit file area.

3. Hospital LMN has 100,000 records in its terminal-digit file area.

LAB ASSIGNMENT 7-4   Assigning Pseudonumbers

OBJECTIVES

At the end of this assignment, the student should be able to:
- Assign pseudonumbers to patients
- Explain the purpose of assigning pseudonumbers

Overview

Pseudonumbers are assigned to any patient who does not have a SSN when it is used as the patient record numbering system. This assignment will familiarize the student with assigning pseudonumbers.

Instructions

1. Assign a pseudonumber to each patient listed below. Refer to Chapter 7 in your textbook to review the purpose of assigning pseudonumbers.

    Pseudonumbers

abc	1	jkl	4	stu	7
def	2	mno	5	vwx	8
ghi	3	pqr	6	yz	9

    NOTE: If the patient has no middle initial, assign 0.

    NOTE: The assigned pseudonumber uses the same format as the SSN (e.g., 000-00-0000).

    EXAMPLE: Mark R. Anderson. DOB 11/1/92. Pseudonumber: 561-11-0192.

(handwritten)
Name   month   day/year
561 – 11 – 0192

227 – 05 – 0330

Student Name _____

Assigning Pseudonumbers

Patient Name and DOB	Pseudonumber
Edward Francis Smart, 5/3/30	
Joseph Kenneth First, 9/18/37	
Eleanor Delores Comp, 7/4/45	
William David Love, 4/15/58	
Sherrie Rebecca Gage, 8/19/67	
Matthew David Brothers, 10/15/89	
Michelle Brittany Ash, 12/30/84	
Robert James Shumaker, 8/7/59	
Michaela Grace, 1/10/87	

LAB ASSIGNMENT 7-5   Assigning Soundex Codes

OBJECTIVES

At the end of this assignment, the student should be able to:

* Assign Soundex codes to patient names
* Explain the reason Soundex codes are assigned to patient names

Overview

The Soundex indexing system allows names that sound alike but are spelled differently to be indexed together. This means that surnames (last names) are indexed so they can be found regardless of spelling. This assignment will familiarize the student with assigning Soundex codes to patient names.

Instructions

1. Review the rules for assigning Soundex codes in Chapter 7 of your textbook.
2. Assign a Soundex code to each patient listed on the following page.
3. To get you started, several codes have been assigned.

Student Name _____

Assigning Soundex Codes

EXAMPLE: To begin the process of assigning a phonetic code for patient Anderson, enter the first letter of the last name followed by a dash (A-). Then, disregarding that letter, assign a number to remaining letters according to the Soundex rules. Assign 5 to the n, 3 to the d, and 6 to the r. Do not assign numbers to vowels or the letters remaining after r (because the maximum length of the code is three numbers).

Anderson	A-536
Condor	
Senator	
Darlington	D-645
Goodyear	
Levy	
Shaw	
Abbott	
Farrell	
Mann	M-500
Jackson	
Biggs	
McCarthy	
Todt	
Gjeljuag	
Lloyd	
Schkolnick	
Skow	
Henman	

Chapter 8

Indexes, Registers, and Health Data Collection

❦ INTRODUCTION

This chapter will familiarize the student with indexes, registers, case abstracting, and health data collection.

LAB ASSIGNMENT 8-1 Case Abstracting

OBJECTIVES

At the end of this assignment, the student should be able to:

- List core data elements for the Uniform Hospital Discharge Data Set (UHDDS)
- Abstract discharged acute care patient records for the purpose of generating indexes (e.g., disease index)

Overview

Case abstracting involves collecting patient information from records and entering data into a computerized abstracting program (or onto paper abstracts for data entry into a computerized abstracting program) to generate indexes (e.g., physician, diagnosis, and procedure) and report data to state and federal agencies. This assignment will familiarize the student with abstracting UHDDS core data elements from discharged acute care patient records.

Instructions

1. Go to the Student Companion website and print one case abstracting form (Figure 8-1) for each patient record to be abstracted (10 total).
2. Refer to Appendix I, where Case01 through Case10 are located.
3. Refer to the Overview of Case Abstracting (Figure 8-2), and review a sample completed abstract (Figure 8-3).
4. Review the Case Abstracting: Walkthrough of Case01 (Figure 8-4).
5. Complete each abstracting form by entering data from Case01–Case10.
6. Submit completed abstracting forms to your instructor for evaluation.

SUNNY VALLEY MEDICAL CENTER ACUTE CARE (INPATIENT) CASE ABSTRACT

01 Hospital Number

02 Patient Date of Birth

Month   Day   Year (YYYY)

03 Patient Gender

1 Male
2 Female
3 Other
4 Unknown

04A Race

1 American Indian/Eskimo/Aleut
2 Asian or Pacific Islander
3 Black
4 White
5 Other
6 Unknown

04B Ethnicity

1 Spanish origin/Hispanic
2 Non-Spanish origin/Non-Hispanic
3 Unknown

05A Living Arrangement

1 Alone
2 With spouse
3 With children
4 With parent or guardian
5 With relative other than spouse
6 With nonrelatives
7 Unknown

05B Marital Status

1 Married
2 Single
3 Divorced
4 Separated
5 Unknown

06 Patient Number

07 Admission Date and Hour

Month   Day   Year (YYYY)

Military Time

08 Type of Admission

1 Scheduled
2 Unscheduled

09 Discharge Date and Time

Month   Day   Year (YYYY)

Military Time

10 Attending Physician Number

11 Operating Physician Number

12 Principal Diagnosis Code

ICD Code

16 Birth Weight of Neonate

Kilograms

Date Abstract Completed

Month   Day   Year (YYYY)

13 Other Diagnosis Code(s)

14 Qualifiers for Other Diagnoses

1 Onset preceded hospital admission
2 Onset followed hospital admission
3 Uncertain whether onset preceded or followed hospital admission

ICD Code

ICD Code

ICD Code

ICD Code

ICD Code

ICD Code

17 Procedures, Dates, and Operating Physician UPIN

Month   Day   Year (YYYY)   UPIN

Month   Day   Year (YYYY)   UPIN

Month   Day   Year (YYYY)   UPIN

Month   Day   Year (YYYY)   UPIN

Month   Day   Year (YYYY)   UPIN

Month   Day   Year (YYYY)   UPIN

Month   Day   Year (YYYY)   UPIN

15 External Cause of Injury Codes

18 Disposition

1 Discharged to home
2 Discharged to acute care hospital
3 Discharged to nursing facility
4 Discharged home to be under the care of a home health service (including hospice)
5 Discharged to other health care facility
6 Left against medical advice (AMA)
7 Alive, other
8 Died

19 Patient's Expected Payment Source

1 Blue Cross/Blue Shield
2 Other commercial insurance
3 Other liability insurance
4 Medicare
5 Medicaid
6 Workers' Compensation
7 Self-insured employer plan
8 Health maintenance organization (HMO)

9 TRICARE
10 CHAMPVA
11 Other government payer
12 Self-pay
13 No charge (e.g., charity, special research, teaching)
14 Other

20 Total Charges

$

Figure 8-1 Case Abstracting Form for Use with ICD-10-CM Codes (also located on the Student Companion website) (Based on California Office of Statewide Health Planning and Development.)

Abstracting involves transferring information from the patient record onto a data entry source document called the case abstract or discharge data abstract. Two methods are typically used:

- *Paper abstract:* prepared for each discharged patient, batched, and sent to the facility's computer center or mailed to a commercial service

- *Online data entry:* abstracted data is entered into a computer and processed by the facility or data is transferred onto a disk and mailed to a commercial service, or data is transmitted to the commercial service using a modem

Advantages of facility-based abstracting systems include:

- Ready access to information from in-house data-processing department

- Less costly than a commercial service

Disadvantages of facility-based abstracting systems include:

- No access to national comparison statistical reports (e.g., comparison of one hospital's infection rate to another's)

- Other departments (e.g., payroll) may take priority when reports are being run

Advantages of a commercial abstracting service include:

- Comparative reports on national and areawide statistics are available

- Such services are in business to serve the health information management department

Disadvantages of a commercial abstracting service include:

- Can be costly (e.g., charge per discharged patient)

- Comparative reports can cost extra

Figure 8-2   Overview of Case Abstracting

SUNNY VALLEY MEDICAL CENTER ACUTE CARE (INPATIENT) CASE ABSTRACT

01 Hospital Number

| 0 | 0 | 0 | 9 | 9 | 9 |

02 Patient Date of Birth

| 0 | 5 | 3 | 0 | Y | Y | Y | Y |

Month Day Year (YYYY)

03 Patient Gender

1 Male
2 Female
3 Other
4 Unknown

2

04A Race

1 American Indian/Eskimo/Aleut
2 Asian or Pacific Islander
3 Black
4 White
5 Other
6 Unknown

3

04B Ethnicity

1 Spanish origin/Hispanic
2 Non-Spanish origin/Non-Hispanic
3 Unknown

2

05A Living Arrangement

1 Alone
2 With spouse
3 With children
4 With parent or guardian
5 With relative other than spouse
6 With nonrelatives
7 Unknown

2

05B Marital Status

1 Married
2 Single
3 Divorced
4 Separated
5 Unknown

1

06 Patient Number

| 1 | 2 | 3 | 4 | 5 | 6 |

07 Admission Date and Hour

| 1 | 0 | 1 | 0 | Y | Y | Y | Y |

Month Day Year (YYYY)

| 1 | 1 | 0 | 0 |

Military Time

08 Type of Admission

1 Scheduled
2 Unscheduled

1

09 Discharge Date and Time

| 1 | 0 | 1 | 3 | Y | Y | Y | Y |

Month Day Year (YYYY)

| 0 | 9 | 0 | 0 |

Military Time

10 Attending Physician Number

| 0 | 0 | 0 | 1 | 4 | 1 |

11 Operating Physician Number

| | | | | | |

12 Principal Diagnosis Code

| I | 2 | 1 | . | 0 | 9 | |

ICD Code

16 Birth Weight of Neonate

| | | | |

Kilograms

Date Abstract Completed

| 1 | 0 | 1 | 3 | Y | Y | Y | Y |

Month Day Year (YYYY)

13 Other Diagnosis Code(s)

14 Qualifiers for Other Diagnoses

1 Onset preceded hospital admission
2 Onset followed hospital admission
3 Uncertain whether onset preceded or followed hospital admission

17 Procedures, Dates, and Operating Physician UPIN

| 4 | A | 0 | 2 | 0 | N | 8 | | 1 | 0 | 1 | 0 | Y | Y | Y | Y | | 4 | 5 | B | 6 | 8 | 0 |

Month Day Year (YYYY) UPIN

| B | 2 | 0 | 1 | 0 | Z | Z | | 1 | 0 | 1 | 0 | Y | Y | Y | Y | | 4 | 5 | B | 6 | 8 | 0 |

Month Day Year (YYYY) UPIN

| I | 2 | 0 | . | 8 | | | ICD Code

| I | 1 | 0 | . | | | | ICD Code

| | | | . | | | | ICD Code

| | | | . | | | | ICD Code

| | | | . | | | | ICD Code

| | | | . | | | | ICD Code

Month Day Year (YYYY) UPIN

15 External Cause of Injury Codes

| | | | . | | | | |

| | | | . | | | | |

| | | | . | | | | |

| | | | . | | | | |

| | | | . | | | | |

18 Disposition

1 Discharged to home
2 Discharged to acute care hospital
3 Discharged to nursing facility
4 Discharged home to be under the care of a home health service (including hospice)
5 Discharged to other health care facility
6 Left against medical advice (AMA)
7 Alive, other
8 Died

1

19 Patient's Expected Payment Source

1 Blue Cross/Blue Shield
2 Other commercial insurance
3 Other liability insurance
4 Medicare
5 Medicaid
6 Workers' Compensation
7 Self-insured employer plan
8 Health maintenance organization (HMO)
9 TRICARE
10 CHAMPVA
11 Other government payer
12 Self-pay
13 No charge (e.g., charity, special research, teaching)
14 Other

1

20 Total Charges

$ | 2 | 8 | , | 9 | 4 | 5 | . | 5 | 9 |

Figure 8-3 Sample Completed Acute Care (Inpatient) Case Abstract (Note: This form is designed for use with ICD-10-CM and ICD-10-PCS codes.)

BLOCK 01:	Enter 000999 as the hospital number.
Block 02:	Enter patient's date of birth in MMDDYYYY format.
	EXAMPLE: 08021957
Block 03:	Enter 1-digit code for the patient's gender.
Block 04A:	Enter 1-digit code for the patient's race.
Block 04B:	Enter 1-digit code for the patient's ethnicity.
	NOTE: If race and ethnicity are not located on face sheet, review patient record.
Block 05A:	Enter 1-digit code for patient's living arrangement.
	NOTE: Review patient record to locate living arrangement.
Block 05B:	Enter 1-digit code for patient's marital status.
Block 06:	Enter 6-digit patient number.
	EXAMPLE: CASE01 Block 07:
	Enter patient's date of admission as MMDDYYYY.
	EXAMPLE: 01012004
	Enter time of admission as military time.
	EXAMPLE: 1300 (1 p.m.)
Block 09:	Enter patient's date of discharge as MMDDYYYY.
	EXAMPLE: 01012004
	Enter time of discharge as military time.
	EXAMPLE: 1300 (1 p.m.)
Block 10:	Enter attending physician UPIN found on the Inpatient Face Sheet.
Block 11:	Enter operating physician's UPIN.
Block 12:	Enter principal diagnosis code.
Block 13:	Enter secondary diagnosis code(s).
Block 14:	Enter the 1-digit number to indicate onset of condition.
	NOTE: Review admission progress note to determine onset.
Block 15:	Enter external cause of injury code, if applicable. Otherwise, leave blank.
Block 16:	If newborn, enter birth weight in kilograms. Otherwise, leave blank.
Block 17:	Enter principal procedure code.
Block 18:	Enter 1-digit number to indicate patient's disposition.
	NOTE: Review discharge progress note or discharge summary to locate disposition.
Block 19:	Enter 1- or 2-digit code to indicate patient's expected payment source.
	NOTE: Expected payment source is primary third-party payer (e.g., BCBS).
Block 20:	Enter charges.
	NOTE: Total charges are not documented in acute care inpatient records. This data will be input by the billing office.

Figure 8-4   Case Abstracting: Walkthrough of Case01

LAB ASSIGNMENT 8-2   Master Patient Index Data Entry

OBJECTIVES

At the end of this assignment, the student should be able to:

- Enter complete and accurate data into a master patient index card
- Explain the purpose of maintaining a master patient index

Overview

Complete and accurate data is entered into an automated master patient index (MPI) or onto MPI cards so that patient information can be easily retrieved. This assignment will familiarize the student with completion of an MPI card.

Instructions

1. Go to the Student Companion website and print the Master Patient Index Form (Figure 8-5).
2. Refer to Appendix I, where Case01 through Case10 are located.
3. Review the sample completed MPI (Figure 8-6).
4. Complete each MPI form for Case01 through Case10 by entering information from each record into each form. Many of the items are found on the face sheet; however, some items such as the patient's age, are found by reviewing the documents contained in the patient's record.
5. Submit completed MPI forms to your instructor for evaluation.

1. LAST NAME	2. FIRST NAME	3. MIDDLE NAME	4. GENDER	5. AGE	6. RACE	7. PATIENT NUMBER

8. ADDRESS			9. DATE OF BIRTH			10. THIRD PARTY PAYERS
			a. MONTH	b. DAY	c. YEAR	

11. MAIDEN NAME	12. PLACE OF BIRTH	13. SOCIAL SECURITY NUMBER (SSN)

14. ADMISSION DATE	15. DISCHARGE DATE	15. PROVIDER	17. ADMIT TYPE	18. DISCHARGE STATUS

Figure 8-5   Sample Blank Master Patient Index Card (also located on the Student Companion website)

1. LAST NAME	2. FIRST NAME	3. MIDDLE NAME	4. GENDER	5. AGE	6. RACE	7. PATIENT NUMBER
LAMBERT	PATRICIA	ANN	F	48	BLACK	123456

8. ADDRESS			9. DATE OF BIRTH			10. THIRD PARTY PAYERS
101 MAIN ST			a. MONTH	b. DAY	c. YEAR	BCBS
ALFRED NY 14802			05	30	YYYY	AETNA

11. MAIDEN NAME	12. PLACE OF BIRTH	13. SOCIAL SECURITY NUMBER (SSN)
SANFORD	ELMIRA, N.Y.	123-56-6789

14. ADMISSION DATE	15. DISCHARGE DATE	15. PROVIDER	17. ADMIT TYPE	18. DISCHARGE STATUS
1010YYYY	1013YYYY	GRIFFITH	3	HOME
0304YYYY	0306YYYY	GRIFFITH	4	HOME

Figure 8-6   Sample Completed Master Patient Index Card

LAB ASSIGNMENT 8-3   Disease, Procedure, and Physician Indexes

OBJECTIVES

At the end of this assignment, the student should be able to:

• Analyze data located on disease, procedure, and physician indexes
• Interpret data from disease, procedure, and physician indexes

Overview

Disease (Figure 8-7), procedure (Figure 8-8), and physician (Figure 8-9) indexes contain data abstracted from patient records and entered into a computerized database, from which the respective index is generated. This lab assignment will allow students to analyze and interpret data found in disease, procedure, and physician indexes.

Instructions

1. Answer each question by reviewing information in the appropriate index.
   a. What is the primary arrangement of the disease index?
   b. What is the primary arrangement of the procedure index?
   c. What is the primary arrangement of the physician index?
   d. How many different attending physicians treated patients listed on the disease index?
   e. How many different attending physicians treated patients listed on the procedure index?
   f. What is the average patient age treated by Dr. James Smith on the physician index?

2. The quality management committee has requested the following information. Determine the correct answer, and identify the index used to locate the information.
   a. Age of the youngest and oldest patient who underwent a culdoscopy.
   b. Secondary diagnoses codes for patients treated for acute poliomyelitis.
   c. Medical record numbers for patients treated by Dr. Jane Thompson.
   d. Medical record numbers of patients treated with salmonella enteritis as primary diagnosis.
   e. Age of the oldest patient treated for acute poliomyelitis by Dr. Jane Thompson.

```
                    Sunny Valley Medical Center
                          Disease Index
Reporting Period        0801YYYY60801YYYY              Date Prepared   08-02-YYYY

                                                                Page  1 of 5
```

Principal Diagnosis	Secondary Diagnoses	Attending Physician	Age	Gender	Payer	Patient Number
SALMONELLA ENTERITIS						
A02.0		138	24	M	BC	236248
A02.0	I10	024	35	M	BC	123456
A02.0		036	42	F	BC	213654
ACUTE POLIOMYELITIS						
A80.9	E11.9	236	80	M	MC	236954
A80.9	E78.5	235	60	F	MD	562159
A80.9	D64.9	138	34	F	WC	236268

Figure 8-7   Disease Index

```
                    Sunny Valley Medical Center

                         Procedure Index
Reporting Period        0301YYYY60301YYYY              Date Prepared   03-02-YYYY

                                                                Page  1 of 5
```

Principal Procedure	Secondary Procedures	Attending Physician	Age	Gender	Payer	Patient Number
BEAM, RADIATION, ABDOMEN, INTRAOPERATIVE						
DW033Z0		248	42	F	01	562359
CULDOSCOPY						
0UJH8ZZ		235	56	F	03	231587
0UJH8ZZ		326	27	F	02	239854
0UJH8ZZ		236	08	F	05	562198
0UJH8ZZ		236	88	F	05	615789
DIVISION, PERINEUM, FEMALE						
0W8NXZZ		326	43	F	03	653218

Figure 8-8   Procedure Index

Sunny Valley Medical Center

Physician Index

Reporting Period   0101YYYY60101YYYY   Date Prepared   01-02-YYYY

Page   1 of 5

Attending Physician	Patient Number	Age	Gender	Payer	Admission Date	Discharge Date	LOS	Principal Diagnosis
JAMES SMITH, M.D.								
024	123456	35	M	BC	1228YYYY	0101YYYY	4	A02.0
024	213654	42	F	BC	1229YYYY	0101YYYY	3	A02.0
024	236248	24	M	BC	1229YYYY	0101YYYY	3	A02.0
JANE THOMSON, M.D.								
025	236268	34	F	WC	1229YYYY	0101YYYY	3	A80.9
025	562159	60	F	MD	1230YYYY	0101YYYY	2	A80.9
025	236954	80	M	MC	1231YYYY	0101YYYY	1	A80.9

Figure 8-9   Physician Index

Chapter 9

Legal Aspects of Health Information Management

🌟 INTRODUCTION

This chapter will familiarize the student with legal aspects of documentation, legislation that impacts health information management, and release of protected health information (PHI).

LAB ASSIGNMENT 9-1   Notice of Privacy Practices

OBJECTIVES

At the end of this assignment, the student should be able to:

- Explain the standards for privacy of health information as established by the HIPAA Privacy Rule
- Analyze the contents of a Privacy Notice

Overview

Patients have a right to the privacy of their health information, and they must be provided with written notice of this right (e.g., Notice of Privacy Practices) when they receive services from health care facilities and providers. This assignment will familiarize the student with the HIPAA Privacy Rule and require the student to analyze a Notice of Privacy Practices.

Instructions

1. Using an Internet browser (e.g., Microsoft Internet Explorer, Google Chrome), go to www.ahima.org.
2. Click on HIM BODY OF KNOWLEDGE.
3. Click the "PRACTICE BRIEFS" folder. Search for the Practice Brief entitled "Notice of Privacy Practices (2013 Update)."
4. Review the practice brief, paying close attention to the section on federal requirements.
5. Review Figure 9-1, Notice of Privacy Practices, and determine whether the notice is complete as compared with the requirements listed in the AHIMA Practice Brief.
6. Prepare a brief summary of the deficiencies you found upon review of the Notice of Privacy Practices found in Figure 9-1.

Sunny Valley Medical Center

NOTICE OF PRIVACY PRACTICES

Effective Date: October 1, 2013

We are required by law to protect the privacy of health information and to provide you with a written copy of this notice outlining the health information privacy practices of our medical center. We are also required to abide by the terms of the notice currently in effect. We have the right to change the terms of this notice and will provide you with this revised notice upon your receiving health care services. The revised notice will be effective for all protected health information. You can also obtain your own copy by calling our office at 607-555-1234. *If you have any questions about this notice or would like further information, please contact: Ima Secret, Privacy Officer, Sunny Valley Medical Center, 100 Main St, Binghamton NY 13901, 607-555-1234.*

PERMITTED DISCLOSURES:

The following is a list of disclosures that will be made without authorization.

Treatment, Payment and Healthcare Operations.

We will only obtain written consent one time to use and disclose your health information for treatment, payment, and business operations. Your health information may be released to your insurance company in the processing of your bill.

Patient Directory and Disclosure to Family and Friends.

You will be asked if you have any objection to including information about yourself in our Patient Directory. You will also be asked if you have any objection to sharing information about your health with your family and friends regarding your care.

Emergencies or Public Need.

We may use or disclose your health information in an emergency or for important public needs.

DISCLOSURES THAT REQUIRE AUTHORIZATION

All other uses and disclosures require authorization and will be made only with your written authorization. You also have the right to revoke the authorization at any time. To revoke a written authorization, please contact the Privacy Officer in writing.

PRIVACY RIGHTS

You have the right to:

- Request restrictions on certain uses and disclosures of information.

- Inspect and copy your health information.

- Receive a paper copy of this notice.

- Special privacy of HIV-related information, alcohol and substance abuse treatment information, mental health information, and genetic information.

Filing a Complaint

If you believe your privacy rights have been violated, you may file a complaint with our Privacy Officer. There will be no retaliation or action taken against you for filing a complaint.

Figure 9-1   Privacy Notice

LAB ASSIGNMENT 9-2 Release of Patient Information

OBJECTIVES

At the end of this assignment, the student should be able to:

- Determine circumstances for which it is appropriate to release patient information
- Communicate a suitable response to the requestor when it has been established that release of patient information is inappropriate

Overview

Facilities must obtain appropriate authorization prior to disclosing patient information; however, HIPAA delineates certain exceptions. This assignment will familiarize the student with the proper release of patient information.

Instructions

1. Review the case scenarios in Figure 9-2, and determine whether patient information should be released.
2. If the patient information should *not* be released, enter a response that would be communicated to the requestor.

1.	The local sheriff enters the medical record department and asks to see the patient record of a recently discharged patient. The patient was involved in a traffic accident and had left the scene. The identification of the agent appears to be in order. Do you release the information? Why or why not?
2.	You are the correspondence secretary and receive an authorization signed by the patient to release medical records to the Aetna Insurance Company. The authorization was signed and dated by the patient on January 27 of this year. According to your records, the patient was admitted to the hospital on January 30 of this year. Do you release the information? Why or why not?
3.	A medical student who is working on her master's degree research project needs to review the medical records of patients who have been diagnosed with myocardial infarction. The facility's policy is that students can review patient information under the supervision of a health information department staff member if the student provides a letter from their instructor indicating that such review is required. The student supplies the letter and agrees to be supervised during the review. Do you allow the student to review the records? Why or why not?
4.	You are served a properly executed *subpoena duces tecum* on a patient discharged last year with the diagnosis of pneumonia. The document states that a copy of the record can be submitted in lieu of your personal appearance in court. Your department routinely uses a record copy service to process requests for information, including *subpoena duces tecum* documents that allow for copies to be sent instead of a court appearance. Do you allow the record copy service to process the release of information to comply with this *subpoena duces tecum*? Why or why not?
5.	The minister of a patient who was recently discharged enters the health information department and states that he needs to view the medical record of a patient who is a member of his congregation. He explains that the patient is in a desperate situation, and he needs to understand the patient's medical situation so he can properly counsel the patient. (The minister also serves as hospital chaplain.) Do you release the information? Why or why not?
6.	Two police detectives arrive in the health information department and properly identify themselves. They inform you that the lab drew blood on an ED patient last night, and the blood vial was properly given to the transporter for the coroner's office. Unfortunately, the vial broke in transport. The detectives are requesting that you make a copy of the blood alcohol level that was documented in the patient's record so they can use it to make the case against the patient that he was driving while under the influence of alcohol. Do you release the information? Why or why not?
7.	The local district attorney arrives in the department with an authorization for release of information that is appropriately completed, signed, and dated by the patient. He is requesting access to the patient's records so he can review them. Do you release the information? Why or why not?
8.	The city police department desk sergeant calls the health information department and requests information of a medical nature on a patient who has been injured in a fight. Do you release the information? Why or why not?
9.	A physician from a neighboring city enters the health information department to review the record of a patient he is now treating. The physician is not on your hospital's medical staff. Do you allow him to review the information? Why or why not?
10.	You receive a telephone call from a hospital emergency department (ED) located in another state. The ED physician states that this is an emergency situation, and he needs to obtain pertinent medical information about a patient currently under treatment. Do you release the information? Why or why not?

Figure 9-2   Release of Information Case Scenarios

LAB ASSIGNMENT 9-3   Release of Information Correspondence Log

OBJECTIVES

At the end of this assignment, the student should be able to:

- Appropriately respond to correspondence requests for release of patient information
- Complete the entries in a correspondence log

Overview

Health information professionals are responsible for releasing patient information. To ensure proper release of patient information, an authorization must be obtained from the patient, and facilities must document information released to fulfill such requests. This assignment will familiarize the student with reviewing correspondence requests for information and entry of released patient information into a correspondence log.

Instructions

1. Go to the Student Companion website and print one copy of the release of information correspondence log form (Figure 9-3).
2. Refer to Appendix I, where Case01 through Case10 are located.
3. Review the requests for patient information (Figures 9-4A through 9-4J) to be used for Case01 through Case10.
4. Determine the following, and enter your responses on the correspondence log:
   a. Type of request
   b. Whether request was appropriately completed
   c. Response form letter to be used
   d. Information released and cost

NOTE: Specific instructions for processing release of information requests and completing the correspondence log are found in Table 9-1.

5. Submit the completed correspondence log to your instructor for evaluation.

Table 9-1 Instructions for Processing Release of Information Requests and Completing the Correspondence Log

Step 1: Review each request for information (Figures 9-4A through 9-4J) to determine the "type of request," and enter the type in column 1 of the correspondence log. Types of requests include:
- Attorney
- Blue Cross
- Commercial Insurance
- Court Order
- Hospital
- Physician
- *Subpoena Duces Tecum*

Step 2: Determine whether copies of records can be released in response to the request. Enter "Yes" or "No" in column 2 of the correspondence log.

NOTE: If you enter "No" on the correspondence log, indicate why records cannot be released. Reasons include:
- Authorization is not HIPAA compliant.
- Authorization is outdated. (This means the date the request was received in the department was more than 90 days after the patient signed/dated the authorization.)
- Authorization predates dates of service.

Step 3: Refer to the response form letter (Figure 9-5) and determine the number(s) that should be marked with an X.
- Select "A" if you are mailing copies of records and will charge for them.
- Select "B" if you are mailing copies of records and no payment is required.
- Select "C" if the patient's authorization for release of information was dated 90 days prior to the health information department receiving it for processing.
- Select "D" if the requestor did not include a HIPAA-compliant authorization signed by the patient or his/her representative.
- Select "E" if the patient's authorization to release information was dated prior to treatment provided.

Step 4: Enter the information released from the record in response to the request.
- Enter "entire record" if every page in the record would be copied.
- Enter the abbreviation for reports copied if the entire record was not copied. Abbreviations include the following:
  - Face sheet (FS)
  - Discharge summary (DS)
  - History & physical examination (HP)
  - Consultation (CON)
  - Progress notes (PN)
  - Doctors orders (DO)
  - Operative report (OP)
  - Laboratory tests (LAB)
  - Radiology reports (XRAY)
  - Nurses notes (NN)
- Enter "none" if you determined that records would not be sent in response to the request.

Step 5: Enter the charge for copies, if applicable.
- Enter "n/c" (no charge) for physician and hospital requests.
- Charge .75 cents per copy for requests from insurance companies and attorneys. To calculate the number of copies, refer to the patient record (because some reports are multiple pages).

NOTE: Pay attention to requests received from insurance companies as they sometimes specify what they will pay for copies of records. In that case, enter the amount specified (and not the 75 cents/page calculation).

CASE	TYPE OF REQUEST	IS REQUEST APPROPRIATE? (IF NO, WHY NOT?)	RESPONSE FORM LETTER SENT	REPORTS RELEASED AND COST
CORRESPONDENCE LOG				
1	Physician	Yes	B	Entire record $0.00
2				
3				
4				
5				
6				
7				
8				
9				
10				

Figure 9-3   Release of Information Correspondence Log (also located on the Student Companion website)

Case01 – Request for Information

Received in Health Information Department for processing on June 1, (this year).

AUTHORIZATION FOR DISCLOSURE OF PROTECTED HEALTH INFORMATION (PHI)

(1) I hereby authorize Sunny Valley Medical Center to disclose/obtain information from the health records of:

Marsha Dennis	02/09/YYYY	(607) 555-7771
Patient Name	Date of Birth (mmddyyyy)	Telephone (w/ area code)
344 Maple Avenue, Alfred NY 14802		Case01
Patient Address		Medical Record Number

(2) Covering the period(s) of health care:

04/27/YYYY	04/29/YYYY		
From (mmddyyyy)	To (mmddyyyy)	From (mmddyyyy)	To (mmddyyyy)

(3) I authorize the following information to be released by Sunny Valley Medical Center (check applicable reports):

❑ Face Sheet	❑ Progress Notes	❑ Pathology Report	❑ Drug Abuse Care
❑ Discharge Summary	❑ Lab Results	❑ Nurses Notes	☒ Other: Entire record
❑ History & Physical Exam	❑ X-ray Reports	❑ HIV Testing Results	
❑ Consultation	❑ Scan Results	❑ Mental Health Care	
❑ Doctors Orders	❑ Operative Report	❑ Alcohol Abuse Care	

This information is to be disclosed to ~~or obtained from~~:

Dr. Raymond Beecher	9 Langston Dr, St. Petersburg, FL 00000	(800) 555-5698
Name of Organization	Address of Organization	Telephone Number
for the purpose of:	follow-up treatment by Dr. Beecher.	

Statement that information used or disclosed may be subject to re-disclosure by the recipient and may no longer be protected by this rule.
(4) I understand that I have a right to revoke this authorization at any time. I understand that if I revoke this authorization I must do so in writing and present my written revocation to the Heath Information Management Department. I understand that the revocation will not apply to information that has already been released in response to this authorization. I understand that the revocation will not apply to my insurance company when the law provides my insurer with the right to contest a claim under my policy. Unless otherwise revoked, this authorization will expire on the following date, event, or condition.

5/25/(next year)			
Expiration Date		Expiration Event	Expiration Condition

If I fail to specify an expiration date, event or condition, this authorization will expire within six (6) months.

Signature of individual and date.
(5) I understand that authorizing the disclosure of this health information is voluntary. I can refuse to sign this authorization. I need not sign this form in order to assure treatment. I understand that I may inspect or copy the information to be used or disclosed, provided in CFR 164.534. I understand that any disclosure of information carries with it the potential for an unauthorized redisclosure and may not be protected by federal confidentiality rules. If I have questions about disclosure of my health information, I can contact the Privacy Officer at Sunny Valley Medical Center.

Signed:

Marsha Dennis	May 25, (this year)
Signature of Patient or Legal Representative	Date

Figure 9-4A   Case01 Request for Information

Case02 – Request for Information

Received in Health Information Department for processing on July 30, (this year).

EMPIRE BLUE CROSS AND BLUE SHIELD of Central New York
344 South Warren Street, Box 4809
Syracuse, New York 13221
315/424-3700

July 15, (this year)

ATTENTION: Health Information Department

                  Sunny Valley Medical Center

Patient: Dilbert Hunter

Service Date: 4/26/YYYY – 4/29/YYYY

Group #:   52656388

Claim #:   02216

Copies of the following provider records are requested for the adjudication of the above-mentioned claim. Under terms of our subscriber contract, the patient has given prior authorization for the release of this information. Please send the following reports:

[X] Final Diagnosis (Face Sheet)

[X] History & Physical Examination

[ ] Progress Notes

[ ] Physician's Orders

[ ] Operative Report

[ ] Ancillary Reports

Please return a copy of this letter with a copy of the records to:

Medical Review

Blue Cross Claims Department

Patient #: 1104272

Thank you.

Sincerely,

Mary Ann Jones

Mary Ann Jones, Claims Reviewer

Figure 9-4B   Case02 Request for Information

Case03 – Request for Information

Received in Health Information Department for processing on May 30, (this year).

AUTHORIZATION FOR DISCLOSURE OF PROTECTED HEALTH INFORMATION (PHI)

(1) I hereby authorize Sunny Valley Medical Center to disclose/obtain information from the health records of:

Erica P. Stanley	04/05/YYYY	(607)555-8818
Patient Name	Date of Birth (mmddyyyy)	Telephone (w/ area code)
23 Langley Drive, Alfred NY 14802		Case03
Patient Address		Medical Record Number

(2) Covering the period(s) of health care:

04/28/YYYY	04/29/YYYY		
From (mmddyyyy)	To (mmddyyyy)	From (mmddyyyy)	To (mmddyyyy)

(3) I authorize the following information to be released by Sunny Valley Medical Center (check applicable reports):

☒ Face Sheet	☐ Progress Notes	☐ Pathology Report	☐ Drug Abuse Care
☐ Discharge Summary	☒ Lab Results	☐ Nurses Notes	☐ Other:
☒ History & Physical Exam	☒ X-ray Reports	☐ HIV Testing Results	
☐ Consultation	☐ Scan Results	☐ Mental Health Care	
☐ Doctors Orders	☐ Operative Report	☐ Alcohol Abuse Care	

This information is to be disclosed to ~~or obtained from~~:

Abdul Raish, M.D.	1421 Lincoln Avenue New York, NY 10035	(800) 555-8951
Name of Organization	Address of Organization	Telephone Number

for the purpose of: treatment by Dr. Raish.

Statement that information used or disclosed may be subject to re-disclosure by the recipient and may no longer be protected by this rule.

(4) I understand that I have a right to revoke this authorization at any time. I understand that if I revoke this authorization I must do so in writing and present my written revocation to the Heath Information Management Department. I understand that the revocation will not apply to information that has already been released in response to this authorization. I understand that the revocation will not apply to my insurance company when the law provides my insurer with the right to contest a claim under my policy. Unless otherwise revoked, this authorization will expire on the following date, event, or condition.

5/1/(next year)		
Expiration Date	Expiration Event	Expiration Condition

If I fail to specify an expiration date, event or condition, this authorization will expire within six (6) months.

Signature of individual and date.

(5) I understand that authorizing the disclosure of this health information is voluntary. I can refuse to sign this authorization. I need not sign this form in order to assure treatment. I understand that I may inspect or copy the information to be used or disclosed, provided in CFR 164.534. I understand that any disclosure of information carries with it the potential for an unauthorized redisclosure and may not be protected by federal confidentiality rules. If I have questions about disclosure of my health information, I can contact the Privacy Officer at Sunny Valley Medical Center.

Signed:

Erica P. Stanley	May 1, (this year)
Signature of Patient or Legal Representative	Date

Figure 9-4C   Case03 Request for Information

Case04 – Request for Information
Received in Health Information Department for processing on August 30, (this year).

DWYER & DWYER, P.C.

ATTORNEYS AT LAW

PARK PLACE PROFESSIONAL BUILDING

OLEAN, NY 14760

716/373-1920

Joseph C. Dwyer & Elaine N. Dwyer   **Practice Limited to Civil Trial Law**
Barbara L. Laferty, Legal Assistant

August 16, (this year)

Sunny Valley Medical Center
Binghamton, NY 13901
ATTN: Records Room

RE: Our Client: Mary C. Howe

Date of Injury: 04/29/YYYY

Gentlemen:

We have been retained by the above to represent the above-named with regard to an injury which occurred on the above date, resulting in personal injuries. It is our understanding that our client was treated at your institution either as an outpatient or inpatient. We respectfully request that you forward to us copies of the hospital records, excluding only TPR, fluid, and laboratory reports. We specifically need the nurse's notes.

Would you please have your billing office send us an original bill as to hospital services rendered but not indicating on it what, if anything, has been paid to date. Please enclose any statement for your customary charges in providing these records. Thank you kindly for your cooperation and assistance.

Yours very truly,

DWYER & DWYER, P.C.

By:

Joseph C. Dwyer

JCD:cd

Figure 9-4D   Case04 Request for Information

Case05 – Request for Information
Received in Health Information Department for processing on August 9, (this year).

HOSPITAL FOR JOINT DISEASES & MEDICAL CENTER (HJD&MC), 1919 MADISON AVENUE, NEW YORK 10035

DATE July 14, (this year)   NAME GIBBON, Andrew   PATIENT # Case05

TO SUNNY VALLEY MEDICAL CENTER, BINGHAMTON, NY

DEAR SIRS:

We have been informed that the above-named patient was treated in your institution on or about 1/1/YYYY. May we obtain from you a resume of your findings, including the radiology reports, operations or other treatment provided?

Very truly yours,
MEDICAL RECORD DEPARTMENT

AUTHORIZATION FOR DISCLOSURE OF PROTECTED HEALTH INFORMATION (PHI)

(1) I hereby authorize Sunny Valley Medical Center to disclose/obtain information from the health records of:

Andrew Gibbon	08/19/YYYY	(607) 555-4500
Patient Name	Date of Birth (mmddyyyy)	Telephone (w/ area code)
22 Market Street, Alfred NY 14802		Case05
Patient Address		Medical Record Number

(2) Covering the period(s) of health care:

January YYYY			
From (mmddyyyy)	To (mmddyyyy)	From (mmddyyyy)	To (mmddyyyy)

(3) I authorize the following information to be released by Sunny Valley Medical Center (check applicable reports):

☒ Face Sheet	☐ Progress Notes	☐ Pathology Report	☐ Drug Abuse Care
☐ Discharge Summary	☒ Lab Results	☐ Nurses Notes	☐ Other:
☒ History & Physical Exam	☒ X-ray Reports	☐ HIV Testing Results	
☐ Consultation	☐ Scan Results	☐ Mental Health Care	
☐ Doctors Orders	☐ Operative Report	☐ Alcohol Abuse Care	

This information is to be disclosed to ~~or obtained from~~:

HJD&MC	1919 Madison Avenue, New York, NY 10035	(800) 555-9567
Name of Organization	Address of Organization	Telephone Number
for the purpose of:	treatment by Dr. HJD&MC.	

Statement that information used or disclosed may be subject to re-disclosure by the recipient and may no longer be protected by this rule.

(4) I understand that I have a right to revoke this authorization at any time. I understand that if I revoke this authorization I must do so in writing and present my written revocation to the Heath Information Management Department. I understand that the revocation will not apply to information that has already been released in response to this authorization. I understand that the revocation will not apply to my insurance company when the law provides my insurer with the right to contest a claim under my policy. Unless otherwise revoked, this authorization will expire on the following date, event, or condition.

5/1/(next year)		
Expiration Date	Expiration Event	Expiration Condition
If I fail to specify an expiration date, event or condition, this authorization will expire within six (6) months.		

Signature of individual and date.

(5) I understand that authorizing the disclosure of this health information is voluntary. I can refuse to sign this authorization. I need not sign this form in order to assure treatment. I understand that I may inspect or copy the information to be used or disclosed, provided in CFR 164.534. I understand that any disclosure of information carries with it the potential for an unauthorized redisclosure and may not be protected by federal confidentiality rules. If I have questions about disclosure of my health information, I can contact the Privacy Officer at Sunny Valley Medical Center.

Signed:

Andrew Gibbon	May 1, (this year)
Signature of Patient or Legal Representative	Date

Figure 9-4E   Case05 Request for Information

Case06 – Request for Information
Received in Health Information Department for processing on October 15, (this year).

PRUDENTIAL

The Prudential Insurance Company of America

August 15, (this year)

AUTHORIZATION TO RELEASE INFORMATION

TO: <u>Sunny Valley Medical Center, Binghamton, NY</u>

For purposes of evaluating a claim, you are authorized to permit the Prudential Insurance Company of America and its authorized representatives to view or obtain a copy of ALL EXISTING RECORDS (including those of psychiatric, drug, or alcohol treatment) pertaining to the examination, medical and dental treatment, history, prescriptions, employment, and insurance coverage of <u>Charles Benson</u>.

This authorization specifically covers a period of hospitalization or medical care and treatment during <u>4/24/YYYY through 4/29/YYYY</u>. This information is for the sole use of Prudential's representatives or the group policy holder or contract holder involved in processing the claim and will not be furnished in an identifiable form to any other persons without my written consent unless expressly permitted or required by law.

I understand that this authorization may be revoked by written notice to Prudential, but this will not apply to information already released. If not revoked, this authorization will be valid while the claim is pending or a maximum of one year from the date it is signed.

I have been furnished a copy of this authorization and acknowledge receipt. I also agree that a photographic copy shall be as valid as the original.

Limitations, if any:

DATE <u>August 15, (this year)</u>
SIGNED: *Charles Benson*

Figure 9-4F   Case06 Request for Information

Case07 – Request for Information
Received in Health Information Department for processing on May 5, (this year).

BLUE CROSS & BLUE SHIELD   **A MEDICARE CARRIER**

UTICA, NEW YORK 13502

DATE: April 30, (this year)

TO: Sunny Valley Medical Center, Binghamton, NY

ATTN: Health Information Department

PATIENT: Holley E. Hoover

DOB: 01/15/YYYY

ADMISSION: 04/30/YYYY

We request the following information to process the above patient's claim:

1.   Face sheet
2.   Surgical procedures performed
3.   History of condition
4.   Discharge summary

Please send a statement for clerical services with this information, and we will be glad to promptly send you a check. Thank you for your prompt cooperation.

Jean Lewis

Claims Examiner

Figure 9-4G   Case07 Request for Information

Case08 – Request for Information
Received in Health Information Department for processing on November 1, (this year).

ADAM ATTORNEY
15 MAIN STREET
ALBANY NY 00000
PHONE: (518) 555-1234

JOHN DOE,)	
Petitioner,)	***SUBPOENA DUCES TECUM***
)	
vs.)	
)	
RICHARD ROE, M.D.)	
Respondent.)	Case No. _____ NY-895623591 _____
)	

TO: Sunny Valley Medical Center
             100 Main St
             Binghamton, NY 13901

RE: Molly P. Mason
DOB: 3/1/YYYY

YOU ARE COMMANDED to produce at the <u>County Courthouse, 15 Main Street, Room 14A, Binghamton, NY 13901</u> on November 15, (this year) at 9 A.M., a complete copy of your medical records, pertaining to the above-referenced individual who has requested the Division of Professional Licensing to conduct a prelitigation panel review of a claim of medical malpractice. **Attendance is not required if records are timely forwarded to the indicated address.**

DATED this <u>twenty-fifth</u> day of <u>October</u> (this year).

By: *Petra Lyons*

Clerk of the Court

Figure 9-4H   Case08 Request for Information

Case09 – Request for Information
Received in Health Information Department for processing on November 15, (this year).

ADAM ATTORNEY
15 MAIN STREET
ALBANY NY 00000
PHONE: (518) 555-1234

DAVID LUCK,   )
Petitioner,   )   ***COURT ORDERED SUBPOENA***
)   ***DUCES TECUM***
vs.   )
)
ALAN GHANN, M.D.   )
Respondent.   )   Case No. ____ NY-895623591
)

TO: Sunny Valley Medical Center
       100 Main St
       Binghamton, NY 13901

RE: David Luck
DOB: 11/21/YYYY

YOU ARE COMMANDED to produce at the <u>County Courthouse, 15 Main Street, Room 14A, Binghamton, NY 13901</u> on November 25, (this year) at 9 A.M., a complete copy of your medical records, pertaining to the above-referenced individual who has requested the Division of Professional Licensing to conduct a prelitigation panel review of a claim of medical malpractice. **Attendance is not required if records are timely forwarded to the indicated address.**

DATED this <u>fifth</u> day of <u>November</u> (this year).

By: *Petra Lyons*
                                        Clerk of the Court

Figure 9-4l   Case09 Request for Information

Case 10 – Request for Information

Received in Health Information Department for processing on October 5, (this year).

Authorization for Release of Confidential HIV-Related Information

Name and address of facility/provider obtaining release:

Sunny Valley Medical Center, 100 Main Street, Binghamton, NY 13901

Name of person whose HIV-related information will be released:

Paula P. Paulson

Name(s) and address(es) of person(s) signing this form (if other than above):

Relationship to person whose HIV information will be released (if other than above):

Name(s) and address(es) of person(s) who will be given HIV-related information:

Michael Diamond, M.D., 1423 Main Street, Wellsville NY 14895

Reason for release of HIV-related information:

To provide historical perspective of HIV status for physician's office record.

Time during which release is authorized: From: 4/26/YYYY   To: 5/1/YYYY

The Facility/Provider obtaining this release must complete the following:

Exceptions, if any, to the right to revoke consent for disclosure: (for example cannot revoke if disclosure has already been made.) N/A

Description of the consequences, if any, of failing to consent to disclosure upon treatment, payment, enrollment, or eligibility for benefits: N/A

(Note: Federal privacy regulations may restrict some consequences.)

My questions about this form have been answered. I know that I do not have to allow release of HIV-related information, and that I can change my mind at any time and revoke my authorization by writing the facility/provider obtaining this release.

Oct 1, (this year)   *Paula P. Paulson*
_____   _____
Date   Signature

Figure 9-4J   Case10 Request for Information

SUNNY VALLEY MEDICAL CENTER
BINGHAMTON NEW YORK 13901
Health Information Department
(607) 555-1234

RE: _____

Your request for copies of patient records on the above-named patient has been received.

Please comply with the following checked items:

A. _____   Please consider this an invoice in the amount of $____.
             Copies of requested patient records are enclosed.

B. _____   Copies of requested patient records are enclosed; no
             payment is required.

C. _____   Authorizations for release of information must be dated
             within 90 days of receipt. Attached is a HIPAA-compliant
             form. Please have the patient complete and sign, and return
             in the enclosed self-addressed stamped envelope (SASE).

D. _____   To process the request for information, we must have a
             HIPAA-compliant authorization signed by the patient or
             his/her representative. Attached is a HIPAA-compliant form.
             Please have the patient complete and sign, and return in the
             SASE.

E. _____   The patient's authorization to release information was dated
             prior to treatment. It is against policy to release such patient
             information. Attached is a HIPAA-compliant form. Please
             have the patient complete and sign, and return in the SASE.

Sincerely,

Debra Director, RHIA

Health Information Department

Figure 9-5   Response Form Letter

LAB ASSIGNMENT 9-4   Telephone Calls for Release of Information Processing

OBJECTIVES

At the end of this assignment, the student should be able to:

- Explain the release of information processing protocol for responding to telephone requests for patient information
- Appropriately respond to verbal requests for patient information

Overview

Health information professionals receive numerous telephone requests for patient information. This assignment will familiarize students with the appropriate response to a verbal request for patient information.

Instructions

1. Carefully read the telephone simulations in Figure 9-6.
2. Respond to the following questions about each telephone simulation.

Simulation #1:

- How would you rate the RHIT's greeting?
- Did the RHIT respond appropriately to the patient's request?
- Do you agree with the RHIT's reason for not releasing records immediately to the new physician? Why or why not?
- What is the significance of the RHIT using the patient's name during the conversation?
- What would you have said differently?

Simulation #2:

- How would you rate the MA's phone response?
- Did the MA respond appropriately to the request?
- What would you have said differently?

Simulation #3:

- Critique Barbara's greeting.
- Determine how you would handle this situation if you were Barbara. What would you have done differently, if anything, from the onset? Given the situation, what would you do next?

Simulation #4:

- What information can be released over the telephone?

SIMULATION #1: The caller is a patient who requests that the health records from her recent hospitalization be forwarded to her new physician in Billings, Montana. The patient, Janice McDonald, has relocated to a suburb of Billings, Montana.

THE TELEPHONE IN THE HEALTH INFORMATION DEPARTMENT RINGS THREE TIMES AND THE REGISTERED HEALTH INFORMATION TECHNICIAN (RHIT) ANSWERS THE PHONE.

RHIT: [professional tone of voice] "Good afternoon (morning). Health information department. May I help you?"

JANICE: [questioning tone of voice] "Hi! Ummm, this is Janice McDonald. I've moved to Montana and want to get my latest inpatient records sent to my new doctor. Can you do that?"

RHIT: [friendly tone of voice] "Sure, Ms. McDonald. I'll just need to send you a release of information authorization form. You'll need to complete it, sign it, and date it. Then, return it in the envelope provided."

JANICE: [confused tone of voice] "Oh. I'm seeing the new doctor next week. Do you think that you can just send the records to him?"

RHIT: [polite tone of voice] "I'm sorry, Ms. McDonald. Your health records are confidential and we cannot release copies without your written authorization."

JANICE: [resigned tone of voice] "Oh, okay. I guess that will have to do."

RHIT: [reassuring tone of voice] "Ms. McDonald, the department is really just trying to maintain privacy of your records. If you like, I can fax the authorization form to you. Then, you could overnight express it to the department. We can't accept a fax of the completed form because we need your original signature. That's hospital policy."

JANICE: [pleased tone of voice] "Oh! That would be great. I'll call my new doctor and get his fax number and give you a call back with it. Okay?"

RHIT: [friendly tone of voice] "That would be just fine, Ms. McDonald."

THE CONVERSATION IS ENDED. THE RHIT HANGS UP THE PHONE.

Figure 9-6   Telephone Simulations

(Continues)

SIMULATION #2: Joe Turner from the State Farm Insurance Company is an angry insurance agent who calls to inform the medical assistant (MA) at the physician's office that the company had mailed a proper authorization three weeks ago for release of records on a recently discharged patient.

THE TELEPHONE RINGS SIX TIMES BEFORE THE MEDICAL ASSISTANT (MA) ANSWERS THE PHONE.

MA: [quick, professional tone of voice] "Good afternoon (morning). Doctor's office."

TURNER: [brusk tone of voice] "Hello. I'm calling to find out why the records I requested three weeks ago have not been sent to me yet. Oh. This is Joe Turner from State Farm Insurance Company."

MA: [courteous tone of voice — recognizes an impatient person] "Could you tell me the name of the patient, please?"

TURNER: [brusk tone of voice] "Mary Jones. Her birth date is 10/02/55. She was discharged on September 1 of this year. I need copies of the doctor's notes in order to get the claim paid. She has called me several times this past couple of weeks. I guess the office keeps sending bills for her to pay and she is as disgusted as I am about this situation!"

MA: [courteous tone of voice] "Mr. Turner, would you like to hold while I check this or could I call you back?"

TURNER: [brusk tone of voice] "No way am I going to let you off the hook. I'll hold!"

MA: [courteous tone of voice — but showing signs of wear] "No problem, Mr. Turner. I'll be with you in a couple of minutes."

ONE MINUTE PASSES AND THE MA TAKES MR. TURNER OFF HOLD.

MA: [pleasant tone of voice] "Mr. Turner, I checked our correspondence log and found that copies of Mary Jones' records were forwarded to your attention last week. You should have them."

TURNER: [impatient tone of voice] "Well, I don't! Oh . . . I guess they were placed on my desk while I wasn't looking. Here they are. Sorry about that. Goodbye."

THE CALLER HANGS UP.

Figure 9-6   Telephone Simulations (*Continued*)

(*Continues*)

SIMULATION #3: Barbara Allen is a new health information technology graduate hired by the medical center's health information management department. This is her first day on the job.

THE TELEPHONE RINGS TWICE, IS ANSWERED BY THE DEPARTMENT SECRETARY, AND THE CALL IS FORWARDED TO BARBARA ALLEN, CORRESPONDENCE TECHNICIAN.

BARBARA: "Correspondence section. May I help you?"

DOCTOR: "Hello, this is Dr. Ahbibe from Breyne's Clinic in Columbia, New Mexico. We have a patient here by the name of Garrick Tanner who was admitted for status epilepticus. We need a past history for this patient and all pertinent documents sent to us immediately. The seizure activity is progressing in frequency and the patient is unable to provide information about drug allergies."

BARBARA: "Would you hold while I pull the patient's record?"

DOCTOR: "Certainly."

Several minutes pass as Barbara searches by checking the MPI and retrieving the record. Upon inspection of the record, she realizes that this is a "sealed file" because of a pending lawsuit. She also notes that Garrick Tanner has an extensive history of cocaine abuse that has been the main cause of his seizures. She closes the record, confused as to how she should handle this situation.

SIMULATION #4: Susie Sits is answering the telephone for the correspondence technician who is on break. Susie usually works in the discharge analysis section of the health information department.

THE TELEPHONE RINGS TWICE, AND SUSIE PICKS UP.

SUSIE: "Good morning, health information management department. Susie Sits speaking."

DOCTOR: "This is Dr. Jones' office calling from Phoenix, Arizona. Could you please give me the final diagnosis for Alfred Peoples, who was recently discharged from your facility?"

SUSIE: "Well, just hold a minute and I will get everything you need."

The doctor is on hold for three minutes while Susie pulls the health record.

SUSIE: "Hello, I think I have everything you need. Mr. Peoples was a patient in our alcohol rehab unit last month. . . ."

Figure 9-6   Telephone Simulations (*Continued*)

LAB ASSIGNMENT 9-5   Statement of Confidentiality

OBJECTIVES

At the end of this assignment, the student should be able to:
- Explain the purpose of a confidentiality statement
- Sign a statement of confidentiality

Overview

Health information students will have access to protected health information when completing professional practice experiences and course assignments. It is essential that patient confidentiality be maintained at all times. In this assignment, the student will review and sign a statement of confidentiality.

Instructions

1. Go to the Student Companion website and print the statement of confidentiality form (Figure 9-7).
2. Review the statement of confidentiality.
3. Sign and date the statement of confidentiality, and have a witness (e.g., proctor, supervisor) sign and date the form.
4. Submit the completed form to your instructor.

PERSONAL HEALTH INFORMATION PLEDGE OF CONFIDENTIALITY

In consideration of my status as a student at _____ and/or association with health care facilities that provide professional practice experiences, and as an integral part of the terms and conditions of association, I hereby agree, pledge and undertake that I will not at any time access or use personal health information, or reveal or disclose to any persons within or outside the provider organization, any personal health information except as may be required in the course of my duties and responsibilities and in accordance with applicable legislation, and corporate and departmental policies governing proper release of information.

I understand that my obligations outlined above will continue after my association with the School and/or facility ends.

I further understand that my obligations concerning the protection of the confidentiality of personal health information relate to all personal health information whether I acquired the information through my association with the School and/or facility.

I also understand that unauthorized use or disclosure of such information will result in a disciplinary action up to and including involuntary expulsion from the School, the imposition of fines pursuant to relevant state and federal legislation, and a report to my professional regulatory body.

_____   _____
Date Signed   Signature of Student

                                     _____
                                     Student's Printed Name

_____   _____
Date Signed   Signature of Witness

Figure 9-7 Confidentiality Statement (also located on the Student Companion website)

Chapter 10

Introduction to Coding and Reimbursement

🖋 INTRODUCTION

This chapter will familiarize the student with classification systems, third-party payers, and reimbursement systems.

LAB ASSIGNMENT 10-1 Hospital Financial Reports

OBJECTIVES

At the end of this assignment, the student should be able to:

- Interpret the information in a hospital financial report
- Analyze a hospital financial report to calculate reimbursement amounts

Overview

Software is used to assign each inpatient to a diagnosis-related group (DRG) according to principal diagnosis code, patient's discharge status, and other factors that impact the DRG assignment. For this assignment, the student will review a hospital financial report and calculate the total payment that the facility will receive based on DRG assignment.

Instructions

1. Review Table 10-1 (Base Payment Amount per DRG) and Figure 10-1 (Sunny Valley Medical Center Financial Report).
2. Complete the financial report in Figure 10-1 by using information from Table 10-1 to:
   a. Determine the base rate for each DRG listed
   b. Calculate the total reimbursement rate (base rate times the number of cases equals reimbursement amount)

Table 10-1 Base Payment Amount per DRG

DRG	Base Payment Amount
368	$ 3,421.55
372	$ 2,730.16
423	$ 4,730.28
467	$ 1,349.05

Sunny Valley Medical Center Financial Report – June YYYY				
Date	DRG Assignment	Base Payment	Number of Cases	Reimbursement
June 1	423	$	25	$
June 4	368	$	32	$
June 5	372	$	15	$
June 10	372	$	41	$
June 15	372	$	11	$
June 19	372	$	27	$
June 25	467	$	31	$
			Total for June YYYY	$

Figure 10-1 Sunny Valley Medical Center Financial Report

LAB ASSIGNMENT 10-2   Updating Clinic Encounter Form

OBJECTIVES

At the end of this assignment, the student should be able to:

* Analyze the contents of a clinic encounter form
* Revise a clinic encounter form with up-to-date information

Overview

ICD-10-CM/PCS, CPT, and HCPCS codes are updated annually, which means that providers must review and revise encounter forms on an annual basis. This assignment will require students to review a clinic encounter form to update and revise the codes.

Instructions

1. Review the encounter form (Figure 10-2) currently in use.
2. Using current editions of the ICD-10-CM, CPT, and HCPCS Level II coding manuals, verify each code, and edit those that have changed.

SUNNY VALLEY MEDICAL CENTER OUTPATIENT CLINIC

Patient Name:	Provider Number:
Address:	Primary Insurance:
Reason for Encounter:	Appointment Time:
Encounter Number:	Date:

CODE	DESCRIPTION	CODE	DESCRIPTION
Office Visits		**Laboratory**	
99201	New Patient - level 1	81001	Urinalysis with microscopy
99202	New Patient - level 2	82044	Urine—Microalbumin Semiquantitative
99303	New Patient - level 3	82947	Blood Glucose Quantitative
99204	New Patient - level 4	85014	Hematocrit
99205	New Patient - level 5	85611	Protime
99211	Established Patient - level 1	86580	PPD
99212	Established Patient - level 2	87060	Strep Screen
99213	Established Patient - level 3		
99214	Established Patient - level 4		
99215	Established Patient - level 5		
Procedures		**Diagnosis**	
58300	IUD Insertion	J20.9	Bronchitis, acute
93005	Electrocardiogram	J20.9	Bronchitis, chronic
92552	Audiometry	R07.9	Chest Pain
92567	Tympanometry	R05	Cough
94650	IPPB treatment	I10.0	Hypertension
94010	Spirometry	H66.90	Otitis
94760	Pulse Oximetry	M54	Pain, back
		M25.50	Pain, joint

Next Appointment: _____

Provider Signature: _____

Figure 10-2   Sunny Valley Medical Center Outpatient Clinic Encounter Form

LAB ASSIGNMENT 10-3   ICD-10-CM and ICD-10-PCS Resources

OBJECTIVES

At the end of this assignment, the student should be able to:

* Identify resources for ICD-10-CM and ICD-10-PCS.

Overview

ICD-10 was implemented in 1994 by WHO member states. ICD-10-CM and ICD-10-PCS were implemented in the United States on October 1, 2015. The National Center for Health Statistics is responsible for maintaining and updating ICD-10-CM, while the Centers for Medicare and Medicaid Services is the agency that maintains and updates ICD-10-PCS.

Instructions

1. Using an Internet browser (e.g., Microsoft Internet Explorer, Google Chrome), go to www.cdc.gov.
2. Search on ICD-10-CM and review the information found on the website regarding ICD-10-CM.
3. Using an Internet browser (e.g., Microsoft Internet Explorer, Google Chrome), go to www.cms.gov.
4. Search on ICD-10-PCS and review the information found on the website regarding ICD-10-PCS.
5. Prepare a two-page summary of information about ICD-10-CM/ICD-10-PCS.
   a. Purpose of ICD-10-CM/ICD-10-PCS
   b. Resources found on the websites that pertain to ICD-10-CM and ICD-10-PCS.

Appendix I

Case 01 through Case 10

This appendix contains 10 inpatient medical records, which students will use to complete assignments in Chapters 6, 8, and 9. Selected forms are located on the Student Companion website at www.Cengage.com, so students can review in an online format.

Case 01

<table>
<tr>
<td colspan="4">
SUNNY VALLEY MEDICAL CENTER
100 MAIN ST, SUNNY VALLEY, NY 14802
(607) 555-1234
HOSPITAL #: 000999
</td>
<td colspan="4" align="right">INPATIENT FACE SHEET</td>
</tr>
</table>

PATIENT NAME AND ADDRESS				GENDER	RACE	MARITAL STATUS	PATIENT NO.
DENNIS, Marsha 344 Maple Avenue Sunny Valley, NY 14802				F	W	M	Case01

				DATE OF BIRTH	MAIDEN NAME	OCCUPATION
				02/09/YYYY	Taylor	Unemployed

ADMISSION DATE	TIME	DISCHARGE DATE	TIME	LENGTH OF STAY	TELEPHONE NUMBER
04/27/YYYY	0800	04/29/YYYY	1335	02 DAYS	(607)555-7771

GUARANTOR NAME AND ADDRESS	NEXT OF KIN NAME AND ADDRESS
DENNIS, Dennis 344 Maple Avenue Sunny Valley, NY 14802	DENNIS, Dennis 344 Maple Avenue Sunny Valley, NY 14802

GUARANTOR TELEPHONE NO.	RELATIONSHIP TO PATIENT	NEXT OF KIN TELEPHONE NUMBER	RELATIONSHIP TO PATIENT
(607)555-7771	Husband	(607)555-7771	Husband

ADMITTING PHYSICIAN	SERVICE	ADMIT TYPE	ROOM NUMBER/BED
Donald Thompson, MD	Surgical	3	0603/01

ATTENDING PHYSICIAN	ATTENDING PHYSICIAN UPIN	ADMITTING DIAGNOSIS	
Donald Thompson, MD	100B01	Abnormal Pap Smear	

PRIMARY INSURER	POLICY AND GROUP NUMBER	SECONDARY INSURER	POLICY AND GROUP NUMBER
BC/BS of WNY	6350088		

DIAGNOSES AND PROCEDURES	ICD-10-CM/PCS
PRINCIPAL DIAGNOSIS	
Acute and chronic cervicitis with squamous metaplasia	N72 N87.1
SECONDARY DIAGNOSES	
PRINCIPAL PROCEDURE	
D & C	0UDB7ZZ
SECONDARY PROCEDURE(S)	
Cold Cone	0UBC7ZZ
TOTAL CHARGES: $ 4,954.40	

DISCHARGE INSTRUCTIONS					
ACTIVITY:	☐ Bedrest	☐ Light	☐ Usual	☐ Unlimited	☐ Other:
DIET:	☐ Regular	☐ Low Cholesterol	☐ Low Salt	☐ ADA	☐ _____ Calorie
FOLLOW-UP:	☐ Call for appointment	☐ Office appointment on _____		☐ Other:	
SPECIAL INSTRUCTIONS:					
ATTENDING PHYSICIAN AUTHENTICATION:					

DENNIS, Marsha   Admission: 04-27-YYYY   CONSENT TO ADMISSION
Case01   DOB: 02/09/YYYY
Dr. Thompson   Room: 0603

I, *Marsha Dennis*_____ hereby consent to admission to the Sunny Valley Medical Center (SVMC), and I
further consent to such routine hospital care, diagnostic procedures, and medical treatment that the medical and
professional staff of SVMC may deem necessary or advisable. I authorize the use of medical information obtained
about me as specified above and the disclosure of such information to my referring physician(s). This form has been
fully explained to me, and I understand its contents. I further understand that no guarantees have been made to me
as to the results of treatments or examinations done at the SVMC.

Marsha Dennis   4-27-YYYY
_____   _____
Signature of Patient   Date

_____   _____
Signature of Parent/Legal Guardian for Minor   Date

_____
Relationship to Minor
Mary M Adams   4-27-YYYY
_____   _____
WITNESS: Sunny Valley Medical Center Staff Member Date

CONSENT TO RELEASE INFORMATION FOR REIMBURSEMENT PURPOSES

In order to permit reimbursement, upon request, the Sunny Valley Medical Center (SVMC) may disclose such
treatment information pertaining to my hospitalization to any corporation, organization, or agent thereof, which is,
or may be liable under contract to the SVMC or to me, or to any of my family members or other person, for
payment of all or part of the SVMC's charges for services rendered to me (e.g., the patient's health insurance carrier).
I understand that the purpose of any release of information is to facilitate reimbursement for services rendered. In
addition, in the event that my health insurance program includes utilization review of services provided during this
admission, I authorize SVMC to release information as is necessary to permit the review. This authorization will
expire once the reimbursement for services rendered is complete.

Marsha Dennis   4-27-YYYY
_____   _____
Signature of Patient   Date

_____   _____
Signature of Parent/Legal Guardian for Minor   Date

_____
Relationship to Minor
Mary M Adams   4-27-YYYY
_____   _____
WITNESS: Sunny Valley Medical Center Staff Member Date

SUNNY VALLEY MEDICAL CENTER ■ 100 MAIN ST, SUNNY VALLEY, NY 14802 ■ (607) 555-1234

DENNIS, Marsha	Admission: 04-27-YYYY	ADVANCE DIRECTIVE
Case01	DOB: 02/09/YYYY	
Dr. Thompson	Room: 0603	

Your answers to the following questions will assist your Physician and the Hospital to respect your wishes regarding your medical care. This information will become a part of your medical record.

	YES	NO	PATIENT'S INITIALS
1. Have you been provided with a copy of the information called "Patient Rights Regarding Health Care Decision?"	X		MD
2. Have you prepared a "Living Will?" If yes, please provide the Hospital with a copy for your medical record.		X	MD
3. Have you prepared a Durable Power of Attorney for Health Care? If yes, please provide the Hospital with a copy for your medical record.		X	MD
4. Have you provided this facility with an Advance Directive on a prior admission and is it still in effect? If yes, Admitting Office to contact Medical Records to obtain a copy for the medical record.		X	MD
5. Do you desire to execute a Living Will/Durable Power of Attorney? If yes, refer to in order: a. Physician b. Social Service c. Volunteer Service		X	MD

HOSPITAL STAFF DIRECTIONS: Check when each step is completed.

1. ___✓___ Verify the above questions where answered and actions taken where required.

2. ___✓___ If the "Patient Rights" information was provided to someone other than the patient, state reason:

_____

_____   _____
Name of Individual Receiving Information   Relationship to Patient

3. ___✓___ If information was provided in a language other than English, specify language and method.

4. ___✓___ Verify patient was advised on how to obtain additional information on Advance Directives.

5. ___✓___ Verify the Patient/Family Member/Legal Representative was asked to provide the Hospital with a copy of the Advance Directive which will be retained in the medical record.

File this form in the medical record and give a copy to the patient.

Name of Patient (Name of Individual giving information if different from Patient)

Marsha Dennis   *April 27, YYYY*
_____   _____
Signature of Patient   Date

Mary M. Adams   April 27, YYYY
_____   _____
Signature of Hospital Representative   Date

SUNNY VALLEY MEDICAL CENTER ■ 100 MAIN ST, SUNNY VALLEY, NY 14802 ■ (607) 555-1234

DENNIS, Marsha Case01 Dr. Thompson	Admission: 04-27-YYYY DOB: 02/09/YYYY Room: 0603	PROGRESS NOTES

Date	(Please skip one line between days)
04-27-YYYY	Pre-Anes: Patient cleared for general anesthesia. D. Galloway, MD
1328	
04-27-YYYY	Post-Anes: No apparent anesthesia complications. No N + V. Awake.
1430	Satisfactory condition.
04-27-YYYY	Under general anesthesia a D&C and cone was done without
1200	anesthetic or operative complications. Patient has oxycel packing, vag.
	gauze pack & foley catheter. D. Thompson, MD
04-28-YYYY	Patient is doing fine. Packing & cath in until tomorrow. Please
0900	discharge tomorrow. Incidentally DRG note says discharge is
	anticipated for today. During precertification it was necessary for
	me to get doctor approval, which I did for surgery the day of
	admission, one day in hospital, the day after surgery, and discharge
	the following day, which is the plan.
04-29-YYYY	Packing & Foley out. May go home today. Shall call with Path
1000	report.

DENNIS, Marsha Case01 Dr. Thompson		Admission: 04-27-YYYY DOB: 02/09/YYYY Room: 0603	DOCTORS ORDERS
Date	Time	Physician's signature required for each order. (Please skip one line between dates.)	
4/22/YYYY	0830	1. For AM admit 04 -27 -YYYY	
		2. Pre Cert # 139-129-62143	
		3. Urinalysis	
		4. Urine preg test	
		5. Chest x-ray done 04-22-YYYY	
		6. EKG done	
		7. NPO after MN 04-26-YYYY	
			Donald Thompson
04-27-YYYY	0830	Admit to Surgical Unit. N.P.O. Perineal shave prep	
		Start IV w / 5 % gluc. In Ringers Lactate @ 125 ML/hr	
		Premeds by Anesthesia	
		To O.R. about 1000 AM. For d & C and Cone	
		T.O. Dr. Thompson/L. Mosher LPN	Donald Thompson
04-27-YYYY	1515	Diet as tol.	
		Bed rest today. Up tomorrow.	
		Tylenol w/ cod. PRN.	
		Connect foley to straight drainage.	
		Discharge from RR @ 1455	
			Donald Thompson
04-27-YYYY	1525	DC IV when finished	
04-29-YYYY	1335	DC Foley. Discharge home.	
			Donald Thompson

DENNIS, Marsha	Admission: 04-27-YYYY	Consent for Operation(s) and/or
Case01	DOB: 02/09/YYYY	Procedure(s) and Anesthesia
Dr. Thompson	Room: 0603	

PERMISSION. I hereby authorize Dr. _Thompson_ , or associates of his/her choice at the

Sunny Valley Medical Center (the "Hospital") to perform upon _Marsha Dennis_

the following operation(s) and/or procedure(s): _Remove conical section of cervix & D&C_

including such photography, videotaping, televising or other observation of the operation(s)/procedure(s) as may be purposeful for the advance of medical knowledge and/or education, with the understanding that the patient's identity will remain anonymous.

EXPLANATION OF PROCEDURE, RISKS, BENEFITS, ALTERNATIVES. Dr. _Thompson_

has fully explained to me the nature and purposes of the operation(s)/procedures named above and has also informed me of expected benefits and complications, attendant discomforts and risks that may arise, as well as possible alternatives to the proposed treatment. I have been given an opportunity to ask questions and all my questions have been answered fully and satisfactorily.

UNFORESEEN CONDITIONS. I understand that during the course of the operation(s) or procedure(s), unforeseen conditions may arise which necessitate procedures in addition to or different from those contemplated. I, therefore, consent to the performance of additional operations and procedures which the above-named physician or his/her associates or assistants may consider necessary.

ANESTHESIA. I further consent to the administration of such anesthesia as may be considered necessary by the above-named physician or his/her associates or assistants. I recognize that there are always risks to life and health associated with anesthesia. Such risks have been fully explained to me and I have been given an opportunity to ask questions and all my questions have been answered fully and satisfactorily.

SPECIMENS. Any organs or tissues surgically removed may be examined and retained by the Hospital for medical, scientific or educational purposes and such tissues or parts may be disposed of in accordance with accustomed practice and applicable State laws and/or regulations.

NO GUARANTEES. I acknowledge that no guarantees or assurances have been made to me concerning the operation(s) or procedure(s) described above.

MEDICAL DEVICE TRACKING. I hereby authorize the release of my Social Security number to the manufacturer of the medical device(s) I receive, if applicable, in accordance with federal law and regulations which may be used to help locate me if a need arises with regard to this medical device. I release the Sunny Valley Medical Center from any liability that might result from the release of this information.*

UNDERSTANDING OF THIS FORM. I confirm that I have read this form, fully understand its contents, and that all blank spaces above have been completed prior to my signing. I have crossed out any paragraphs above that do not pertain to me.

Patient/Relative/Guardian*

| _Marsha Dennis_ | Marsha Dennis |
| Signature | Print Name |

Relationship, if other than patient signed:

Witness:

| _William Preston_ | William Preston |
| Signature | Print Name |

Date: _4/27/YYYY_

*The signature of the patient must be obtained unless the patient is an unemancipated minor under the age of 18 or is otherwise incompetent to sign.

PHYSICIAN'S CERTIFICATION. I hereby certify that I have explained the nature, purpose, benefits, risks of and alternatives to the operation(s)/procedure(s), have offered to answer any questions and have fully answered all such questions. I believe that the patient (relative/guardian) fully understands what I have explained and answered.

PHYSICIAN:

| _Donald Thompson, MD_ | _4/27/YYYY_ |
| Signature | Date |

SUNNY VALLEY MEDICAL CENTER ■ 100 MAIN ST, SUNNY VALLEY, NY 14802 ■ (607) 555-1234

ANESTHESIA RECORD

DENNIS, Marsha	Admission: 04-27-YYYY
Case01	DOB: 02/09/YYYY
Dr. Thompson	Room: 0603

PROCEDURE(S):	D&C. Cold cone.	ANESTHESIA	START 1322	STOP 1415
SURGEON(S):	Thompson	PROCEDURE	1325	1340
DATE OF SURGERY:	4/27/YYYY	ROOM TIME	IN: 1300	OUT: 1420

PRE-PROCEDURE

- ☑ Patient Identified
- ☑ ID band verified
- ☑ Patient questioned
- ☑ Chart reviewed
- ☑ Consent form signed
- ☑ Patient reassessed prior to anesthesia (ready to proceed)
- ☑ Peri-operative pain management discussed with patient/guardian (plan of care completed)
- Pre-Anesthetic State:
- ☑ Awake ☑ Anxious ☐ Calm
- ☐ Lethargic ☐ Uncooperative
- ☐ Unresponsive
- ☐ Other: _____
- ☑ Anesthesia machine #5626984 checked
- ☑ Secured with safety belt
- ☑ Arm secured on board ☑ Left ☐ Right

MONITORS/EQUIPMENT

- ☑ Stethoscope
- ☐ Precordial
- ☐ Suprasternal
- ☐ Esoph
- ☑ Non-invasive B/P
- ☐ V-lead ECG
- ☑ Continuous ECG
- ☐ ST Analysis
- ☑ Pulse oximeter
- ☐ End tidal CO_2
- ☑ Nerve stimulator: ☐ Ulnar ☐ Tibial ☐ Facial
- ☑ Oxygen monitor
- ☐ Cell Saver
- ☑ ET agent analyzer
- ☐ B/S ☐ TEE
- ☐ Fluid/Blood warmer
- ☐ Temp:
- ☐ BIS
- ☐ ICS
- ☑ NG/OG tube
- ☐ FHT monitor
- ☑ Foley catheter
- ☐ EEG
- ☐ Airway humidifier
- ☐ Evoked potential: ☐ SSEP ☐ BAEP ☐ MEP
- ☐ Arterial line _____ ☐ CVP _____

ANESTHETIC TECHNIQUES

- GA Induction: ☑ IV ☐ Pre-O2 ☐ RSI ☐ PR
- ☐ Cricoid pressure ☐ Inhalation ☐ IM
- GA Maintenance: ☐ TIVA ☐ Inhalation
- ☑ Inhalation/IV ☐ GA/Regional Comb.

Regional:
- Epidural: ☐ Thoracic ☐ Lumbar ☐ Caudal
- ☐ Femoral ☐ Auxiliary ☐ Interscalene
- ☐ CSE ☐ Bier ☐ SAB ☐ Ankle
- ☐ Continuous Spinal ☐ Cervical Plexus

Regional Techniques: ☐ See Remarks
- ☐ Position _____ ☐ Prep _____
- ☐ Site _____ ☐ Needle _____
- ☐ LA _____ ☐ Narcotic _____
- ☐ Additive _____ ☐ Test dose Rx ___

AIRWAY MANAGEMENT

- ☑ Oral ETT ☐ LTA ☐ RAE
- ☐ Nasal ETT ☐ LMA #
- ☐ Stylet ☐ LMA Fastrach # ____
- ☐ DVL ☐ LMA ProSeal # ____
- ☐ EMG ETT ☐ Bougie
- ☐ Armored ETT ☐ LIS
- ☑ Breath sounds = bilateral
- ☐ Cuffed – min occ pres with ☑ air ☐ NS
- ☐ Uncuffed – leaks at _____ cm H_2O
- ☑ Oral airway ☐ Nasal airway ☐ Bite block
- Circuit: ☐ Circle system ☐ NRB ☐ Bain
- ☐ Via tracheotomy/stoma ☐ Mask case
- ☐ Nasal cannula ☑ Simple O_2 mask
- Nebulizer: _____
- Nerve Block(s): _____

TIME:	15	30	45	15	30	45	15	30	45	15	30	45	15	30	45	TOTALS
AGENTS																
☐ Des ☐ Iso ☐ Sevo ☐ Halo (%)																
☑ Air (L/min)		2.5	2.5	X												
☑ Oxygen (L/min)	66	2	2	66												
☑ N2O (L/min)		2.5	2.5	X												
☑ Forane (%)		1/3	2/3	2/0	X											
☑ Anectine (mg)																
☑ Pentothal (mg)		100	100	100	X											226
FLUIDS																
Urine																
EBL																
Gastric																

SYMBOLS

☒⊼ BP cuff pressure

⊥ Arterial line pressure

× Mean arterial pressure

● Pulse

○ Spontaneous Respirations

∅ Assisted Respirations

T Tourniquet

MONITORS																
☑ ECG																
☑ % Oxygen Inspired (FI0₂)		98	98	98	98											
☑ End Tidal CO_2			44	44	44											
☑ Temp: ☐ C ☑ F		98			98											
☑ BP Monitor																

PERI-OP MEDS

	200															
	180															
	160															
	140	⌄	⌄	⌄												
	120				⌄	⌄										
	100			•	•	•										
	80	•	•	⌃	⌃											
	60	⌃	⌃			⌃										
	40															
	20	○	○	○	○	○										
	10															

VENT																
Tidal Volume (ml)																
Respiratory Rate		SA	SA	SA	SA											
Peak Pressure (cm H_2O)																
☐ PEEP ☐ CPAP (cm H_2O)																

Position: Lithotomy

Mask. S32 Nasal airway, rt nostril. S20 Oral tubing.
Intake D5LR 1000. Total 650 cc. S18 gu. left.

Surgeon	Thompson
Assistant	
Scrub Nurse	Mary Marks, RN
Circulating Nurse	Cynthia Lewis, RN
Signature of Anesthesiologist or C.R.N.A.	Don Galloway, M.D.

Time of Delivery: _____

Gender: ☐ M ☐ F

Apgars: ___/___

DENNIS, Marsha Case01 Dr. Thompson	Admission: 04-27-YYYY DOB: 02/09/YYYY Room: 0603	PRE-ANESTHESIA AND POST-ANESTHESIA RECORD

PRE-ANESTHESIA EVALUATION

HISTORY TAKEN FROM:	☑ Patient ☐ Parent/ Guardian ☐ Significant Other ☑ Chart ☐ Poor Historian ☐ Language Barrier

PROPOSED PROCEDURE:	D&C. Cold cone.	DATE OF SURGERY:	4/27/YYYY

AGE	GENDER	HEIGHT	WEIGHT	BLOOD PRESSURE	PULSE	RESPIRATIONS	TEMPERATURE	O2 SAT%
54	☐ Male ☑ Female	5'5"	145	130/80	75	22	98.6	96

PREVIOUS ANESTHESIA:	☑ None
PREVIOUS SURGERY:	☑ None
CURRENT MEDICATIONS:	☑ None
FAMILY HX – ANES. PROBLEMS:	☑ None
ALLERGIES:	☑ None

AIRWAY	☐ MP1 ☐ MP2 ☐ MP3 ☐ MP4 ☐ Unrestricted neck ROM ☐ T-M distance = _____
(Enter X in appropriate boxes.)	☐ Obesity ☐ ↓ neck ROM ☐ History of difficult airway ☐ Short muscular neck
	☐ Teeth poor repair ☐ Teeth chipped/loose ☐ Edentulous ☐ Facial hair

BODY SYSTEM	COMMENTS	DIAGNOSTIC STUDIES
RESPIRATORY	☑ WNL Tobacco Use: ☐ Yes ☑ No ☐ Quit ___ Packs/Day for ___ Years	ECG CHEST X-RAY Negative PULMONARY STUDIES
CARDIOVASCULAR	☑ WNL Pre-procedure Cardiac Assessment:	LABORATORY STUDIES PT/PTT/INR: T&S / T&C:
GASTROINTESTINAL	☑ WNL Ethanol Use: ☐ Yes ☑ No ☐ Quit Frequency ___ ☐ History of Ethanol abuse	HCG: 13.2 UA
Abnormal pap smear		OTHER DIAGNOSTIC TESTS Hct 38.4
MUSCULOSKELETAL	☑ WNL	PLANNED ANESTHESIA/MONITORS ECG. ETCO2. O2. Temp. O2 Sat. BP monitor.
GENITOURINARY	☐ WNL	
OTHER	☐ WNL	PRE-ANESTHESIA MEDICATION
ASA risk classification 1		
PREGNANCY	☐ WNL ☐ AROM ☐ SROM ☐ Pitocin Drip ☐ Induction ☐ MgDrip EDC: ___ Weeks Gestation: ___ G: ___ P: ___	
		SIGNATURE OF ANESTHESIOLOGIST OR C.R.N.A. Don Galloway, M.D.

POST-ANESTHESIA EVALUATION

CONTROLLED MEDICATIONS

Location	Time	B/P	O2Sat	Pulse	Respirations	Temperature	Medication	Used	Destroyed	Returned
Room	1630	142/84	96	90	14	98.6				

☑ Awake ☐ Mask O2 ☐ Somnolent ☐ Unarousable ☐ Oral/nasal airway
☑ Stable ☐ NC O2 ☐ Unstable ☐ T-Piece ☐ Intubated ☐ Ventilator
☐ Regional – dermatome level: ☐ Continuous epidural analgesia
☐ Direct admit to hospital room ☑ No anesthesia related complications noted
☐ See progress notes for anesthesia related concerns ☑ Satisfactory postanesthesia/analgesia recovery

SIGNATURE OF ANESTHESIOLOGIST OR C.R.N.A.
Don Galloway, M.D.

DENNIS, Marsha	Admission: 04-27-YYYY	OPERATIVE REPORT
Case01	DOB: 02/09/YYYY	
Dr. Thompson	Room: 0603	

DATE OF SURGERY: 4-27-YYYY

PREOPERATIVE DIAGNOSIS: Abnormal Papanicolaou smear

POSTOPERATIVE DIAGNOSIS: Squamous dysplasia
Acute and chronic cervicitis with squamous metaplasia

OPERATION PERFORMED: Dilatation and curettage and conization

SURGEON: Dr. Thompson

ANESTHETIC: General

COMPLICATIONS: None

OPERATIVE NOTE: The patient was anesthetized, placed in lithotomy position and prepped and draped in the usual manner for vaginal surgery. The cervix was painted with Schiller's stain delineating the iodine negative Schiller positive area. The cervix was then grasped with a single toothed tenaculum at 3 and 9 o'clock outside of the unstained area of the cervix and an area of excisional cone biopsy was done in such a way as to incl 1.rle all the iodine negative areas. The conization specimen was labeled with suture at 12 o'clock and sent to Pathology in saline for processing. The uterine cavity was then sounded to a depth of 4+ inches and the endometrial cavity curetted with a sharp curette. A very scanty amount of endometrium was obtained and sent to Pathology as specimen ®2. Oxycel pack was then placed in the defect left by the cone and because of the size of the cone it was necessary to close the angles with interrupted sutures of 1 chromic catgut. A vaginal packing was placed in the vagina to hold the Oxycel pack. A Foley catheter was placed in the bladder. There was no significant bleeding. The patient withstood the procedure well and was returned to the Recovery Room in good condition. No anesthetic or operative complications.

DD: 04-28-YYYY

DT: 04-29-YYYY

Donald Thompson, MD
_____
Donald Thompson, M.D.

```
DENNIS, Marsha        Admission: 04-27-YYYY        PATHOLOGY REPORT
Case01                DOB: 02/09/YYYY
Dr. Thompson          Room: 0603
```

Date of Surgery: 4/27/YYYY

OPERATION: Cold cone cervix. D&C.

SPECIMEN: #1. Cone cervix suture @ 1200
             #2. Uterus curettements

GROSS

Number one consists of a cervical cone which measures 3.4 cm in diameter x 2.5 cm in greatest thickness. The mucosal surface is reddened and slightly irregular noted especially involving the inferior portion of the mucosa. The specimen is cut into thin parallel sections and entirely submitted as indicated on the diagram below labeled as "A," "B," "C," and "D." A portion of suture is attached to the specimen which is designated as "1200." Number two submitted as "uterine curettings" consists of approximately .5 grams of fragmented pink-tan and purple-tan tissue which is entirely submitted as "E."

MICROSCOPIC

Sections "A," "B," "C," and "D" are all similar showing portions of cervix including the squamocolumnar junction. There is acute and chronic cervicitis and focal squamous metaplasia of the endocervix including squamous metaplasia effecting some endocervical glands. In the region of the squamocolumnar junction, the squamous epithelium shows some cells with enlarged hyperchromatic nuclei and there is a mild decrease in maturation with some mild disorganization. In some regions, the upper levels or even the entire epithelium is absent. This seems to extend out on the ectocervical side of the squamocolumnar junction and is not obviously in the margin, however, in some regions the margins are incomplete. Multiple levels are examined. The dysplasia is most advanced in the sections labeled "C." Section "E" shows fragments of endometrium containing convoluted nonsecretory glands. The stroma consists of spindle- and polygonal-type cells.

DIAGNOSIS

#1. "CONE CERVIX:" MILD TO MODERATE SQUAMOUS DYSPLASIA. ACUTE AND CHRONIC CERVICITIS WITH SQUAMOUS METAPLASIA.

#2. "UTERINE CURETTEMENTS:" FRAGMENTS OF NONSECRETORY PHASE ENDOMETRIUM.

DD: 04-29-YYYY

DT: 04-30-YYYY

Albert Gardner, M.D.
Albert Gardner, M.D.

DENNIS, Marsha
Case01
Dr. Thompson

Admission: 04-27-YYYY
DOB: 02/09/YYYY
Room: 0603

RECOVERY ROOM RECORD

DATE: 4/27/YYYY   **TIME:** 1420

OPERATION: D&C. Cold cone.

ANESTHESIA: General

AIRWAY: N/A

O₂ USED: ☒ YES ☐ NO
ROUTE: Mask @ 6L/min.

TIME	MEDICATIONS	SITE

INTAKE	AMOUNT
300 D5L R Left hand	
IV site w/o redness or edema	
250 D5L. R on discharge	
TOTAL	50 cc

OUTPUT	AMOUNT
CATHETER Clear light yellow	10 cc
LEVINE N/A	
HEMOVAC N/A	
TOTAL	10 cc

DISCHARGE STATUS

ROOM: 0603   **TIME:** 1455

CONDITION: Satisfactory

TRANSFERRED BY Stretcher

R.R. NURSE: Sally James, RN

PREOP VISIT:

POSTOP VISIT: Report given to Dr. Galloway at 1500 by S. James, R.N.

Graph — O₂ readings along top rows: 210, 190, 170 marked "O2 100% 100% 100% 100% 100% 100% 97% 98% 98% 97%". Temperature/BP/pulse plot symbols across time columns 0–60, 15–60.

Thermoscan probe. Oral mode q9 adm.

POSTANESTHESIA RECOVERY SCORE		Adm	30 min	1 hr	2 hr	Disch
Moves 4 extremities voluntarily or on command (2) Moves 2 extremities voluntarily or on command (1) Moves 0 extremities voluntarily or on command (0)	Activity	2	2	2	2	2
Able to deep breathe and cough freely (2) Dyspnea or limited breathing (1) Apneic (0)	Respiration	2	2	2	2	2
BP ± 20% of preanesthetic level BP + 20% of preanesthetic level BP + 50% of preanesthetic level	Circulation	2	2	2	2	2
Fully awake (2) Arouseable on calling (1) Not responding (0)	Consciousness	2	2	2	2	2
Pink (2) Pale, dusky, blotchy, jaundiced, other (1) Cyanotic (0)	Color	2	2	2	2	2

COMMENTS & OBSERVATIONS:

Dinamap BP monitor R arm q5min.

Pt awake on arrival to RR with respirations deep, easy and regular.

2" vaginal packing in place as reported by circulating nurse.

Foley draining small amount yellow urine.

Mary Crawford, RN
SIGNATURE OF RECOVERY ROOM NURSE

LABORATORY DATA

DENNIS, Marsha
Case01
Dr. Thompson

Admission: 04-27-YYYY
DOB: 02/09/YYYY
Room: 0603

SPECIMEN COLLECTED: 04-22-YYYY

SPECIMEN RECEIVED: 04-22-YYYY

TEST	RESULT	FLAG	REFERENCE
URINALYSIS			
DIPSTICK ONLY			
COLOR	CLOUDY YELLOW		
SP GRAVITY	1.025		≤ 1.030
GLUCOSE	110		≤ 125 mg/dl
BILIRUBIN	NEG		≤ 0.8 mg/dl
KETONE	TRACE		≤ 10 mg/dl
BLOOD	0.03		0.06 mg/dl hgb
PH	5.0		5-8.0
PROTEIN	NORMAL		≤ 30 mg/dl
UROBILINOGEN	NORMAL		≤ -1 mg/dl
NITRITES	NEG		NEG
LEUKOCYTE	NEG		≤ 15 WBC/hpf
W.B.C.	5-10		≤ 5/hpf
R.B.C.	RARE		≤ 5/hpf
BACT.	4f		1+ (≤ 20/hpf)
URINE PREGNANCY TEST			
	NEG		

End of Report

DENNIS, Marsha	Admission: 04-27-YYYY	RADIOLOGY REPORT
Case01	DOB: 02/09/YYYY	
Dr. Thompson	Room: 0603	

Date Requested: 04-22-YYYY
Pre-op: 04-27-YYYY

CHEST: PA and lateral views show that the heart, lungs, thorax, and mediastinum are normal.

DD: 04-22-YYYY

DT: 04-22-YYYY

Philip Rogers
_____
Philip Rogers, M.D., Radiologist

DENNIS, Marsha   Admission: 04-27-YYYY   **EKG REPORT**
Case01   DOB: 02/09/YYYY
Dr. Thompson   Room: 0603

Date of EKG: *04-22-YYYY*   Time of EKG: *10:56:20*

Rate	*66*	
PR	*184*	
QRSD	*60*	
QT	*363*	*Normal.*
QTC	*380*	
-- Axis --		
P	*76*	
QRS	*79*	
T	*71*	

Bella Kaplan

Bella Kaplan, M.D.

Case 02

SUNNY VALLEY MEDICAL CENTER 100 MAIN ST, SUNNY VALLEY, NY 14802 (607) 555-1234 HOSPITAL #: 000999				INPATIENT FACE SHEET		

PATIENT NAME AND ADDRESS		GENDER	RACE	MARITAL STATUS	PATIENT NO.
HUNTER, Dilbert 543 Yukon Trail Sunny Valley, NY 14802		M	W	M	Case02

DATE OF BIRTH	MAIDEN NAME	OCCUPATION
09-22-YYYY	N/A	Unemployed

ADMISSION DATE	TIME	DISCHARGE DATE	TIME	LENGTH OF STAY	TELEPHONE NUMBER
04-26-YYYY	15:20	04-29-YYYY	10:10	03 DAYS	(607) 555-6632

GUARANTOR NAME AND ADDRESS	NEXT OF KIN NAME AND ADDRESS
Hunter, Anita 543 Yukon Trail Sunny Valley, NY 14802	Hunter, Anita 543 Yukon Trail Sunny Valley, NY 14802

GUARANTOR TELEPHONE NO.	RELATIONSHIP TO PATIENT	NEXT OF KIN TELEPHONE NUMBER	RELATIONSHIP TO PATIENT
(607) 555-6632	Wife	(607) 555-6632	Wife

ADMITTING PHYSICIAN	SERVICE	ADMIT TYPE	ROOM NUMBER/BED
William Ruddy, MD	Medical	2	0366/01

ATTENDING PHYSICIAN	ATTENDING PHYSICIAN UPIN	ADMITTING DIAGNOSIS
William Ruddy, MD	100T32	Rule out pneumonia.

PRIMARY INSURER	POLICY AND GROUP NUMBER	SECONDARY INSURER	POLICY AND GROUP NUMBER
Empire Plan	352656388		

DIAGNOSES AND PROCEDURES	ICD-10-CM/PCS
PRINCIPAL DIAGNOSIS	
Acute Bronchitis	J44.0
SECONDARY DIAGNOSES	
Asthma	J44.9
COPD	I10
↑ B.P.	
PRINCIPAL PROCEDURE	
SECONDARY PROCEDURES	
TOTAL CHARGES: $ 2,692.74	

ACTIVITY:	☐ Bedrest	☑ Light	☐ Usual	☐ Unlimited	☐ Other:
DIET:	☐ Regular	☐ Low Cholesterol	☑ Low Salt	☐ ADA	☐ _____ Calorie
FOLLOW-UP:	☐ Call for appointment	☐ Office appointment on _____		☐ Other:	

SPECIAL INSTRUCTIONS:

Signature of Attending Physician: William Ruddy, MD

HUNTER, Dilbert	Admission: 04-26-YYYY
Case 02	DOB: 09-22-YYYY
Dr. Ruddy	ROOM: 0366

CONSENT TO ADMISSION

I, _Dilbert Hunter_ hereby consent to admission to the Sunny Valley Medical Center (SVMC), and I further consent to such routine hospital care, diagnostic procedures, and medical treatment that the medical and professional staff of SVMC may deem necessary or advisable. I authorize the use of medical information obtained about me as specified above and the disclosure of such information to my referring physician(s). This form has been fully explained to me, and I understand its contents. I further understand that no guarantees have been made to me as to the results of treatments or examinations done at the SVMC.

Dilbert Hunter   _April 26, YYYY_

Signature of Patient   Date

Signature of Parent/Legal Guardian for Minor   Date

Relationship to Minor

Andrea Witteman   _April 26, yyyy_

WITNESS: Sunny Valley Medical Center Staff Member   Date

CONSENT TO RELEASE INFORMATION FOR REIMBURSEMENT PURPOSES

In order to permit reimbursement, upon request, the Sunny Valley Medical Center (SVMC) may disclose such treatment information pertaining to my hospitalization to any corporation, organization, or agent thereof, which is, or may be liable under contract to the SVMC or to me, or to any of my family members or other person, for payment of all or part of the SVMC's charges for services rendered to me (e.g., the patient's health insurance carrier). I understand that the purpose of any release of information is to facilitate reimbursement for services rendered. In addition, in the event that my health insurance program includes utilization review of services provided during this admission, I authorize SVMC to release information as is necessary to permit the review. This authorization will expire once the reimbursement for services rendered is complete.

Dilbert Hunter   _April 26, YYYY_

Signature of Patient   Date

Signature of Parent/Legal Guardian for Minor   Date

Relationship to Minor

Andrea Witteman   _April 26, yyyy_

WITNESS: Sunny Valley Medical Center Staff Member   Date

SUNNY VALLEY MEDICAL CENTER ■ 100 MAIN ST, SUNNY VALLEY, NY 14802 ■ (607) 555-1234

HUNTER, Dilbert	Admission: 04-26-YYYY	ADVANCE DIRECTIVE
Case02	DOB: 09-22-YYYY	
Dr. Ruddy	ROOM: 0366	

Your answers to the following questions will assist your Physician and the Hospital to respect your wishes regarding your medical care. This information will become a part of your medical record.

	YES	NO	PATIENT'S INITIALS
1. Have you been provided with a copy of the information called "Patient Rights Regarding Health Care Decision?"	X		DH
2. Have you prepared a "Living Will?" If yes, please provide the Hospital with a copy for your medical record.		X	DH
3. Have you prepared a Durable Power of Attorney for Health Care? If yes, please provide the Hospital with a copy for your medical record.		X	DH
4. Have you provided this facility with an Advance Directive on a prior admission and is it still in effect? If yes, Admitting Office to contact Medical Records to obtain a copy for the medical record.		X	DH
5. Do you desire to execute a Living Will/Durable Power of Attorney? If yes, refer to in order: a. Physician b. Social Service c. Volunteer Service		X	DH

HOSPITAL STAFF DIRECTIONS: Check when each step is completed.

1. ✓ Verify the above questions where answered and actions taken where required.
2. ✓ If the "Patient Rights" information was provided to someone other than the patient, state reason:

_____

_____ _____
Name of Individual Receiving Information   Relationship to Patient

3. ✓ If information was provided in a language other than English, specify language and method.
4. ✓ Verify patient was advised on how to obtain additional information on Advance Directives.
5. ✓ Verify the Patient/Family Member/Legal Representative was asked to provide the Hospital with a copy of the Advance Directive which will be retained in the medical record.

File this form in the medical record and give a copy to the patient.

Name of Patient (Name of Individual giving information if different from Patient)

Dilbert Hunter   April 26, YYYY
_____   _____
Signature of Patient   Date

Andrea Witteman   April 26, yyyy
_____   _____
Signature of Hospital Representative   Date

SUNNY VALLEY MEDICAL CENTER ■ 100 MAIN ST, SUNNY VALLEY, NY 14802 ■ (607) 555-1234

HUNTER, Dilbert	Admission: 04-26-YYYY	HISTORY & PHYSICAL EXAM
Case 02	DOB: 09-22-YYYY	
Dr. Ruddy	ROOM: 0366	

CHIEF COMPLAINT: Shortness of breath.

HISTORY OF PRESENT ILLNESS: The patient is a 55 yr. old gentleman with severe COPD with asthma and hypertension, who had developed an acute bronchitis about a week ago and five days ago was started on Ampicillin taking his usual 500 mg. t.i.d. This did not help, and he was started on a Medrol Dose-Pak but he had already been taking Prednisone. The patient had increasing shortness of breath the last 24 hours and came in. He had to stop four times to walk from the parking lot into the office due to increasing shortness of breath. He has some orthopnea, paroxysmal nocturnal dyspnea with it, which is typical for a flare up of his COPD with asthma and especially if infected. The patient has severe allergies to nonsteroidals causing him almost an anaphylactic type of reaction and with severe shortness of breath and had one respiratory arrest requiring intubation for that particular problem.

PAST MEDICAL HISTORY: General health has been good when he is in between his breathing attacks. Childhood diseases-no rheumatic or scarlet fever. Adult diseases-no TB or diabetes. Has had recurrent pneumonias. Operations: hemorrhoidectomy.

MEDICATIONS: At this time include Lasix 40 mg. daily. Calan 80 mg. t.i.d. Prednisone 10 mg. daily. Vasotec 10 mg. daily. Theolair 250 b.i.d. Allopurinol 300 mg. daily. Proventil and Azmacort 2 puffs q. i .d.

ALLERGIES: Nonsteroidal antiinflammatory drugs, including aspirin.

SOCIAL HISTORY: Does not smoke or drink.

FAMILY HISTORY: Noncontributory.

REVIEW OF SYSTEMS: Head: no headaches, seizures or convulsions. EENT reveals rhinorrhea and allergies, particularly with sinusitis. Chest and heart: see HPI. GI: no nausea, diarrhea, constipation. GU: no dysuria, hematuria, nocturia. Extremities: no edema. Has a lot of arthritic problems getting along with Tylenol at this time.

GENERAL APPEARANCE: The patient is a middle-aged gentleman who is short of breath at rest.

VITAL SIGNS: Temperature is 97, pulse is 60, respirations 24, blood pressure 146/68. Weight 254 lbs.

SKIN: Normal color and texture. No petechiae or ecchymoses.

HEENT: Normal cephalic. No mastoid or cranial tenderness. Eyes, pupils equal and reactive to light and accommodation. Extra-ocular muscle function intact. Funduscopic examination within normal limits. Ears: no inflammation or bulging of the drums. Nose: no inflammation, though there is same clear rhinorrhea. Mouth: no inflammation or exudate.

NECK: Supple. No adenopathy. Trachea in the midline. Thyroid normal. Carotids 2/4 with no bruits.

CHEST: Symmetrical.

LUNGS: There are wheezes heard throughout the lung fields with rhonchi and rales at the right base.

HEART: Regular rhythm. S1 2/4, S2 2/4, with no S3, S4 or murmurs.

BACK: No CVA or spinal tenderness.

ABDOMEN: Soft. No organomegaly, masses, or tenderness to palpation or percussion. Normal bowel sounds.

GENITALIA: Normal external genitalia.

RECTAL: Good sphincter tone. No mucosal masses. Stool hemoccult negative. Prostate 2+ with no nodules.

EXTREMITIES: Peripheral pulses 2+. No edema, cyanosis or clubbing.

NEUROLOGIC: Within normal limits.

IMPRESSION: 1) Asthma with acute bronchitis and bronchospasm.

2) Hypertension.

DD: 04-26-YYYY

DT: 04-27-YYYY

William Ruddy, MD
_____
William Ruddy, MD

HUNTER, Dilbert	Admission: 04-26-YYYY	PROGRESS NOTES
Case 02	DOB: 09-22-YYYY	
Dr. Ruddy	ROOM: 0366	

Date	(Please skip one line between dates.)
4/26/YYYY	Chief Complaint: Shortness of breath.
	Dx: COPD, asthma, acute brohchitis.
	Plan of Treatment: See physician orders.
	Discharge Plan: Home. William Ruddy, MD
4/27/YYYY	Pt. is less SOB today but still has considerable wheezing. Will cont same meds
	until I get results of culture and sensitivity. William Ruddy, MD

HUNTER, Dilbert		Admission: 04-26-YYYY	DOCTORS ORDERS
Case 02		DOB: 09-22-YYYY	
Dr. Ruddy		ROOM: 0366	

Date	Time	Physician's signature required for each order. (Please skip one line between dates.)
4/26/YYYY	1525	Sputum C & S. CBC, UA, ABG Rx and call CXR; NAS diet; Saline Lock
		Ancef 1 gm q 8°
		Solumedrol 125mg q 6° IV
		Calan 80mg Tid
		Vasotic 10mg daily
		Theodur 300mg Bid (q 12°)
		Allopurinol 300mg daily
		Proventil and Azmacort puffs qid – do own Rx William Ruddy, MD
		R.A.V. V.O. Dr. Ruddy/J.Anderson, RN
4/26/YYYY	1720	D/C ABC. Do RA oximetry. R.A.V. T.O. Dr. Ruddy/E. Blossom RN
4/26/YYYY	1720	O2 2L/Ne R.A.V. T.O. Dr. Ruddy/E. Blossom RN
4/27/YYYY	1320	Tylenol 650mg po q 4° prn pain R.A.V. T.O. Dr. Ruddy/H. Figgs RN
4/28/YYYY	1020	1) D/C IV
		2) Ceftin 250mg P.O. Bid
		3) Prednisone 20mg P.O. William Ruddy, MD
		4) Walk hall as tolerated R.A.V. T.O. Dr. Ruddy/E. Blossom RN
		William Ruddy, MD
4/28/YYYY	0900	DC O2 R.A.V. T.O. Dr. Ruddy/H. Figgs RN
4/29/YYYY	1200	Discharge home – dict later William Ruddy, MD

SUNNY VALLEY MEDICAL CENTER ■ 100 MAIN ST, SUNNY VALLEY, NY 14802 ■ (607) 555-1234

```
HUNTER, Dilbert      Admission: 04-26-YYYY              LABORATORY DATA
Case02               DOB: 09-22-YYYY
Dr. Ruddy            ROOM: 0366
```

SPECIMEN COLLECTED: 04-26-YYYY   **SPECIMEN RECEIVED:** 04-26-YYYY

URINALYSIS

URINE DIPSTICK

COLOR	STRAW	
SP GRAVITY	1.010	1.001-1.030
GLUCOSE	NEGATIVE	< 125 mg/dl
BILIRUBIN	NEGATIVE	NEG
KETONE	NEGATIVE	NEG mg/dl
BLOOD	NEGATIVE	NEG
PH	7.5	4.5-8.0
PROTEIN	NEGATIVE	NEG mg/dl
UROBILINOGEN	NORMAL	NORMAL-1.0 mg/dl
NITRITES	NEGATIVE	NEG
LEUKOCYTES	NEGATIVE	NEG
WBC	RARE	0-5 /HPF
RBC	--	0-5 /HPF
EPI CELLS	RARE	/HPF
BACTERIA	--	/HPF
CASTS.	--	< 1 HYALINE/HPF

End of Report

HUNTER, Dilbert   Admission: 04-26-YYYY   LABORATORY DATA

Case 02   DOB: 09-22-YYYY

Dr. Ruddy   ROOM: 0366

SPECIMEN COLLECTED: 04-26-YYYY   SPECIMEN RECEIVED: 04-26-YYYY

CBC c̄ DIFF

TEST	RESULT	FLAG	REFERENCE
WBC	7.4		4.5-11.0 thous/UL
RBC	5.02	**L**	5.2-5.4 mill/UL
HGB	15.0		11.7-16.1 g/dl
HCT	45.8		35.0-47.0 %
MCV	91.2		85-99 fL.
MCHC	32.8	**L**	33-37
RDW	15.2	**H**	11.4-14.5
Platelets	165		130-400 thous/UL
MPV	8.4		7.4-10.4
LYMPH %	21.1		20.5-51.1
MONO %	7.8		1.7-9.3
GRAN %	71.1		42.2-75.2
LYMPH x 10^3	1.6		1.2-3.4
MONO x 10^3	.6	**H**	0.11-0.59
GRAN x 10^3	5.3		1.4-6.5
EOS x 10^3	< .7		0.0-0.7
BASO x 10^3	< .2		0.0-0.2
ANISO	SLIGHT		

End of Report

HUNTER, Dilbert	Admission: 04-26-YYYY	RADIOLOGY REPORT
Case02	DOB: 09-22-YYYY	
Dr. Ruddy	ROOM: 0366	

Initial Diagnosis/History: COPD

Date Requested: 04-26-YYYY

Transport: ☑ Wheelchair   ☐ Stretcher   ☐ O$_2$ ☐ IV
           ☑ IP   ☐ OP   ☐ ER
           ☐ PRE OP   ☐ OR/RR   ☐ Portable

CHEST: PA and lateral views reveals the heart and mediastinum to be normal. The lungs are hyperinflated with flattening of the diaphragms and disorganization of the interstitial markings secondary to chronic disease. There is also some old pleural thickening at the left base laterally. Since our previous study of 4-30-YYYY, an area of atelectasis has developed in the middle lobe. I do not know if this is of any current significance. No areas of consolidation or any pleural effusions are visible.

DD: 04-26-YYYY

Philip Rogers
_____
Philip Rogers

DT: 04-27-YYYY

HUNTER, Dilbert	Admission: 04-26-YYYY	
Case02	DOB: 09-22-YYYY	MEDICATION ADMINISTRATION RECORD
Dr. Ruddy	ROOM: 0366	

SPECIAL INSTRUCTIONS:

MEDICATION (dose and route)	DATE: 04-26 TIME	INITIALS	DATE: 04-27 TIME	INITIALS	DATE: 04-28 TIME	INITIALS	DATE: 04-29 TIME	INITIALS
ANCEF 1GM Q 8°	0800	VT	0800	VT	0800	HF		
	1600	JD	1600	OR	D/c			
	2400	P.S.	2400	P.S.	D/c			
SOLUMEDROL 125 MG IV 1 6°	0600	GPW	0600	GPW	0600	GPW		
	1200	GPW	1200	VT	D/c			
	1800	JD	1800	OR	D/c			
	2400	GPW	2400	GPW	D/c			
CALAN 80 MG TID	0800	VT	0800	VT	0800	HF	0800	HF
	1300	VT	1300	VT	1300	HF	D/c	
	1800	JD	1800	JD	1800	OR	1800	JD
VASOTEC 10MG DAILY	0800	JD	0800	JD	0800	HF	0800	HF
THEODUR 300MG Q 12°	0800	JD	0800	JD	0800	HF	0800	HF
	2000	JD	2000	JD	2000	OR	2000	JD
ALLOPURINOL 300MG DAILY	0800	JD	0800	JD	0800	HF	0800	HF
SALINE FLUSH P̄ EACH USE	0800	JD	0800	JD	D/c			
CEFTIN 250 mg PO BID	0800	HF	0800	HF	0800	HF	0800	HF
	1600	JD	1600	JD	1600	JD	D/c	

INITIALS	SIGNATURE AND TITLE		INITIALS	SIGNATURE AND TITLE		INITIALS	SIGNATURE AND TITLE
VT	VERA SOUTH, EN		GPW	G. P. WELL, RN			
OR	ORA RICHARDS, RN		P.S.	P. SMALL, RN			
JD	JANE DOBBS, RN						
HF	H. Figgs RN						

SUNNY VALLEY MEDICAL CENTER ■ 100 MAIN ST, SUNNY VALLEY, NY 14802 ■ (607) 555-1234

| HUNTER, Dilbert
Case02
Dr. Ruddy | Admission: 04-26-YYYY
DOB: 09-22-YYYY
ROOM: 0366 | PATIENT PROPERTY RECORD |

I understand that while the facility will be responsible for items deposited in the safe, I must be responsible for all items retained by me at the bedside. (Dentures kept at the bedside will be labeled, but the facility cannot assure responsibility for them.) I also recognize that the hospital cannot be held responsible for items brought in to me after this form has been completed and signed.

Dilbert Hunter
_____
Signature of Patient

Andrea Witteman
_____
Signature of Witness

April 26, YYYY
_____
Date

April 26, YYYY
_____
Date

- -

I have no money or valuables that I wish to deposit for safekeeping. I do not hold the facility responsible for any other money or valuables that I am retaining or will have brought in to me.

I have been advised that it is recommended that I retain no more than $5.00 at the bedside.

Dilbert Hunter
_____
Signature of Patient

Andrea Witteman
_____
Signature of Witness

April 26, YYYY
_____
Date

April 26, YYYY
_____
Date

- -

I have deposited valuables in the facility safe. The envelope number is _____.

_____
Signature of Patient

_____
Signature of Person Accepting Property

_____
Date

_____
Date

- -

I understand that medications I have brought to the facility will be handled as recommended by my physician. This may include storage, disposal, or administration.

_____
Signature of Patient

_____
Signature of Witness

_____
Date

_____
Date

Case 03

SUNNY VALLEY MEDICAL CENTER
100 MAIN ST, SUNNY VALLEY, NY 14802
(607) 555-1234
HOSPITAL #: 000999

INPATIENT FACE SHEET

PATIENT NAME AND ADDRESS				GENDER	RACE	MARITAL STATUS	PATIENT NO.
STANLEY, Erica P.				F	W	M	Case03
23 Langley Drive				DATE OF BIRTH	MAIDEN NAME		OCCUPATION
Sunny Valley, NY 14802				04-05-YYYY	Holland		Homemaker

ADMISSION DATE	TIME	DISCHARGE DATE	TIME	LENGTH OF STAY	TELEPHONE NUMBER
04-28-YYYY	06:20	04-29-YYYY	10:20	01 DAY	(607)555-8818

GUARANTOR NAME AND ADDRESS	NEXT OF KIN NAME AND ADDRESS
Stanley, Robert	Stanley, Robert
23 Langley Drive	23 Langley Drive
Sunny Valley, NY 14802	Sunny Valley, NY 14802

GUARANTOR TELEPHONE NO.	RELATIONSHIP TO PATIENT	NEXT OF KIN TELEPHONE NUMBER	RELATIONSHIP TO PATIENT
(607)555-8818	Husband	(607)555-8818	Husband

ADMITTING PHYSICIAN	SERVICE	ADMIT TYPE	ROOM NUMBER/BED
E.W. Wylie, MD	Surgical	03	0255/01

ATTENDING PHYSICIAN	ATTENDING PHYSICIAN UPIN	ADMITTING DIAGNOSIS	
E.W. Wylie, MD	100D43	Gallbladder disease	

PRIMARY INSURER	POLICY AND GROUP NUMBER	SECONDARY INSURER	POLICY AND GROUP NUMBER
Medicaid	329130095		

DIAGNOSES AND PROCEDURES	ICD-10-CM/PCS
PRINCIPAL DIAGNOSIS	
chronic acalculus cholecystitis	K81.1
SECONDARY DIAGNOSES	
PRINCIPAL PROCEDURE	
Laparoscopic cholecystectomy	0FT44ZZ
SECONDARY PROCEDURES	
TOTAL CHARGES: $ 3,500.50	

ACTIVITY: ☐ Bedrest ☒ Light ☐ Usual ☐ Unlimited ☒ Other: Don't lift heavy or stairs

DIET: ☒ Regular ☐ Low Cholesterol ☐ Low Salt ☐ ADA ☐ _____ Calorie

FOLLOW-UP: ☐ Call for appointment ☒ Office appointment in ≥ WKS ☒ Other: Dr. Winslow in one wk

SPECIAL INSTRUCTIONS: May shower.

SIGNATURE OF ATTENDING PHYSICIAN: E Wylie, M.D.

STANLEY, Erica P.   Admission: 04-28-YYYY
Case03   DOB: 04-05-YYYY
Dr. Wylie   ROOM: 0255

CONSENT TO ADMISSION

I, _Erica P. Stanley_ hereby consent to admission to the Sunny Valley Medical Center (SVMC), and I further consent to such routine hospital care, diagnostic procedures, and medical treatment that the medical and professional staff of SVMC may deem necessary or advisable. I authorize the use of medical information obtained about me as specified above and the disclosure of such information to my referring physician(s). This form has been fully explained to me, and I understand its contents. I further understand that no guarantees have been made to me as to the results of treatments or examinations done at the SVMC.

Erica P. Stanley _____ _April 28, YYYY_ _____
Signature of Patient   Date

_____ _____
Signature of Parent/Legal Guardian for Minor   Date

_____
Relationship to Minor

Andrea Witteman _____ _April 28, YYYY_ _____
WITNESS: Sunny Valley Medical Center Staff Member   Date

CONSENT TO RELEASE INFORMATION FOR REIMBURSEMENT PURPOSES

In order to permit reimbursement, upon request, the Sunny Valley Medical Center (SVMC) may disclose such treatment information pertaining to my hospitalization to any corporation, organization, or agent thereof, which is, or may be liable under contract to the SVMC or to me, or to any of my family members or other person, for payment of all or part of the SVMC's charges for services rendered to me (e.g., the patient's health insurance carrier). I understand that the purpose of any release of information is to facilitate reimbursement for services rendered. In addition, in the event that my health insurance program includes utilization review of services provided during this admission, I authorize SVMC to release information as is necessary to permit the review. This authorization will expire once the reimbursement for services rendered is complete.

Erica P. Stanley _____ _April 28, YYYY_ _____
Signature of Patient   Date

_____ _____
Signature of Parent/Legal Guardian for Minor   Date

_____
Relationship to Minor

Andrea Witteman _____ _April 28, YYYY_ _____
WITNESS: Sunny Valley Medical Center Staff Member   Date

SUNNY VALLEY MEDICAL CENTER ■ 100 MAIN ST, SUNNY VALLEY, NY 14802 ■ (607) 555-1234

STANLEY, Erica P.	Admission: 04-28-YYYY	ADVANCE DIRECTIVE
Case03	DOB: 04-05-YYYY	
Dr. Wylie	ROOM: 0255	

Your answers to the following questions will assist your Physician and the Hospital to respect your wishes regarding your medical care. This information will become a part of your medical record.

	YES	NO	PATIENT'S INITIALS
1. Have you been provided with a copy of the information called "Patient Rights Regarding Health Care Decision?"	X		EPS
2. Have you prepared a "Living Will?" If yes, please provide the Hospital with a copy for your medical record.		X	EPS
3. Have you prepared a Durable Power of Attorney for Health Care? If yes, please provide the Hospital with a copy for your medical record.		X	EPS
4. Have you provided this facility with an Advance Directive on a prior admission and is it still in effect? If yes, Admitting Office to contact Medical Records to obtain a copy for the medical record.		X	EPS
5. Do you desire to execute a Living Will/Durable Power of Attorney? If yes, refer to in order: a. Physician b. Social Service c. Volunteer Service		X	EPS

HOSPITAL STAFF DIRECTIONS: Check when each step is completed.

1. ____✓____ Verify the above questions where answered and actions taken where required.

2. ____✓____ If the "Patient Rights" information was provided to someone other than the patient, state reason:

_____

_____

Name of Individual Receiving Information   Relationship to Patient

3. ____✓____ If information was provided in a language other than English, specify language and method.

4. ____✓____ Verify patient was advised on how to obtain additional information on Advance Directives.

5. ____✓____ Verify the Patient/Family Member/Legal Representative was asked to provide the Hospital with a copy of the Advance Directive which will be retained in the medical record.

File this form in the medical record, and give a copy to the patient.

_____
Name of Patient (Name of Individual giving information if different from Patient)
Erica P. Stanley   *April 28, YYYY*

_____
Signature of Patient   Date
Andrea Witteman   *April 28, YYYY*

_____
Signature of Hospital Representative   Date

SUNNY VALLEY MEDICAL CENTER ■ 100 MAIN ST, SUNNY VALLEY, NY 14802 ■ (607) 555-1234

STANLEY, Erica P.	Admission: 04-28-YYYY	HISTORY & PHYSICAL EXAM
Case03	DOB: 04-05-YYYY	
Dr. Wylie	ROOM: 0255	

CHIEF COMPLAINT: Chronic acalculus cholecystitis

HISTORY OF PRESENT ILLNESS: The patient is a 52-year-old white female who, for about 1 year, has been very symptomatic to the point that even water starts to make her have right upper quadrant pain. She had problems with all sorts of foods, fried foods, gravies, and this causes right upper quadrant pains and sometimes nausea radiating around the costal margin straight through to the back underneath the scapula on the right side, very reproducible. Dr. Will ams saw her and obtained an ultra-sound which showed some very subtle thickening of the gallbladder wall but the ultra-sound findings were equivocal. It was suggested that if there were appropriate clinical symptoms that a cholecystokinin HIDA scan might be helpful. Under the circumstances patient is not really anxious to undergo the test in case she gets more pain and with her symptoms being as reproducible as they are, she probably has chronic acalculus gallbladder disease and I think she is getting this every day with every meal it seems a little ridiculous: to try and produce this again so I am going to go ahead and plan for a laparoscopic cholecystectomy with IOC and she understands the procedure as I have explained it to her and agrees to it the way I have explained it to her. I told her that sometimes open procedure is necessary for reasons of safety or bleeding, etc. and I have given her a pamphlet that explains the entire procedure for her to read. She understands and agrees to this the way I have explained it to her.

PAST MEDICAL HISTORY: Reveals that she is allergic to CODEINE AND ASPIRIN. She has been taking Bancap for pain which periodically helps. She has had bilateral implants in her eye and she has had bilateral Stapes operations on her ears and she has had a TAH and BSO. She has had an appendectomy. She has no other known medical illnesses.

SYSTEMIC REVIEW: Consistent with HPI and PMH and otherwise unremarkable.

FAMILY HISTORY: Reveals cancer in the family but nothing hereditary. There is colon cancer, pelvic cancer, etc. She has one daughter who has epilepsy. No bleeding problems or anesthesia problems. No other hereditary problems noted in the family.

SOCIAL HISTORY: She smokes 1/2 pack of cigarettes a day and does not take any alcohol. She is a housewife, married, living at home with her grandchild whom she is taking care of.

At the time of admission, she is a well developed, well nourished, white female in no acute distress. Vital signs are stable. She is afebrile, pleasant, cooperative, and well oriented.

HEENT: Reveals normal cephalic skull. Pupils are round, regular, and reactive to light and accommodation. Extra-ocular movements are intact. Nose and throat - benign.

NECK: Supple. No masses, thyroidomegaly, or adenopathy. She has 2+/4+ bilateral, carotid pulses with good upstrokes. No supraclavicular adenopathy on either side.

CHEST: Clear to auscultation bilaterally.

CARDIAC: Regular sinus rhythm with no murmurs or gallops heard.

BREASTS: Free of any dominant masses or nodules bilaterally.

AXILLA: Free of any adenopathy.

ABDOMEN: Soft. No hernias, masses, or organomegaly. She has some tenderness over the gallbladder in the right upper quadrant area but no rigidity, guarding, or rebound. She has normal bowel sounds.

PELVIC: Deferred today.

PULSES: Equal bilaterally.

NEURO: Within normal limits grossly.

EXTREMITIES: Full range of motion bilaterally with no pain or edema.

IMPRESSION: Chronic acalculus cholecystitis apparently quite symptomatic. The patient will be admitted for a laparoscopic cholecystectomy under antibiotic prophylaxis as noted above as AM admission.

DD: 04-28-YYYY

DT: 04-28-YYYY

E.W. Wylie, M.D.

E.W. Wylie, M.D.

STANLEY, Erica P.	Admission: 04-28-YYYY	PROGRESS NOTES
Case 03	DOB: 04-05-YYYY	
Dr. Wylie	ROOM: 0255	

Date	(Please skip one line between dates.)
4/28/YYYY	cc: chronic acalculus cholecystitis.
0700	Plan of Treatment: Laparosopic cholecystomy.
	Discharge Plan: Home - No services needed. E.W. Wylie, M.D.
04-28-yyyy	Anesthesia Pre Op Note
0715	This 52 y o w female scheduled for Lap Chole. PMHx: ⊕ tobacco hx. ⊕ Past Surgical Hx - appendectomy, total abdominal hysterectomy.
	Cataracts, bilaterally. Bilateral stapes repair. Meds preop. Alergies: Codeine, ASA, ASA II.
	Plan and GETA, Risks, Benefits, Options Explained. Understood and agreed upon.
	Don Galloway, M.D.
04-28-YYYY	Brief Op. note
1400	Laparoscopic cholecystectomy done under A.E.T. over
	without pain or complications. E.B.L. min. Pt. tolerated the
	procedure well & left the O.R. in satisfactory condition.
04-28-YYYY	POST OP
1439	Awake, Aert, vital signs stable. Normal pulse, pressure.
	Abd. soft, w/o distention. Wound is clean and dry. No
	Problems.
	E.W. Wylie, M.D.

STANLEY, Erica P.		Admission: 04-28-YYYY DOB: 04-05-YYYY ROOM: 0255

DOCTORS ORDERS

Date	Time	Physician's signature required for each order. (Please skip one line between dates.)
04-28-YYYY	0800	**Allergies:** codeine, ASA E Wylie, M.D.
04-28-YYYY	0805	PATIENT NAME: Stanley, Erica
		AGE: 52
		ADMIT TO GEN. SURGERY: a.m. admit
		CONDITION: satisfactory
		OUT OF BED, AD LIB.
		DIET: N.S.D.
		US – ROUTINE done in lab 4/23 hj
		CBC, UA, RPR, BUN, GLUCOSE, LYTES → pre-op
		EKG 04-23-YYYY → pre-op
		CHEST X-RAY done 04-23 → pre-op
		SHAVE & PREP for laparoscopic cholecystectomy
		FOR OR ON: 04-28-YYYY
		NPO
		M/N OF 04-27-YYYY
		anes. will pre-op.
		IN SAME DAY SURGERY: Begin IV of lactate ringers at 125 CC PER Hr.
		Ancef IV, on ad to O.R. placed transderm- scop
		Patch behind ear A.S.A.P.
		Measure for thigh-high TED's
		Bilateral mammogram
		E Wylie, M.D.

STANLEY, Erica P.		Admission: 04-28-YYYY
Case 03		DOB: 04-05-YYYY
Dr. Wylie		ROOM: 0255

DOCTORS ORDERS

Date	Time	Physician's signature required for each order. (Please skip one line between dates.)
04-28-YYYY	1530	POST OP ORDERS
		1. Routine post-op vital signs
		2. OOB ad lib
		3. Surg. clear liq diet to house diet ad lib
		4. P.O.R.T.
		5. D5 ½ NS w/2 0mEq KCL/L at 100ml/hr
		May d/c when tolerating PO fluids
		6. Cefazolin 1 gm at 1900 hr. and 0300 hr.
		7. May cath., if needed.
		8. Nalbuphine (Nubain) 20 mg IM/IV q3h prn pain, if Toradol is not sufficient
		9. ~~Meperidine 75 mg and Hydroxyzine 25 mg IM q4h prn pain if nalbuphine not sufficient.~~
		10. Percocet 1 P.O. q4h with food prn pain.
		11. Prochlorperasinze (copazine) 10mg IM/IV q6h prn nausea.
		12. Flurazepam (Dalmane) 30mg P.O. qhs prn sleep.
		13. Acetaminophen 650mg. P.O. temp of 101 degrees or above
		14. MOM 30 ml P.O. qhs prn constipation.
		15. Bisacodyl suppository or fleet enema bid prn "gas" or constipation.
		16. Toradol 30 mg IM, q6h, XX doses, then d/c
		E Wylie, M.D.
4-28-YYYY	1430	Discharge from PACU 1430 R.A.V. T.O. Dr. Wylie per H. Figgs RN
4-28-YYYY	0900	Cancel mammogram pre-op (scheduled for 5-18-YYYY at 10:30 am)
		R.A.V. T.O. Dr. Wylie/ Ross, RN
		E Wylie, M.D.

STANLEY, Erica P. Case03 Dr. Wylie		Admission: 04-28-YYYY DOB: 04-05-YYYY ROOM: 0255	DOCTORS ORDERS
Date	**Time**		**Physician's signature required for each order. (Please skip one line between dates.)**
4-28-YYYY	1530		Pt. See Dr. Wilson in one wk and me in two.
			E Wylie, M.D.
4-29-YYYY			Pt. may d/c today
			S&D done. Discharge home.
			E Wylie, M.D.

STANLEY, Erica P.	Admission: 04-28-YYYY	
Case 03	DOB: 04-05-YYYY	Consent for Operation(s) and/or
Dr. Wylie	ROOM: 0255	Procedure(s) and Anesthesia

PERMISSION. I hereby authorize Dr. _Wylie_ , or associates of his/her choice at the

Sunny Valley Medical Center (the "Hospital") to perform upon _Erica P. Stanley_

the following operation(s) and/or procedure(s): _Laparoscopic cholecystectomy_

including such photography, videotaping, televising or other observation of the operation(s)/procedure(s) as may be purposeful for the advance of medical knowledge and/or education, with the understanding that the patient's identity will remain anonymous.

EXPLANATION OF PROCEDURE, RISKS, BENEFITS, ALTERNATIVES. Dr. _Wylie_

has fully explained to me the nature and purposes of the operation(s)/procedures named above and has also informed me of expected benefits and complications, attendant discomforts and risks that may arise, as well as possible alternatives to the proposed treatment. I have been given an opportunity to ask questions and all my questions have been answered fully and satisfactorily.

UNFORESEEN CONDITIONS. I understand that during the course of the operation(s) or procedure(s), unforeseen conditions may arise which necessitate procedures in addition to or different from those contemplated. I, therefore, consent to the performance of additional operations and procedures which the above-named physician or his/her associates or assistants may consider necessary.

ANESTHESIA. I further consent to the administration of such anesthesia as may be considered necessary by the above-named physician or his/her associates or assistants. I recognize that there are always risks to life and health associated with anesthesia. Such risks have been fully explained to me and I have been given an opportunity to ask questions and all my questions have been answered fully and satisfactorily.

SPECIMENS. Any organs or tissues surgically removed may be examined and retained by the Hospital for medical, scientific or educational purposes and such tissues or parts may be disposed of in accordance with accustomed practice and applicable State laws and/or regulations.

NO GUARANTEES. I acknowledge that no guarantees or assurances have been made to me concerning the operation(s) or procedure(s) described above.

MEDICAL DEVICE TRACKING. I hereby authorize the release of my Social Security number to the manufacturer of the medical device(s) I receive, if applicable, in accordance with federal law and regulations which may be used to help locate me if a need arises with regard to this medical device. I release the Sunny Valley Medical Center from any liability that might result from the release of this information.*

UNDERSTANDING OF THIS FORM. I confirm that I have read this form, fully understand its contents, and that all blank spaces above have been completed prior to my signing. I have crossed out any paragraphs above that do not pertain to me.

Patient/Relative/Guardian*

Erica P. Stanley	Erica P. Stanley
Signature	Print Name

Relationship, if other than patient signed:

Witness:

Shirley Thompson	Shirley Thompson
Signature	Print Name

Date: _April 28, YYYY_

*The signature of the patient must be obtained unless the patient is an unemancipated minor under the age of 18 or is otherwise incompetent to sign.

PHYSICIAN'S CERTIFICATION. I hereby certify that I have explained the nature, purpose, benefits, risks of and alternatives to the operation(s)/procedure(s), have offered to answer any questions and have fully answered all such questions. I believe that the patient (relative/guardian) fully understands what I have explained and answered.

PHYSICIAN: _E Wylie, M.D._   _April 28, YYYY_

Signature	Date

SUNNY VALLEY MEDICAL CENTER ■ 100 MAIN ST, SUNNY VALLEY, NY 14802 ■ (607) 555-1234

STANLEY, Erica P.	Admission: 04-28-YYYY		ANESTHESIA RECORD
Case03	DOB: 04-05-YYYY		
Dr. Wylie	ROOM: 0255		

			START	STOP
PROCEDURE(S):	*Laparoscopic cholecystectomy*	ANESTHESIA	1219, 1228	1345
SURGEON(S):	*Wylie*	PROCEDURE	1248	1331
DATE OF SURGERY:	04/28/YYYY	ROOM TIME	IN: 1200	OUT: 1345

PRE-PROCEDURE

- ☑ Patient Identified   ☑ ID band verified
- ☑ Patient questioned   ☑ Chart reviewed
- ☑ Consent form signed
- ☑ Patient reassessed prior to anesthesia (ready to proceed)
- ☑ Peri-operative pain management discussed with patient/guardian (plan of care completed)
- Pre-Anesthetic State:
- ☐ Awake   ☑ Anxious   ☐ Calm
- ☐ Lethargic   ☐ Uncooperative
- ☐ Unresponsive
- ☐ Other: _____
- ☑ Anesthesia machine #5626984 checked
- ☑ Secured with safety belt
- ☑ Arm secured on board   ☑ Left   ☐ Right

MONITORS/EQUIPMENT

- ☑ Stethoscope   ☐ Precordial
- ☐ Suprasternal   ☐ Esoph
- ☑ Non-invasive B/P   ☐ V-lead ECG
- ☑ Continuous ECG   ☐ ST Analysis
- ☑ Pulse oximeter   ☑ End tidal CO$_2$
- ☐ Nerve stimulator: ☐ Ulnar ☐ Tibial ☐ Facial
- ☑ Oxygen monitor   ☐ Cell Saver
- ☑ ET agent analyzer   ☐ B/S   ☐ TEE
- ☐ Fluid/Blood warmer   ☐ Temp:
- ☐ BIS   ☐ ICS
- ☑ NG/OG tube   ☐ FHT monitor
- ☑ Foley catheter   ☐ EEG
- ☐ Airway humidifier
- ☐ Evoked potential: ☐ SSEP ☐ BAEP ☐ MEP
- ☐ Arterial line _____   ☐ CVP _____

ANESTHETIC TECHNIQUES

- GA Induction: ☑ IV ☐ Pre-O$_2$ ☐ RSI ☐ PR
- ☐ Cricoid pressure ☐ Inhalation   ☐ IM
- GA Maintenance: ☐ TIVA   ☐ Inhalation
- ☑ Inhalation/IV   ☐ GA/Regional Comb.
- Regional:
- Epidural : ☐ Thoracic ☐ Lumbar ☐ Caudal
- ☐ Femoral ☐ Auxiliary ☐ Interscalene
- ☐ CSE ☐ Bier ☐ SAB ☐ Ankle
- ☐ Continuous Spinal ☐ Cervical Plexus
- Regional Techniques:
- ☐ Position _____   ☐ See Remarks
- ☐ Site _____   ☐ Prep _____
- ☐ LA _____   ☐ Needle _____
- ☐ Additive _____   ☐ Narcotic _____
- ☐ Test dose Rx _____

AIRWAY MANAGEMENT

- ☑ Oral ETT   ☐ LTA   ☐ RAE
- ☐ Nasal ETT   ☐ LMA # _____
- ☐ Stylet   ☐ LMA Fastrach # ____
- ☐ DVL   ☐ LMA ProSeal # ____
- ☐ EMG ETT   ☐ Bougie
- ☐ Armored ETT   ☐ LIS
- ☑ Breath sounds = bilateral
- ☐ Cuffed – min occ pres with ☑ air ☐ NS
- ☐ Uncuffed – leaks at _____ cm H$_2$O
- ☑ Oral airway ☐ Nasal airway ☐ Bite block
- Circuit: ☐ Circle system ☐ NRB ☐ Bain
- ☐ Via tracheotomy/stoma ☐ Mask case
- ☐ Nasal cannula ☑ Simple O$_2$ mask
- Nebulizer: _____
- Nerve Block(s): _____

TIME:		15	30	45	15	30	45	15	30	45	15	30	45	15	30	45	TOTALS
☐ Des ☐ Iso ☐ Sevo ☐ Halo (%)																	
☑ Air (L/min)		/	/	/	/	/ ∗											
☑ Oxygen (L/min)		10 /	/	/	/	/	2/12										
☑ Tracrium mg				5													
☑ Forane (%)		.25	.25	.25	25	.25											
☑ Anectine (mg)		150	120	120	150	150	x										
☑ Pentothal (mg)		100															226

FLUIDS

Urine	foley
EBL	
Gastric	

SYMBOLS

∨∧
BP cuff pressure

⊥
Arterial line pressure

× Mean arterial pressure

● Pulse

○ Spontaneous Respirations

∅ Assisted Respirations

T Tourniquet

MONITORS

☑ ECG										
☑ % Oxygen Inspired (FIO$_2$)			98	98	98	98				
☑ ETCO$_2$				49	49	49				
☑ Temp: ☐ C ☑ F			98			98				
☑ BP Monitor										

PERI-OP MEDS

Atropine .4	200								
Ketorolec 60	180								
Sublimage 3 cc	160								
Tacrium 5 mg	140	∨	∨	∨					
D-Tubo 2.5 mg	120				∨	∨	∨	∨	
	100			•	•	•	•	•	
	80		•	•	∧	∧		∧	
	60	•	•	∧	∧		∧		∧
	40	∧	∧			∧		∧	
	20	○	○	○	○	○	○	○	○
	10								

VENT

Tidal Volume (ml)							
Respiratory Rate		SV	SV	SV	SV	SV	
Peak Pressure (cm H$_2$O)							
☐ PEEP ☐ CPAP (cm H$_2$O)							

Time of Delivery: _____

Gender: ☐ M ☐ F

Apgars: ____/____

Position: *lithotomy*	Surgeon *Wylie*
	Assistant *Johnson*
Pt ID, chart and machine ☑ed. Pt. brought to OR no. 2 Monitors applied. Pt preoxygenated. IV induction smooth. Laryngoscopy $1QT.CV MAC3.0 intubation $17.52 MOP BS = BS. DETCO2 cuff palpable. Tube taped 20 cm. Eyes taped. OA. Thermovent OG.	Scrub Nurse *Mary Marks, RN*
	Circulating Nurse *Cynthie Lewis, RcN*
	Signature of Anesthesiologist or C.R.N.A. *Don Galloway, M.D.*

STANLEY, Erica P. Case03 Dr. Wylie	Admission: 04-28-YYYY DOB: 04-05-YYYY ROOM: 0255	PRE-ANESTHESIA AND POST-ANESTHESIA RECORD

PRE-ANESTHESIA EVALUATION

HISTORY TAKEN FROM:	☑ Patient	☐ Parent/ Guardian	☐ Significant Other	☑ Chart	☐ Poor Historian	☐ Language Barrier

PROPOSED PROCEDURE:					DATE OF SURGERY:	04/28/YYYY

AGE	GENDER	HEIGHT	WEIGHT	BLOOD PRESSURE	PULSE	RESPIRATIONS	TEMPERATURE	O2 SAT%
52	☐ Male ☑ Female	5' ½"	112#	98/68	75	18	98.6	96

PREVIOUS ANESTHESIA:	☐ None	GETA without complications.
PREVIOUS SURGERY:	☐ None	Appendectomy. TAH. Cataract x 2. Both ear stap-y.
CURRENT MEDICATIONS:	☑ None	
FAMILY HX – ANES. PROBLEMS:	☑ None	
ALLERGIES	☐ None	Codeine. ASA.

AIRWAY	☐ MP1	☐ MP2	☐ MP3	☐ MP4	☐ Unrestricted neck ROM	☐ T-M distance = _____
(Enter X in appropriate boxes.)	☐ Obesity		☐ ↓ neck ROM	☐ History of difficult airway	☐ Short muscular neck	
	☐ Teeth poor repair	☐ Teeth chipped/loose	☑ Edentulous		☐ Facial hair	

BODY SYSTEM	COMMENTS	DIAGNOSTIC STUDIES
RESPIRATORY ☑ WNL	Tobacco Use: ☑ Yes ☑ No ☐ Quit ½ Packs/Day for 32 Years Adequate oral airway. Negative asthma, bronchitis, URI.	ECG CHEST X-RAY WNL PULMONARY STUDIES
CARDIOVASCULAR ☑ WNL	Pre-procedure Cardiac Assessment: Negative hypertension, MI, CHF, arrhythmia, angina. Good exercise tolerance. Regular rhythm. No carotid bruits. Positive CTA. Negative SEM.	LABORATORY STUDIES PT/PTT/INR: T&S / T&C:
GASTROINTESTINAL ☑ WNL	Ethanol Use: ☐ Yes ☑ No ☐ Quit Frequency _____ ☐ History of Ethanol abuse	HCG: 15.0 UA
		OTHER DIAGNOSTIC TESTS Hct 43.3
MUSCULOSKELETAL ☑ WNL Full cervical ROM.		**PLANNED ANESTHESIA/MONITORS** ECG. ETCO2. O2. Temp. O2 Sat. BP monitor.
GENITOURINARY ☐ WNL		
OTHER ☐ WNL Negative seizures, stroke. Negative D.M., thyroid, kidney, coag, PUD, hepatitis. ASA risk class. 2		**PRE-ANESTHESIA MEDICATION**
PREGNANCY ☐ WNL	☐ AROM ☐ SROM ☐ Pitocin Drip ☐ Induction ☐ MgDrip EDC: _____ Weeks Gestation: _____ G: ____ P: ____	
Plan: GETA, Risks, Benefits, options, explained, understood and agreed upon.		**SIGNATURE OF ANESTHESIOLOGIST OR C.R.N.A.** Don Galloway, M.D.

POST-ANESTHESIA EVALUATION

CONTROLLED MEDICATIONS

Location	Time	B/P	O2Sat	Pulse	Respirations	Temperature	Medication	Used	Destroyed	Returned
Recovery Room	1345	125/50	99	85	18	97.1				

☑ Awake	☐ Mask O2	☐ Somnolent	☐ Unarousable ☐ Oral/nasal airway
☑ Stable	☐ NC O2	☐ Unstable	☐ T-Piece ☐ Intubated ☐ Ventilator
☐ Regional – dermatome level:		☐ Continuous epidural analgesia	
☐ Direct admit to hospital room		☑ No anesthesia related complications noted	
☐ See progress notes for anesthesia related concerns		☑ Satisfactory postanesthesia/analgesia recovery	

Pt experiencing nausea. Gave pt 10 mg Reglan.

SIGNATURE OF ANESTHESIOLOGIST OR C.R.N.A.
Don Galloway, M.D.

STANLEY, Erica P. Admission: 04-28-YYYY
Case03 DOB: 04-05-YYYY
Dr. Wylie ROOM: 0255

RECOVERY ROOM RECORD

DATE:	4/28/YYYY	TIME:	1345

OPERATION: Laparoscopy cholecyst.

ANESTHESIA: General

AIRWAY: N/A

O₂ USED: ☒ YES ☐ NO

ROUTE: 4 French cath, d/c 1414

TIME	MEDICATIONS	SITE
	Scopolamine patch	behind
	(intact)	left ear

INTAKE	AMOUNT
700 cc LR, L distal forearm	
site w/o edema or redness	
iV intact & infusing at disch.	
TOTAL	200 cc

OUTPUT	AMOUNT
CATHETER N/A	
LEVINE N/A	
HEMOVAC N/A	
TOTAL	

DISCHARGE STATUS

ROOM:	0255	TIME:	1450

CONDITION: Satisfactory

TRANSFERRED BY Stretcher

R.R. NURSE: Sally James, RN

PREOP VISIT:

POSTOP VISIT: Report to Dr. Galloway at 1445 by S. James, R.N.

POSTANESTHESIA RECOVERY SCORE

		Adm	30 min	1 hr	2 hr	Disch
Moves 4 extremities voluntarily or on command (2) / Moves 2 extremities voluntarily or on command (1) / Moves 0 extremities voluntarily or on command (0)	Activity	2	2	2	2	2
Able to deep breathe and cough freely (2) / Dyspnea or limited breathing (1) / Apneic (0)	Respiration	2	2	2	2	2
BP ± 20% of preanesthetic level / BP + 20% of preanesthetic level / BP + 50% of preanesthetic level	Circulation	2	2	2	2	2
Fully awake (2) / Arouseable on calling (1) / Not responding (0)	Consciousness	2	2	2	2	2
Pink (2) / Pale, dusky, blotchy, jaundiced, other (1) / Cyanotic (0)	Color	2	2	2	2	2

COMMENTS & OBSERVATIONS:

Resp easy, spont at arrival. Four band-aids dry and intact over wounds. c/o nausea at arrival. Dry Emesis. DB encouraged and good compliance 1350. Pt admits to stomach settling a little now. Resting, eyes closed.

Mary Crawford, RN
SIGNATURE OF RECOVERY ROOM NURSE

SUNNY VALLEY MEDICAL CENTER ▪ 100 MAIN ST, SUNNY VALLEY, NY 14802 ▪ (607) 555-1234

STANLEY, Erica P.   Admission: 04-28-YYYY
Case03   DOB: 04-05-YYYY   LABORATORY DATA
Dr. Wylie   ROOM: 0255

SPECIMEN COLLECTED: 04-23-YYYY   **SPECIMEN RECEIVED:** Blood

TEST	RESULT	FLAG	REFERENCE
Sodium	142		136-147 meq/L
Potassium	3.9		3.6-5.0 mmol/L
Chloride	102		99-110 mmol/L
CO2	29		24-32 mg/dl
Glucose	95		70-110 mg/dl
Urea Nitrogen	6	**L**	7-18 mg/dl

End of Report

STANLEY, Erica P.   Admission: 04-28-YYYY   LABORATORY DATA
Case03   DOB: 04-05-YYYY
Dr. Wylie   ROOM: 0255

SPECIMEN COLLECTED: 04-23-YYYY   SPECIMEN RECEIVED: 04-23-YYYY

TEST	RESULT	FLAG	REFERENCE
URINALYSIS			
DIPSTICK ONLY			
COLOR	CLOUDY YELLOW		
SP GRAVITY	1.025		≤ 1.030
GLUCOSE	110		≤ 125 mg/dl
BILIRUBIN	NEG		≤ 0.8 mg/dl
KETONE	TRACE		≤ 10 mg/dl
BLOOD	0.03		0.06 mg/dl hgb
PH	5.0		5-8.0
PROTEIN	NORMAL		≤ 30 mg/dl
UROBILINOGEN	NORMAL		≤ -1 mg/dl
NITRITES	NEG		NEG
LEUKOCYTE	NEG		≤ 15 WBC/hpf
W.B.C.	5-10		≤ 5/hpf
R.B.C.	RARE		≤ 5/hpf
BACT.	4f		1+ (≤ 20/hpf)
URINE PREGNANCY TEST			
	NEG		

End of Report

RADIOLOGY REPORT

STANLEY, Erica P.   Admission: 04-28-YYYY

Case03   DOB: 04-05-YYYY

Dr. Wylie   ROOM: 0255

Initial Diagnosis/History: Preoperative chest X-ray.

Date Requested: 04-23-YYYY

Transport:	☐ Wheelchair	☐ Stretcher	☐ O$_2$	☐ IV
	☑ IP	☐ OP	☐ ER	
	☑ PRE OP	☐ OR/RR	☐ Portable	

CHEST: PA and lateral views show that the heart, lungs, thorax and mediastinum are normal.

DD: 04-23-YYYY

DT: 04-24-YYYY

Philip Rogers, M.D.
_____
Philip Rogers, M.D., Radiologist

```
STANLEY, Erica P.        Admission: 04-28-YYYY        RADIOLOGY REPORT
Case03                   DOB: 04-05-YYYY
Dr. Wylie                ROOM: 0255
```

Initial Diagnosis/History: Screening mammogram, bilateral.

Date Requested: 04-23-YYYY

Transport: ☐ Wheelchair   ☐ Stretcher   ☐ O$_2$ ☐ IV
              ☑ IP   ☐ OP   ☐ ER
              ☑ PRE OP   ☐ OR/RR   ☐ Portable

BILATERAL MAMMOGRAM: Normal.

DD: 04-23-YYYY

DT: 04-24-YYYY   *Philip Rogers, M.D.*
                                       _____
                                       Philip Rogers, M.D., Radiologist

STANLEY, Erica P.   Admission: 04-28-YYYY   EKG REPORT
Case03   DOB: 04-05-YYYY
Dr. Wylie   ROOM: 0255

Date of EKG: 04-23-YYYY   Time of EKG: 13:56:20

Rate   66
PR   184
QRSD   60
QT   363   Normal.
QTC   380
-- Axis --
P   76
QRS   79
T   71

Bella Kaplan
Bella Kaplan, M.D.

Case 04

SUNNY VALLEY MEDICAL CENTER 100 MAIN ST, SUNNY VALLEY, NY 14802 (607) 555-1234 HOSPITAL #: 000999			INPATIENT FACE SHEET			

PATIENT NAME AND ADDRESS		GENDER	RACE	MARITAL STATUS		PATIENT NO.
HOWE, Mary C. 55 Upland Drive Sunny Valley, New York 14802		F	W	S		Case04

			DATE OF BIRTH	MAIDEN NAME		OCCUPATION
			03-31-YYYY	Same		Student

ADMISSION DATE	TIME	DISCHARGE DATE	TIME	LENGTH OF STAY	TELEPHONE NUMBER
04-29-YYYY	09:00	04-29-YYYY	16:00	01 DAY	(607)555-1511

GUARANTOR NAME AND ADDRESS	NEXT OF KIN NAME AND ADDRESS
Howe, Shirley 55 Upland Drive Sunny Valley, New York 14802	HOWE, Shirley 55 Upland Drive Sunny Valley, New York 14802

GUARANTOR TELEPHONE NO.	RELATIONSHIP TO PATIENT	NEXT OF KIN TELEPHONE NUMBER	RELATIONSHIP TO PATIENT
(607)555-1511	Mother	(607)555-1511	Mother

ADMITTING PHYSICIAN	SERVICE	ADMIT TYPE	ROOM NUMBER/BED
Donald Thompson, MD	Surgical	3	0254/02

ATTENDING PHYSICIAN	ATTENDING PHYSICIAN UPIN	ADMITTING DIAGNOSIS	
Donald Thompson, MD	100B01	Nasal Fracture	

PRIMARY INSURER	POLICY AND GROUP NUMBER	SECONDARY INSURER	POLICY AND GROUP NUMBER
Empire Plan	857062234		

DIAGNOSES AND PROCEDURES	ICD-10-CM/PCS
PRINCIPAL DIAGNOSIS	
Nasal Fx	S022XXA
SECONDARY DIAGNOSES	
Nasal Laceration	S0120XA
	V892XXA
PRINCIPAL PROCEDURE	
Nasal Septal Fx Reduction	0NSB0ZZ
SECONDARY PROCEDURES	
Closure Nasal Laceration	09QKXZZ
TOTAL CHARGES: $ 1,850.75	

ACTIVITY:	☐ Bedrest	☑ Light	☐ Usual	☐ Unlimited	☐ Other:
DIET:	☑ Regular	☐ Low Cholesterol	☐ Low Salt	☐ ADA	☐ _____ Calorie
FOLLOW-UP:	☑ Call for appointment	☐ Office appointment on ____		☐ Other:	

SPECIAL INSTRUCTIONS: *Do not blow nose*

Signature of Attending Physician: *Donald Thompson, MD*

HOWE, Mary C.	Admission: 04-29-YYYY	CONSENT TO ADMISSION
Case 04	DOB: 03-31-YYYY	
Dr. Thompson	ROOM: 0254	

I, _Mary C. Howe_ hereby consent to admission to the Sunny Valley Medical Center (SVMC), and I further consent to such routine hospital care, diagnostic procedures, and medical treatment that the medical and professional staff of SVMC may deem necessary or advisable. I authorize the use of medical information obtained about me as specified above and the disclosure of such information to my referring physician(s). This form has been fully explained to me, and I understand its contents. I further understand that no guarantees have been made to me as to the results of treatments or examinations done at the SVMC.

Mary C. Howe

April 29, YYYY

Signature of Patient — Date

Shirley Howe

April 29, YYYY

Signature of Parent/Legal Guardian for Minor — Date

Mother

Relationship to Minor

Andrea Witteman

April 29, YYYY

WITNESS: Sunny Valley Medical Center Staff Member — Date

CONSENT TO RELEASE INFORMATION FOR REIMBURSEMENT PURPOSES

In order to permit reimbursement, upon request, the Sunny Valley Medical Center (SVMC) may disclose such treatment information pertaining to my hospitalization to any corporation, organization, or agent thereof, which is, or may be liable under contract to the SVMC or to me, or to any of my family members or other person, for payment of all or part of the SVMC's charges for services rendered to me (e.g., the patient's health insurance carrier). I understand that the purpose of any release of information is to facilitate reimbursement for services rendered. In addition, in the event that my health insurance program includes utilization review of services provided during this admission, I authorize SVMC to release information as is necessary to permit the review. This authorization will expire once the reimbursement for services rendered is complete.

Mary C. Howe

April 29, YYYY

Signature of Patient — Date

Shirley Howe

April 29, YYYY

Signature of Parent/Legal Guardian for Minor — Date

Mother

Relationship to Minor

Andrea Witteman

April 29, YYYY

WITNESS: Sunny Valley Medical Center Staff Member — Date

SUNNY VALLEY MEDICAL CENTER ■ 100 MAIN ST, SUNNY VALLEY, NY 14802 ■ (607) 555-1234

HOWE, Mary C.	Admission: 04-29-YYYY	ADVANCE DIRECTIVE
Case04	DOB: 03-31-YYYY	
Dr. Thompson	ROOM: 0254	

Your answers to the following questions will assist your Physician and the Hospital to respect your wishes regarding your medical care. This information will become a part of your medical record.

	YES	NO	PATIENT'S INITIALS
1. Have you been provided with a copy of the information called "Patient Rights Regarding Health Care Decision?"	X		MCH
2. Have you prepared a "Living Will?" If yes, please provide the Hospital with a copy for your medical record.		X	MCH
3. Have you prepared a Durable Power of Attorney for Health Care? If yes, please provide the Hospital with a copy for your medical record.		X	MCH
4. Have you provided this facility with an Advance Directive on a prior admission and is it still in effect? If yes, Admitting Office to contact Medical Records to obtain a copy for the medical record.		X	MCH
5. Do you desire to execute a Living Will/Durable Power of Attorney? If yes, refer to in order: a. Physician b. Social Service c. Volunteer Service		X	MCH

HOSPITAL STAFF DIRECTIONS: Check when each step is completed.

1. ___✓___ Verify the above questions where answered and actions taken where required.

2. ___✓___ If the "Patient Rights" information was provided to someone other than the patient, state reason:

_____

_____   _____
Name of Individual Receiving Information   Relationship to Patient

3. ___✓___ If information was provided in a language other than English, specify language and method.

4. ___✓___ Verify patient was advised on how to obtain additional information on Advance Directives.

5. ___✓___ Verify the Patient/Family Member/Legal Representative was asked to provide the Hospital with a copy of the Advance Directive which will be retained in the medical record.

File this form in the medical record, and give a copy to the patient.

_____
Name of Patient (Name of Individual giving information if different from Patient)
Mary C. Howe   *April 29, YYYY*
_____   _____
Signature of Patient   Date
Andrea Witteman   *April 29, YYYY*
_____   _____
Signature of Hospital Representative   Date

SUNNY VALLEY MEDICAL CENTER ■ 100 MAIN ST, SUNNY VALLEY, NY 14802 ■ (607) 555-1234

HOWE, Mary C. Admission: 04-29-YYYY	SHORT STAY RECORD
Case 04 DOB: 03-31-YYYY	
Dr. Thompson ROOM: 0254	

CHIEF COMPLAINT AND HISTORY:	**HEART:**
S/P MVA. Hit steering wheel. Nose hurts.	S1, S2 within normal limits.
PERTINENT PAST HISTORY:	**LUNGS:**
Asthma. S/P cleft surgery.	Clear without wheezing.
MEDICATIONS:	**ABDOMEN:**
Ventolin p.r.n.	Within normal limits.
FAMILY HISTORY:	**ENDOCRINE:**
Mother has Parkinson Disease. Asthma.	Neck negative. Groin, and axilla deferred.
REVIEW OF SYSTEMS:	**GENITALIA:**
Nonessential except asthma – last attack.	Deferred.
ALLERGIES:	**EXTREMITIES**
Negative.	Full range of motion.
PHYSICAL EXAMINATION	**NEUROLOGIC:**
GENERAL: 18 yo white female.	Oriented x 3.
EENT:	**DIAGNOSIS:**
PERRLA.	S/P M.V.A. Nasal fx.
	PLAN:
	Reduction of nasal fx.
	Donald Thompson, M.D.

HOWE, Mary C.	Admission: 04-29-YYYY	PROGRESS NOTES
Case04	DOB: 03-31-YYYY	
Dr. Thompson	ROOM: 0254	

Date	Time	Physician's signature required for each order. (Please skip one line between dates.)
4-29-yyyy	1000	Preanesthesia eval: 18 y/o WF for closed reduction of nasal fracture. Smokes, asthma, ASA II. Explained GA
		and risks. Indicates understanding of risks, answered questions and concerns.
		Don Galloway, M.D.
4-29-yyyy	1415	Postanesthesia eval: Tolerated GA well, no complications, sleeping, stable.
		Don Galloway, M.D.
4/29/yyyy	1400	Short Op Note:
		Preop Dx: Nasal septal fx. Nasal laceration.
		Postop Dx: Same.
		Procedure: Open reduction, nasal septal fx. Closure, nasal lacerations.
		Anesthesia: General, oral.
		Patient tolerated well.
		Donald Thompson, MD

HOWE, Mary C.		Admission: 04-29-YYYY
Case04		DOB: 03-31-YYYY
Dr. Thompson		ROOM: 0254

DOCTORS ORDERS

Date	Time	Physician's signature required for each order. (Please skip one line between dates.)
04/29/YYYY	0930	PRE-OP ORDERS
		1) ~~Admit to S.D.S. or~~ AM Admit.
		2) Diet: NPO
		3) Allergies: ∅
		4) CBC, UA
		5) I.V. D5 LR at 75 cc/hr *Wait until OR anesthesia to start IV*
		6) Solumedrol 125 mg I.V. PUSH
		7) Antibiotics: *Keflex 500 mg*
		8) PRE-MED: As per anesthesia.
		9) Pre Op Rinse. (Labeled for home use BID)
		10) Old Chart: Yes ~~or No~~.
		Donald Thompson, MD
4/29/YYYY	1155	*Post op*
		Diet – regular
		Toradil 30 mg IM q4h PRN severe pain
		Codeine 1 or 2 q4h PRN moderate pain
		Tylenol 650 mg q4h PRN mild pain
		Donald Thompson, MD
4/29/YYYY	1115	*Discharge from PACU at 1115. R.A.V. T.O. Dr. Thompson/B. Densmore, RN*
		Donald Thompson, MD
4/29/YY	1150	*Clarify IV – D5LR 25 cc/hr Donald Thompson, MD*
		R.A.V. T.O. Dr. Thompson/C. Smith, RN
4/29/YY	1500	*D/C IV. Discharge home. Donald Thompson, MD*

HOWE, Mary C. Case 04 Dr. Thompson	Admission: 04-29-YYYY DOB: 03-31-YYYY ROOM: 0254	Consent for Operation(s) and/or Procedure(s) and Anesthesia

PERMISSION. I hereby authorize Dr. _Thompson_ , or associates of his/her choice at the

Sunny Valley Medical Center (the "Hospital") to perform upon _Mary C. Howe_

the following operation(s) and/or procedure(s): _Nasal Septal Fx Reduction /Closure Nasal Laceration_

including such photography, videotaping, televising or other observation of the operation(s)/procedure(s) as may be purposeful for the advance of medical knowledge and/or education, with the understanding that the patient's identity will remain anonymous.

EXPLANATION OF PROCEDURE, RISKS, BENEFITS, ALTERNATIVES. Dr. _Thompson_

has fully explained to me the nature and purposes of the operation(s)/procedures named above and has also informed me of expected benefits and complications, attendant discomforts and risks that may arise, as well as possible alternatives to the proposed treatment. I have been given an opportunity to ask questions and all my questions have been answered fully and satisfactorily.

UNFORESEEN CONDITIONS. I understand that during the course of the operation(s) or procedure(s), unforeseen conditions may arise which necessitate procedures in addition to or different from those contemplated. I, therefore, consent to the performance of additional operations and procedures which the above-named physician or his/her associates or assistants may consider necessary.

ANESTHESIA. I further consent to the administration of such anesthesia as may be considered necessary by the above-named physician or his/her associates or assistants. I recognize that there are always risks to life and health associated with anesthesia. Such risks have been fully explained to me and I have been given an opportunity to ask questions and all my questions have been answered fully and satisfactorily.

SPECIMENS. Any organs or tissues surgically removed may be examined and retained by the Hospital for medical, scientific or educational purposes and such tissues or parts may be disposed of in accordance with accustomed practice and applicable State laws and/or regulations.

NO GUARANTEES. I acknowledge that no guarantees or assurances have been made to me concerning the operation(s) or procedure(s) described above.

MEDICAL DEVICE TRACKING. I hereby authorize the release of my Social Security number to the manufacturer of the medical device(s) I receive, if applicable, in accordance with federal law and regulations which may be used to help locate me if a need arises with regard to this medical device. I release The Sunny Valley Medical Center from any liability that might result from the release of this information.*

UNDERSTANDING OF THIS FORM. I confirm that I have read this form, fully understand its contents, and that all blank spaces above have been completed prior to my signing. I have crossed out any paragraphs above that do not pertain to me.

Patient/Relative/Guardian*

Mary C. HOWE   Mary C. Howe
Signature   Print Name

Relationship, if other than patient signed:

Witness:

Shirley Thompson   Shirley Thompson
Signature   Print Name

Date: _April 29, YYYY_

*The signature of the patient must be obtained unless the patient is an unemancipated minor under the age of 18 or is otherwise incompetent to sign.

PHYSICIAN'S CERTIFICATION. I hereby certify that I have explained the nature, purpose, benefits, risks of and alternatives to the operation(s)/ procedure(s), have offered to answer any questions and have fully answered all such questions. I believe that the patient (relative/guardian) fully understands what I have explained and answered.

PHYSICIAN: _Donald Thompson, MD_

Signature   April 29, YYYY

Date

SUNNY VALLEY MEDICAL CENTER ■ 100 MAIN ST, SUNNY VALLEY, NY 14802 ■ (607) 555-1234

ANESTHESIA RECORD

HOWE, Mary C.	Admission: 04-29-YYYY
Case 04	DOB: 03-31-YYYY
Dr. Thompson	ROOM: 0254

PROCEDURE(S):	Nasal Septal Fx Reduction	ANESTHESIA	START 0945	STOP 1015
SURGEON(S):	Donald Thompson	PROCEDURE	0950	1015
DATE OF SURGERY:	4/29/YYYY	ROOM TIME	IN: 0930	OUT: 1030

PRE-PROCEDURE
- ☑ Patient Identified   ☑ ID band verified
- ☑ Patient questioned   ☑ Chart reviewed
- ☑ Consent form signed
- ☑ Patient reassessed prior to anesthesia (ready to proceed)
- ☑ Peri-operative pain management discussed with patient/guardian (plan of care completed)
- Pre-Anesthetic State:
- ☑ Awake   ☑ Anxious   ☐ Calm
- ☐ Lethargic   ☐ Uncooperative
- ☐ Unresponsive
- ☐ Other: _____
- ☑ Anesthesia machine #5626984 checked
- ☑ Secured with safety belt
- ☑ Arm secured on board   ☑ Left   ☐ Right

MONITORS/EQUIPMENT
- ☑ Stethoscope   ☐ Precordial
- ☐ Suprasternal   ☐ Esoph
- ☑ Non-invasive B/P   ☐ V-lead ECG
- ☑ Continuous ECG   ☐ ST Analysis
- ☑ Pulse oximeter   ☐ End tidal CO$_2$
- ☐ Nerve stimulator: ☐ Ulnar   ☐ Tibial   ☐ Facial
- ☑ Oxygen monitor   ☐ Cell Saver
- ☐ ET agent analyzer   ☐ B/S   ☐ TEE
- ☐ Fluid/Blood warmer   ☐ Temp:
- ☐ BIS   ☐ ICS
- ☐ NG/OG tube   ☐ FHT monitor
- ☑ Foley catheter   ☐ EEG
- ☐ Airway humidifier
- ☐ Evoked potential: ☐ SSEP ☐ BAEP ☐ MEP
- ☐ Arterial line _____   ☐ CVP _____

ANESTHESTIC TECHNIQUES
- GA Induction: ☑ IV ☐ Pre-O$_2$ ☐ RSI ☐ PR
- ☐ Cricoid pressure ☐ Inhalation ☐ IM
- GA Maintenance: ☐ TIVA ☐ Inhalation
- ☑ Inhalation/IV ☐ GA/Regional Comb.
- Regional:
- Epidural : ☑ Thoracic ☐ Lumbar ☐ Caudal
- ☐ Femoral ☐ Auxiliary ☐ Interscalene
- ☐ CSE ☐ Bier ☐ SAB ☐ Ankle
- ☐ Continuous Spinal ☐ Cervical Plexus
- Regional Techniques: ☐ See Remarks
- ☐ Position _____ ☐ Prep _____
- ☐ Site _____ ☐ Needle _____
- ☐ LA _____ ☐ Narcotic _____
- ☐ Additive _____ ☐ Test dose Rx ___

AIRWAY MANAGEMENT
- ☑ Oral ETT   ☐ LTA   ☐ RAE
- ☐ Nasal ETT   ☐ LMA # ____
- ☐ Stylet   ☐ LMA Fastrach # ____
- ☐ DVL   ☐ LMA ProSeal # ____
- ☐ EMG ETT   ☐ Bougie
- ☐ Armored ETT   ☐ LIS
- ☑ Breath sounds = bilateral
- ☑ Cuffed – min occ pres with ☑ air ☐ NS
- ☐ Uncuffed – leaks at _____ cm H$_2$O
- ☑ Oral airway ☐ Nasal airway ☐ Bite block
- Circuit: ☐ Circle system ☐ NRB ☐ Bain
- ☐ Via tracheotomy/stoma ☐ Mask case
- ☐ Nasal cannula ☑ Simple O$_2$ mask
- Nebulizer: _____
- Nerve Block(s): _____

TIME:	15	30	45	15	30	45	15	30	45	15	30	45	15	30	45	TOTALS
AGENTS																
☐ Des ☐ Iso ☐ Sevo ☐ Halo (%)																
☑ N^{2}O ☑ Air (L/min)		2.5	2.5	✗												
☑ Oxygen (L/min)	66	2	2	66												
☑ N$_2$O (L/min)																
☑ Forane (%)		1/5	2/5	2/0	✗											
☑ Anectine (mg)																
☑ Pentothal (mg)		100	100	100	✗											226
FLUIDS																
Urine																
EBL																
Gastric																
MONITORS																
☑ ECG																
☑ % Oxygen Inspired (FIO$_2$)		98	98	98	98											
☑ End Tidal CO$_2$			49	49	49											
☑ Temp: ☐ C ☑ F		98			98											
☑ BP Monitor																

SYMBOLS

∨∧ BP cuff pressure

⊥ Arterial line pressure

✗ Mean arterial pressure

● Pulse

○ Spontaneous Respirations

∅ Assisted Respirations

T Tourniquet

Time of Delivery: _____

Gender: ☐ M ☐ F

Apgars: ___ / ___

PERI-OP MEDS graph (200–10 scale)

VENT
	15	30	45	15	30	45
Tidal Volume (ml)						
Respiratory Rate		sa	sa	sa	sa	
Peak Pressure (cm H$_2$O)						
☐ PEEP ☐ CPAP (cm H$_2$O)						

Position:	LIthogomy	Surgeon	Thompson
		Assistant	
#20 Oral tubing. Intake DSLR 1000.		Scrub Nurse	Mary Marks, RN
Total 650 cc. #18 gu, left.		Circulating Nurse	Cynthia Lewis, RN
		Signature of Anesthesiologist or C.R.N.A.	Don Galloway, M.D.

HOWE, Mary C. Case04 Dr. Thompson	Admission: 04-29-YYYY DOB: 03-31-YYYY ROOM: 0254	PRE-ANESTHESIA AND POST-ANESTHESIA RECORD

PRE-ANESTHESIA EVALUATION

HISTORY TAKEN FROM: ☑ Patient ☐ Parent/ Guardian ☐ Significant Other ☑ Chart ☐ Poor Historian ☐ Language Barrier

PROPOSED PROCEDURE: **DATE OF SURGERY:** 04-29-YYYY

AGE	GENDER	HEIGHT	WEIGHT	BLOOD PRESSURE	PULSE	RESPIRATIONS	TEMPERATURE	O2 SAT%
18	☐ Male ☑ Female	5 ft 2 in	100	105065	70	18	98.6	98

PREVIOUS ANESTHESIA: ☑ None

PREVIOUS SURGERY: ☑ None

CURRENT MEDICATIONS: ☑ None

FAMILY HX – ANES. PROBLEMS: ☑ None

ALLERGIES: ☑ None

AIRWAY (Enter ✗ in appropriate boxes.)
☐ MP1 ☐ MP2 ☐ MP3 ☐ MP4 ☐ Unrestricted neck ROM ☐ T-M distance = ____
☐ Obesity ☐ ↓ neck ROM ☐ History of difficult airway ☐ Short muscular neck
☐ Teeth poor repair ☐ Teeth chipped/loose ☐ Edentulous ☐ Facial hair

BODY SYSTEM / COMMENTS

RESPIRATORY ☑ WNL Tobacco Use: ☐ Yes ☑ No ☐ Quit ____ Packs/Day for ____ Years

CARDIOVASCULAR ☑ WNL Pre-procedure Cardiac Assessment:

GASTROINTESTINAL ☑ WNL Ethanol Use: ☐ Yes ☑ No ☐ Quit Frequency ____ ☐ History of Ethanol abuse

MUSCULOSKELETAL ☑ WNL

GENITOURINARY ☐ WNL

OTHER ☐ WNL ASA risk classification I

PREGNANCY ☐ WNL ☐ AROM ☐ SROM ☐ Pitocin Drip ☐ Induction ☐ MgDrip EDC: ____ Weeks Gestation: ____ G: ____ P: ____

DIAGNOSTIC STUDIES
ECG
CHEST X-RAY Negative
PULMONARY STUDIES

LABORATORY STUDIES
PT/PTT/INR:
T&S / T&C:
HCG: 13.2
UA

OTHER DIAGNOSTIC TESTS
Hct 38.4

PLANNED ANESTHESIA/MONITORS
ECG. ETCO2. O2. Temp.
O2 Sat. BP monitor.

PRE-ANESTHESIA MEDICATION

SIGNATURE OF ANESTHESIOLOGIST OR C.R.N.A.
Don Galloway, M.D.

POST-ANESTHESIA EVALUATION

Location	Time	B/P	O2Sat	Pulse	Respirations	Temperature
Room	1430	110/70	96	70	18	98.6

☑ Awake ☐ Mask O2 ☐ Somnolent ☐ Unarousable ☐ Oral/nasal airway
☑ Stable ☐ NC O2 ☐ Unstable ☐ T-Piece ☐ Intubated ☐ Ventilator
☐ Regional – dermatome level: ☐ Continuous epidural analgesia
☐ Direct admit to hospital room ☑ No anesthesia related complications noted
☐ See progress notes for anesthesia related concerns ☑ Satisfactory postanesthesia/analgesia recovery

CONTROLLED MEDICATIONS
Medication	Used	Destroyed	Returned

SIGNATURE OF ANESTHESIOLOGIST OR C.R.N.A.
Don Galloway, M.D.

SUNNY VALLEY MEDICAL CENTER ■ 100 MAIN ST, SUNNY VALLEY, NY 14802 ■ (607) 555-1234

RECOVERY ROOM RECORD

HOWE, Mary C.
Case 04
Dr. Thompson

Admission: 04-29-YYYY
DOB: 03-31-YYYY
ROOM: 0254

DATE: 4/29/YYYY **TIME:** 1030
OPERATION: Nasal Septal Fx Reduction
ANESTHESIA: General
AIRWAY: N/A
O₂ USED: ☒ YES ☐ NO
ROUTE: Nasal @ 4 l/min. d/c 1100.

TIME	MEDICATIONS	SITE

INTAKE	AMOUNT
350 D5L R antecubital	
iV site w/o redness or edema	
200 D5L R on discharge	
TOTAL	150 cc

OUTPUT	AMOUNT
CATHETER N/A	
LEVINE N/A	
HEMOVAC N/A	
TOTAL	

DISCHARGE STATUS

ROOM: 0254 **TIME:** 1115
CONDITION: Stable
TRANSFERRED BY: Stretcher
R.R. NURSE: Sally James, RN

PREOP VISIT:

POSTOP VISIT: Report given to Dr. Galloway at 1125 by S. James, R.N.

Dinamap left arm, 15.

POSTANESTHESIA RECOVERY SCORE		Adm	30 min	1 hr	2 hr	Disch
Moves 4 extremities voluntarily or on command (2) / Moves 2 extremities voluntarily or on command (1) / Moves 0 extremities voluntarily or on command (0)	Activity	2	2	2	2	2
Able to deep breathe and cough freely (2) / Dyspnea or limited breathing (1) / Apneic (0)	Respiration	2	2	2	2	2
BP ± 20% of preanesthetic level / BP + 20% of preanesthetic level / BP + 50% of preanesthetic level	Circulation	2	2	2	2	2
Fully awake (2) / Arouseable on calling (1) / Not responding (0)	Consciousness	1	2	2	2	2
Pink (2) / Pale, dusky, blotchy, jaundiced, other (1) / Cyanotic (0)	Color	2	2	2	2	2

COMMENTS & OBSERVATIONS:

Patient arousable on arrival to PACU with respirations deep, easy and regular.

Denver splint in place. Dry hacking cough noted. HOB elevated 30°.

Mary Crawford, RN
SIGNATURE OF RECOVERY ROOM NURSE

HOWE, Mary C.   Admission: 04-29-YYYY   LABORATORY DATA
Case04   DOB: 03-31-YYYY
Dr. Thompson   ROOM: 0254

SPECIMEN COLLECTED: 04-29-YYYY   SPECIMEN RECEIVED: 04-29-YYYY

TEST	RESULT	FLAG	REFERENCE
URINALYSIS			
DIPSTICK ONLY			
COLOR	CLOUDY YELLOW		
SP GRAVITY	1.025		≤ 1.030
GLUCOSE	110		≤ 125 mg/dl
BILIRUBIN	NEG		≤ 0.8 mg/dl
KETONE	TRACE		≤ 10 mg/dl
BLOOD	0.03		0.06 mg/dl hgb
PH	5.0		5-8.0
PROTEIN	NORMAL		≤ 30 mg/dl
UROBILINOGEN	NORMAL		≤ -1 mg/dl
NITRITES	NEG		NEG
LEUKOCYTE	NEG		≤ 15 WBC/hpf
W.B.C.	5-10		≤ 5/hpf
R.B.C.	RARE		≤ 5/hpf
BACT.	4f		1+(≤ 20/hpf)
URINE PREGNANCY TEST			
	NEG		

End of Report

HOWE, Mary C.   Admission: 04-29-YYYY   **LABORATORY DATA**

Case04   DOB: 03-31-YYYY

Dr. Thompson   ROOM: 0254

SPECIMEN COLLECTED: 04-29-YYYY   **SPECIMEN RECEIVED:** 04-29-YYYY

CBC c̄ DIFF

TEST	RESULT	FLAG	REFERENCE
WBC	7.4		4.5-11.0 thous/UL
RBC	5.02	**L**	5.2-5.4 mill/UL
HGB	15.0		11.7-16.1 g/dl
HCT	45.8		35.0-47.0 %
MCV	91.2		85-99 fL.
MCHC	32.8	**L**	33-37
RDW	15.2	**H**	11.4-14.5
Platelets	165		130-400 thous/UL
MPV	8.4		7.4-10.4
LYMPH %	21.1		20.5-51.1
MONO %	7.8		1.7-9.3
GRAN %	71.1		42.2-75.2
LYMPH x 10^3	1.6		1.2-3.4
MONO x 10^3	.6	**H**	0.11-0.59
GRAN x 10^3	5.3		1.4-6.5
EOS x 10^3	< .7		0.0-0.7
BASO x 10^3	< .2		0.0-0.2
ANISO	SLIGHT		

End of Report

Case 05

SUNNY VALLEY MEDICAL CENTER 100 MAIN ST, SUNNY VALLEY, NY 14802 (607) 555-1234 HOSPITAL #: 000999			INPATIENT FACE SHEET		

PATIENT NAME AND ADDRESS		GENDER	RACE	MARITAL STATUS	PATIENT NO.
GIBBON, Andrew 22 Market Street Sunny Valley, NY 14802		M	W	M	Case05
		DATE OF BIRTH		MAIDEN NAME	OCCUPATION
		08-19-YYYY		N/A	Retired

ADMISSION DATE	TIME	DISCHARGE DATE	TIME	LENGTH OF STAY	TELEPHONE NUMBER
04-27-YYYY	13:00	04-29-YYYY	00:00	02 DAYS	(607) 555-4500

GUARANTOR NAME AND ADDRESS		NEXT OF KIN NAME AND ADDRESS	
GIBBON, Andrew 22 Market Street Sunny Valley, NY 14802		GIBBON, Cynthia 22 Market Street Sunny Valley, NY 14802	

GUARANTOR TELEPHONE NO.	RELATIONSHIP TO PATIENT	NEXT OF KIN TELEPHONE NUMBER	RELATIONSHIP TO PATIENT
(607) 555-4500	Self	(607) 555-4500	Wife

ADMITTING PHYSICIAN	SERVICE	ADMIT TYPE	ROOM NUMBER/BED
Alan Norris, MD	Medical	2	0362/02

ATTENDING PHYSICIAN	ATTENDING PHYSICIAN UPIN	ADMITTING DIAGNOSIS	
Alan Norris, MD	100G02	Chest pain	

PRIMARY INSURER	POLICY AND GROUP NUMBER	SECONDARY INSURER	POLICY AND GROUP NUMBER
Medicare			

DIAGNOSES AND PROCEDURES	ICD-10-CM/PCS
PRINCIPAL DIAGNOSIS	
Unstable Angina	I20.0
SECONDARY DIAGNOSES	
Hypertension	I10
Status post myocardial infarction	I25.2
PRINCIPAL PROCEDURE	
SECONDARY PROCEDURES	
TOTAL CHARGES: $ 4,855.65	

ACTIVITY:	☐ Bedrest	☑ Light	☐ Usual	☐ Unlimited	☐ Other:
DIET:	☑ Regular	☐ Low Cholesterol	☐ Low Salt	☐ ADA	☐ _____ Calorie

FOLLOW-UP: ☐ Call for appointment ☐ Office appointment on _____ ☐ Medications: *Procardia, Isordil, Vasotec, Inderal, Aldoril, Aspirin.*

SPECIAL INSTRUCTIONS: *See Dr. Derby next week Do not take Dyazide until you see Dr. Derby.*

Signature of Attending Physician: *Alan Norris, MD*

```
GIBBON, Andrew        Admission: 04-27-YYYY        CONSENT TO ADMISSION
Case05                DOB: 08-19-YYYY
Dr. Norris            ROOM: 0362
```

I, _Andrew Gibbon_ hereby consent to admission to the Sunny Valley Medical Center (SVMC), and I further consent to such routine hospital care, diagnostic procedures, and medical treatment that the medical and professional staff of SVMC may deem necessary or advisable. I authorize the use of medical information obtained about me as specified above and the disclosure of such information to my referring physician(s). This form has been fully explained to me, and I understand its contents. I further understand that no guarantees have been made to me as to the results of treatments or examinations done at the SVMC.

Andrew Gibbon   _April 27, YYYY_
_____   _____
Signature of Patient   Date

_____   _____
Signature of Parent/Legal Guardian for Minor   Date

_____
Relationship to Minor

Andrea Witteman   _April 27, yyyy_
_____   _____
WITNESS: Sunny Valley Medical Center Staff Member   Date

CONSENT TO RELEASE INFORMATION FOR REIMBURSEMENT PURPOSES

In order to permit reimbursement, upon request, the Sunny Valley Medical Center (SVMC) may disclose such treatment information pertaining to my hospitalization to any corporation, organization, or agent thereof, which is, or may be liable under contract to the SVMC or to me, or to any of my family members or other person, for payment of all or part of the SVMC's charges for services rendered to me (e.g., the patient's health insurance carrier). I understand that the purpose of any release of information is to facilitate reimbursement for services rendered. In addition, in the event that my health insurance program includes utilization review of services provided during this admission, I authorize SVMC to release information as is necessary to permit the review. This authorization will expire once the reimbursement for services rendered is complete.

Andrew Gibbon   _April 27, YYYY_
_____   _____
Signature of Patient   Date

_____   _____
Signature of Parent/Legal Guardian for Minor   Date

_____
Relationship to Minor

Andrea Witteman   _April 27, yyyy_
_____   _____
WITNESS: Sunny Valley Medical Center Staff Member   Date

GIBBON, Andrew	Admission: 04-27-YYYY	ADVANCE DIRECTIVE
Case05	DOB: 08-19-YYYY	
Dr. Norris	ROOM: 0362	

Your answers to the following questions will assist your Physician and the Hospital to respect your wishes regarding your medical care. This information will become a part of your medical record.

	YES	NO	PATIENT'S INITIALS
1. Have you been provided with a copy of the information called "Patient Rights Regarding Health Care Decision?"	X		AG
2. Have you prepared a "Living Will?" If yes, please provide the Hospital with a copy for your medical record.		X	AG
3. Have you prepared a Durable Power of Attorney for Health Care? If yes, please provide the Hospital with a copy for your medical record.		X	AG
4. Have you provided this facility with an Advance Directive on a prior admission and is it still in effect? If yes, Admitting Office to contact Medical Records to obtain a copy for the medical record.		X	AG
5. Do you desire to execute a Living Will/Durable Power of Attorney? If yes, refer to in order: a. Physician b. Social Service c. Volunteer Service		X	AG

HOSPITAL STAFF DIRECTIONS: Check when each step is completed.

1. ___✓___ Verify the above questions where answered and actions taken where required.

2. ___✓___ If the "Patient Rights" information was provided to someone other than the patient, state reason:

_____

_____ _____
Name of Individual Receiving Information   Relationship to Patient

3. ___✓___ If information was provided in a language other than English, specify language and method.

4. ___✓___ Verify patient was advised on how to obtain additional information on Advance Directives.

5. ___✓___ Verify the Patient/Family Member/Legal Representative was asked to provide the Hospital with a copy of the Advance Directive which will be retained in the medical record.

File this form in the medical record, and give a copy to the patient.

Name of Patient (Name of Individual giving information if different from Patient)
Andrew Gibbon   _April 27, YYYY_
Signature of Patient   Date

Andrea Witteman   _April 27, yyyy_
Signature of Hospital Representative   Date

SUNNY VALLEY MEDICAL CENTER ■ 100 MAIN ST, SUNNY VALLEY, NY 14802 ■ (607) 555-1234

GIBBON, Andrew	Admission: 04-27-YYYY	HISTORY & PHYSICAL EXAM
Case 05	DOB: 08-19-YYYY	
Dr. Norris	ROOM: 0362	

CHIEF COMPLAINT: 72 yr. old gentleman of Dr. K. Derby's who presents with chest pain.

HISTORY OF PRESENT ILLNESS: Mr. Gibbon is a very cheery sort of fellow. He is very pleasant. He looks as though he probably should be running some sort of hardware store commercial. He states that today while he was preparing breakfast, in the restroom he suffered some chest discomfort. He is a little bit vague as to where his chest really is. He felt it in his back, he felt it in his jaw. He took a couple of Nitroglycerin in sequence three minutes apart and felt better. Apparently this has been occurring a little more frequently recently. All these things are nebulous. If it wasn't for his wife I think he would deny everything. According to her he has been having more frequent episodes and has gained a fair amount of weight over the winter. He had been fairly active. His pastor who is with him and often serves as his spokesman, stated that he had hunted this past fall without having to take any Nitroglycerin. However he said the pace was quite controlled and he really didn't do very much in the way of heavy exercise. The patient has a history of an infarction in 1981. Underwent catheterization. Apparently no surgery was necessary. There is also some question about him having a lot of indigestion from time to time and it is not clear whether it is cardiac or GI. Because of his prior cardiac history, the progression of his chest pain, the uncertainty of its origin, he will be admitted for further evaluation and treatment.

PAST MEDICAL HISTORY: Is essentially that listed above.

MEDICATIONS: He is on Dyazide once a day. Isordil 10 mg. q.i.d. Vasotec 2.5 mg. daily. Aspirin one a day. Propranolol 40 mg. q.i.d.

ALLERGIES: Sulfa.

SOCIAL HISTORY & FAMILY HISTORY: The patient is married. Doesn't smoke, although he had in the past. Doesn't drink. There is no disease common in the family.

REVIEW OF SYSTEMS: Negative.

GENERAL: Reveals a very pleasant 72 yr. old gentleman.

VITAL SIGNS: Temperature of 97.6, pulse is 64, respirations 18, blood pressure 178/94.

HEAD: Normocephalic.

ENT: Eyes -sclera and conjunctiva normal. PERRL, EOM's intact. Fundi reveal arteriolar narrowing. ENT are unremarkable.

NECK: Supple. No thyromegaly. Carotids are 2 out of 4. No bruits, no jugular venous distention.

CHEST: Symmetrical. Clear to auscultation and percussion.

HEART: Regular rhythm without any particular murmurs or gallops.

ABDOMEN: Nontender. No organomegaly. Bowel sounds normal activity. No bruits or masses.

BACK: No CVA tenderness nor tenderness to percussion over the spinous processes.

GENITALIA: Normal male.

RECTAL: Good sphincter tones. Stool is hemoccult negative. Prostate is normal in size.

EXTREMITIES: No cyanosis, clubbing or edema. Pulses equal and full.

NEUROLOGIC: Is physiologic.

IMPRESSION: 1) Chest pain, etiology to be determined

2) Hypertension

PLAN: Outlined in the order sheet.

DD:04-28-YYYY

DT: 04-30-YYYY

Alan Norris, MD

Alan Norris, MD

GIBBON, Andrew	Admission: 04-27-YYYY	PROGRESS NOTES
Case05	DOB: 08-19-YYYY	
Dr. Norris	ROOM: 0362	

Date	(Please skip one line between dates.)
4-27-YY	Chief Complaint: Unstable angina.
	Diagnosis: Unstable angina.
	Plan of Treatment: See orders.
	Discharge Plan: Home – No services needed
	Alan Norris, MD
4/28/YY	Pt has had no pain overnight. Plan to get pt up and walking. Treadmill Thursday if no pain. BG studies today.
	Alan Norris, MD
4/29/YY	Treadmill – pt not able to achieve goal. Shortness of breath.
	Alan Norris, MD

GIBBON, Andrew		Admission: 04-27-YYYY
Case 05		DOB: 08-19-YYYY
Dr. Norris		ROOM: 0362

DOCTORS ORDERS

Date	Time	Physician's signature required for each order. (Please skip one line between dates.)
4-27-YY	1330	TELEMETRY PROTOCOL
		1. Saline lock, insert and flush every 24 hours and PRN
		2. EKG with chest pain x 1
		3. Oxygen 3 1/min. via nasal cannula PRN for chest pain.
		4. Chest Pain: NTG 0.4mg SL q 5 min x 3.
		5. Bradycardia: Atropine 0.5mg IV q 5 min to total of 2mg for symptomatic heart rate
		(Pulse less than 50 or 60 with decreased BP and/or PVC's)
		6. PVC's: Lidocaine 50mg IV push
		Start drip 500cc D5W Lidocaine 2 gm @ 2mg/Min (30cc/hr) for greater
		than 6 PVC's per min or 3 PVC's in a row.
		7. V-Tach: (If patient is hemodynamically stable)
		Lidocaine 50mg IV push.
		Start drip 500cc D5W Lidocaine 2 gm @ 2mg/min (30cc/hr)
		(If unstable) Cardiovert at 50 watt seconds
		8. V-fig: Immediately defibrillate at 200 watt seconds, if not converted:
		Immediately defibrillate at 300 watt seconds, if not converted;
		Immediately defibrillate at 360 watt seconds, if not converted: Start CPR
		Give Epinephrine (1:10,000) 1 mg IC push
		Give Lidocaine as per V-Tach protocol
		9. Asystole/EMD: Begin CPR
		Epinephrine (1:10,000) 1mg IV push
		Atropine 1 mg IV push if no response with Epinephrine
		10. Respiratory arrest: Intubation with mechanical ventilation.
		11. Notify Physician for chest pain or arrhythmias requiring treatment.
		R.A.V. T.O. Dr. Norris/M. Higgin, R.N.
		Alan Norris, MD

GIBBON, Andrew	Admission: 04-27-YYYY	DOCTORS ORDERS
Case05	DOB: 08-19-YYYY	
Dr. Norris	ROOM: 0362	

Date	Time	Physician's signature required for each order. (Please skip one line between dates.)
27 Apr YY	1340	Inderal 40 mg qid
		Procardia XL 60 mg q day
		Isordil 10 mg qid
		Vasotec 25 mg q day
		Schedule for stress test 4/28, 1230 if possible
		GB US R/O stones
		Reg diet
		Up in room
		Alan Norris, MD
27 Apr YY	1645	Reschedule for treadmill for 1230, 29 Apr YY.
		Hepatobiliary scan tomorrow.
		Alan Norris, MD
28 Apr YY	0830	Ambulate in hall ad lib.
		Lytes SCGII in am.
		Alan Norris, MD
28 Apr YY	1610	Inderal 20 mg po qid
		Lytes SCGII in am.
		Alan Norris, MD

```
GIBBON, Andrew        Admission: 04-27-YYYY
Case05                DOB: 08-19-YYYY               LABORATORY DATA
Dr. Norris            ROOM: 0362
```

SPECIMEN COLLECTED: 04-29-YYYY   SPECIMEN RECEIVED: 04-29-YYYY

TEST	RESULT	FLAG	REFERENCE
Glucose	97		70-110 mg/dl
BUN	12		8-25 mg/dl
Creatinine	1.0		0.9-1.4 mg/dl
Sodium	135	**L**	135-145 mmol/L
Potassium	4.2		3.6-5.0 mmol/L
Chloride	97	**L**	99-110 mmol/L
CO2	30		21-31 mmol/L
Calcium	9.3		8.8-10.5 mg/dl
WBC	4.7		4.5-11.0 thous/UL
RBC	5.80		5.2-5.4 mill/UL
HGB	17.0		11.7-16.1 g/dl
HCT	50.1		35.0-47.0 %
Platelets	102	**L**	140-400 thous/UL
Protime	11.4		11.0-13.0
PTT	21		< 32 seconds

End of Report

SUNNY VALLEY MEDICAL CENTER ■ 100 MAIN ST, SUNNY VALLEY, NY 14802 ■ (607) 555-1234

```
GIBBON, Andrew      Admission: 04-27-YYYY
Case05              DOB: 08-19-YYYY              LABORATORY DATA
Dr. Norris          ROOM: 0362
```

SPECIMEN COLLECTED: 04-29-YYYY   **SPECIMEN RECEIVED:** 04-29-YYYY

URINALYSIS

URINE DIPSTICK

COLOR	STRAW	
SP GRAVITY	1.010	1.001-1.030
GLUCOSE	NEGATIVE	< 125 mg/dl
BILIRUBIN	NEGATIVE	NEG
KETONE	NEGATIVE	NEG mg/dl
BLOOD	NEGATIVE	NEG
PH	7.5	4.5-8.0
PROTEIN	NEGATIVE	NEG mg/dl
UROBILINOGEN	NORMAL	NORMAL-1.0 mg/dl
NITRITES	NEGATIVE	NEG
LEUKOCYTES	NEGATIVE	NEG
WBC	RARE	0-5 /HPF
RBC	--	0-5 /HPF
EPI CELLS	RARE	/HPF
BACTERIA	--	/HPF
CASTS.	--	< 1 HYALINE/HPF

End of Report

SUNNY VALLEY MEDICAL CENTER ■ 100 MAIN ST, SUNNY VALLEY, NY 14802 ■ (607) 555-1234

GIBBON, Andrew	Admission: 04-27-YYYY	NUCLEAR MEDICINE REPORT
Case05	DOB: 08-19-YYYY	
Dr. Norris	ROOM: 0362	

Reason for Ultrasound (please initial): *r/o stones*

Date Requested:

Transport: ☑ Wheelchair   ☐ Stretcher   ☐ O$_2$ ☐ IV
               ☑ IP   ☐ OP   ☐ ER
               ☐ PRE OP   ☐ OR/RR   ☐ Portable

HEPATOBILIARY SCAN: Following injection of isotope there is prompt demonstration of the liver, gallbladder, biliary system and small bowel. This would indicate no significant obstruction of either the cystic or the common duct.

CONCLUSION: Normal hepatobiliary scan.

ABDOMINAL ULTRASOUND: Multiple real time images show that the gallbladder is of normal size without evidence of any stones or wall thickening. Portions of the kidneys, spleen, pancreas and upper aorta are demonstrated and are unremarkable.

CONCLUSION: Normal ultrasound

DD: 04-28-YYYY

DT: 04-29-YYYY

D. Lane
_____
D. Lane, M.D.

SUNNY VALLEY MEDICAL CENTER ■ 100 MAIN ST, SUNNY VALLEY, NY 14802 ■ (607) 555-1234

GIBBON, Andrew   Admission: 04-27-YYYY   EKG REPORT
Case05   DOB: 08-19-YYYY
Dr. Norris   ROOM: 0362
                Date of EKG 04-27-YYYY   Time of EKG 11:42:03

Rate   61
PR   158   Abnormal: Old inferior MI
QRSD   64   non specific st-t Changes
QT   383   no old tracings for Comparison
QTC   386   Clinical Correlation needed.
     -- Axis --
P   1
QRS   -27
T   28

                                    Bella Kaplan, M.D.
                                    _____
                                    Name of Physician

GIBBON, Andrew
Case05
Dr. Norris

Admission: 04-27-YYYY
DOB: 08-19-YYYY
ROOM: 0362

TREADMILL STRESS TEST

Date of EKG 04-29-YYYY

Time of EKG 13:00

Protocol	Manual	Time	6:41
Age	72	Rate	116, 78% of Expected Max (148)
Race	Caucasian	BP	13/85
Sex	Male	Stage	3
Ht	66 in.	Speed	3.4
Wt	160 lbs.	Grade	14.0
Opt	362	RPP	156
Rate	92	METS	6.4
BP	110/70		

Inconclusive. Pt developed dyspnea, probably due to
Inderal. No change on EKG to suggest ischemic disease.

Bella Kaplan, M.D.

Name of Physician

Case 06

| SUNNY VALLEY MEDICAL CENTER
100 MAIN ST, SUNNY VALLEY, NY 14802
(607) 555-1234
HOSPITAL #: 000999 | | INPATIENT FACE SHEET | | | |

PATIENT NAME AND ADDRESS		GENDER	RACE	MARITAL STATUS	PATIENT NO.
BENSON, Charles 42 Sherwood Street Sunny Valley, NY 14802		M	W	M	Case06

| | | DATE OF BIRTH | MAIDEN NAME | OCCUPATION | |
| BENSON, Charles ... | | 12-13-YYYY | | Cabinetmaker | |

ADMISSION DATE	TIME	DISCHARGE DATE	TIME	LENGTH OF STAY	TELEPHONE NUMBER
04-24-YYYY	14:30	04-29-YYYY	10:00	5 DAYS	(607) 555-2032

GUARANTOR NAME AND ADDRESS	NEXT OF KIN NAME AND ADDRESS
BENSON, Charles 42 Sherwood Street Sunny Valley, NY 14802	BENSON, Laura 42 Sherwood Street Sunny Valley, NY 14802

GUARANTOR TELEPHONE NO.	RELATIONSHIP TO PATIENT	NEXT OF KIN TELEPHONE NUMBER	RELATIONSHIP TO PATIENT
(607) 555-2032	Self	(607) 555-2032	Wife

ADMITTING PHYSICIAN	SERVICE	ADMIT TYPE	ROOM NUMBER/BED
Thompson MD, Donald	ICU	2	0204/02

ATTENDING PHYSICIAN	ATTENDING PHYSICIAN UPIN	ADMITTING DIAGNOSIS	
Thompson, Donald MD	100B01	Chest Pain	

PRIMARY INSURER	POLICY AND GROUP NUMBER	SECONDARY INSURER	POLICY AND GROUP NUMBER
Medicare	18712166A	AARP	50873240 2

DIAGNOSES AND PROCEDURES	ICD-10-CM/PCS

PRINCIPAL DIAGNOSIS

Costochondritis	M94.0

SECONDARY DIAGNOSES

Arteriosclerotic cardiovascular disease w/ arteriosclerosis Past myocardial infarction Old CVA Status post bypass surgery	I51.9 I52 I70.90 I70.91 I25.2 Z86.79 Z95.1

PRINCIPAL PROCEDURE

SECONDARY PROCEDURES

TOTAL CHARGES: $ 2,335.50

ACTIVITY:	☐ Bedrest	☑ Light	☐ Usual	☐ Unlimited	☐ Other:
DIET:	☐ Regular	☐ Low Cholesterol	☐ Low Salt	☐ ADA	☐ _____ Calorie
FOLLOW-UP:	☑ Call for appointment	☑ Office appointment in <u>one week</u>	☐ Other:		

SPECIAL INSTRUCTIONS: O₂ 4L/min. Albuterol inhaler w/ aerochamber 2 puffs 4 times a day.

Signature of Attending Physician: Donald Thompson, MD

SUNNY VALLEY MEDICAL CENTER ■ 100 MAIN ST, SUNNY VALLEY, NY 14802 ■ (607) 555-1234

BENSON, Charles	Admission: 04-24-YYYY	CONSENT TO ADMISSION
Case 06	DOB: 12-13-YYYY	
Dr. Thompson	ROOM: 0204	

I, _Charles Benson_ hereby consent to admission to the Sunny Valley Medical Center (SVMC), and I further consent to such routine hospital care, diagnostic procedures, and medical treatment that the medical and professional staff of SVMC may deem necessary or advisable. I authorize the use of medical information obtained about me as specified above and the disclosure of such information to my referring physician(s). This form has been fully explained to me, and I understand its contents. I further understand that no guarantees have been made to me as to the results of treatments or examinations done at the SVMC.

Charles Benson   _April 24, YYYY_
_____   _____
Signature of Patient   Date

_____   _____
Signature of Parent/Legal Guardian for Minor   Date

_____
Relationship to Minor

Andrea Witteman   _April 24, YYYY_
_____   _____
WITNESS: Sunny Valley Medical Center Staff Member   Date

CONSENT TO RELEASE INFORMATION FOR REIMBURSEMENT PURPOSES

In order to permit reimbursement, upon request, the Sunny Valley Medical Center (SVMC) may disclose such treatment information pertaining to my hospitalization to any corporation, organization, or agent thereof, which is, or may be liable under contract to the SVMC or to me, or to any of my family members or other person, for payment of all or part of the SVMC's charges for services rendered to me (e.g., the patient's health insurance carrier). I understand that the purpose of any release of information is to facilitate reimbursement for services rendered. In addition, in the event that my health insurance program includes utilization review of services provided during this admission, I authorize SVMC to release information as is necessary to permit the review. This authorization will expire once the reimbursement for services rendered is complete.

Charles Benson   _April 24, YYYY_
_____   _____
Signature of Patient   Date

_____   _____
Signature of Parent/Legal Guardian for Minor   Date

_____
Relationship to Minor

Andrea Witteman   _April 24, YYYY_
_____   _____
WITNESS: Sunny Valley Medical Center Staff Member   Date

SUNNY VALLEY MEDICAL CENTER ■ 100 MAIN ST, SUNNY VALLEY, NY 14802 ■ (607) 555-1234

BENSON, Charles	Admission: 04-24-YYYY	ADVANCE DIRECTIVE
Case 06	DOB: 12-13-YYYY	
Dr. Thompson	ROOM: 0204	

Your answers to the following questions will assist your Physician and the Hospital to respect your wishes regarding your medical care. This information will become a part of your medical record.

	YES	NO	PATIENT'S INITIALS
1. Have you been provided with a copy of the information called "Patient Rights Regarding Health Care Decision?"	X		CB
2. Have you prepared a "Living Will?" If yes, please provide the Hospital with a copy for your medical record.		X	CB
3. Have you prepared a Durable Power of Attorney for Health Care? If yes, please provide the Hospital with a copy for your medical record.		X	CB
4. Have you provided this facility with an Advance Directive on a prior admission and is it still in effect? If yes, Admitting Office to contact Medical Records to obtain a copy for the medical record.		X	CB
5. Do you desire to execute a Living Will/Durable Power of Attorney? If yes, refer to in order: a. Physician b. Social Service c. Volunteer Service		X	CB

HOSPITAL STAFF DIRECTIONS: Check when each step is completed.

1. ___✓___ Verify the above questions where answered and actions taken where required.

2. ___✓___ If the "Patient Rights" information was provided to someone other than the patient, state reason:

_____

_____ _____
Name of Individual Receiving Information   Relationship to Patient

3. ___✓___ If information was provided in a language other than English, specify language and method.

4. ___✓___ Verify patient was advised on how to obtain additional information on Advance Directives.

5. ___✓___ Verify the Patient/Family Member/Legal Representative was asked to provide the Hospital with a copy of the Advance Directive which will be retained in the medical record.

File this form in the medical record, and give a copy to the patient.

_____
Name of Patient (Name of Individual giving information if different from Patient)

CHARLES BENSON   *April 24, YYYY*
_____ _____
Signature of Patient   Date

Andrea Witteman   *April 24, yyyy*
_____ _____
Signature of Hospital Representative   Date

SUNNY VALLEY MEDICAL CENTER ■ 100 MAIN ST, SUNNY VALLEY, NY 14802 ■ (607) 555-1234

BENSON, Charles	Admission: 04-24-YYYY	CONSULTATION REPORT
Case06	DOB: 12-13-YYYY	
Dr. Thompson	ROOM: 0204	

The patient is a 64 yr. old gentleman of Dr. Thompson's who I was asked to see for chest pain.

HISTORY OF PRESENT ILLNESS: Mr. Benson had about a three day history of somewhat progressive, unprovoked chest pain. It varies in its location and description as the history goes on. I don't think this is intentionally being elusive, I just think he can't well describe it. It is not truly substernal, but more left lateral chest wall. It is exacerbated by movement. It is relieved by Nitroglycerin but a varying dosage. Ultimately he ends up getting Morphine. There is no association with food as far as we can tell. The patient does have a prior cardiac history. He says he has had 2-3 heart attacks and equal number of CVA's, apparently leading to some blindness in one of his eyes. He has had coronary artery bypass, triple vessel I am told. He has a prior history of at least two packs per day smoking for years. He is rather overweight. Interestingly he states that his sternotomy never did heal very well. There is no preceding history of cough, fever, chills, or any kind of muscular activity.

PAST MEDICAL HISTORY: Essentially that mentioned above. He has had back surgery. He has also had hernia repairs.

MEDICATIONS: The patient is on Cardizem 60 mg. q.i.d. Lasix 40 mg. a day. Isordil 40 mg. t.i.d Potassium 10 mEq. Daily. Resteril 30 mg. at bedtime. Theophylline 200 mg. 2 b.i.d. Nitro Patch and Coumadin.

ALLERGIES: None

SOCIAL HISTORY & FAMILY HISTORY: The patient is married. No longer smokes. No strong family history of any particular disease. Interestingly, he served honorably in WWII, was exposed to the radiation blasts where he said he and others were exposed to direct radiation while they were trying to sink the ships with nuclear devices. He also has been exposed to a lot of wood dust in his profession as a cabinetmaker.

REVIEW OF SYSTEMS: Noncontributory.

PHYSICAL EXAMINATION: Reveals a 64 yr. old man in no gross distress at the moment. VITAL SIGNS: Temperature 98, pulse 68 and regular, respirations 16, blood pressure 140/100. HEAD: Normocephalic. Eyes sclera and conjunctiva are normal. PERRLA, EOM's intact. Fundi not visualized. ENT are unremarkable. NECK: Supple, no thyromegaly. Carotids are 2 out of 4. No bruits, no JVD. Chest is symmetrical and clear to A&P. HEART: Reveals a regular rhythm, no particular murmurs or gallops. ABDOMEN: Nontender, no organomegaly. Bowel sounds normal activity. No bruits or masses. BACK: No CVAT, tenderness to percussion over the spinous processes. Anterior chest reveals tenderness to palpation over the left pectoralis muscle and it really makes him whine with light palpation. RECTAL, GENITALIA: Deferred at this time. EXTREMITIES: No cyanosis, clubbing or edema. Pulses are equal and full. NEUROLOGIC: Is physiologic.

IMPRESSION: 1) Chest pain, probably chest wall, although the precipitating event is not clear at this time.

              2) ASCVD with history of infarction and CVA's.

RECOMMENDATIONS: I think that if at all possible we ought to put him on NSAIDs, at least temporarily. See if we can't control the discomfort. I am not convinced that there is a cardiac component to this as its presentation is not in pattern. Likewise, there are no changes on the cardiogram and any other objective way of confirming that this is cardiac. Will follow along with you. Thank you for allowing me to participate in his care.

DD: 04-24-YYYY

DT: 04-25-YYYY

Sandra Reese, M.D.
Sandra Reese, M.D.

BENSON, Charles	Admission: 04-24-YYYY	PROGRESS NOTES
Case06	DOB: 12-13-YYYY	
Dr. Thompson	ROOM: 0204	

Date	(Please skip one line between dates.)
4/24	Chief Complaint: Chest pain into left lateral chest wall, shortness of breath, and nausea.
	Diagnosis: Chest pain Unstsable angina. Rule out myocardial infarction.
	Plan of Treatment: iCU observation and work-up. Donald Thompson, MD
04/25	HHN with 0.5 ml proventil/NSS, tolerated well. Breath sounds ↓ clear. Sitting in chair, heart rate 72.
1600	Respirations regular, 18. O2 p+p BLNR. O2 sat. 95%. Rita Childs, R.R.T.
04/25	HHN w/ 0.5 ml proventil and NSS given in mask. Heart rate 84. Respirations regular, 20.
1930	Breath sounds clear, with decreased bases. Patient had good npc, O2 on partial room air. T. Perry, RRT
04-26	Treatment given: HHN with 0.5 ml Proventil/NSS via mask with patient tolerating well.
0715	BS ↓ clear, pulse 64, respirations 16, NPC O2, N/C. L Seraphin RRT
04-26	Pt. doing better. Still complains of L sided chest pain. Will try to gradually remove O2. D. Thompson, MD
04-26	Treatment given: HHN with 0.5 ml Proventil / NSS via mask. Breath sounds ↓ clear.
1100	Pulse 80, respirations 20, NPC O2 on 6L pre O2 on O2 5L port. L Seraphin
04-26	Tx given: MDI with Proventil via aerochamber. Pt. instructed on use + using good technique.
1500	BS ↓ w/ rales at bases. P 80. R 20. No cough. O_2 on a 5L N/C. L Seraphin
04-26	MDI w/ 2 puffs Proventil treatment given via aerochamber. Patient tolderated treatment well. B.S. clear. ↓'d bases.
1910	No cough. O2 on 5 l n.c. pre and post treatment. C. Steinerly, CPT
04-27	MDI w/ 2 puffs proventil via aerochamber gd. Tx tol well. BS clear ↓, no cough. O2 p+p tx 5L N.C. O2 sat. 97%.
0710	R. Rose CPT
04-27	Pt. has less pain. Continue treatment.

BENSON, Charles	Admission: 04-24-YYYY	PROGRESS NOTES
Case 06	DOB: 12-13-YYYY	
Dr. Thompson	ROOM: 0204	

Date	(Please skip one line between dates.)
04-27	Met w/ pt. per multidisciplinary team conference referral by cpt/nursing. Pt. stated to having home O₂ but
0900	unknown is type of set up he has to meet O₂ demands Presently @ 5 LPM. Interview done w/ pt. this am. He has
	liquid O₂ @ home (can go ↑ to 10 lpm) and also has access to an O₂ concentrator (usually goes to 4-5 pm). Pt also
	has E-portable tanks. Pt. utilizes a portable O₂ demand system on a sensor he described as supply/demand by
	by sensoring constant need w/ rest/activity. Pt. utilizes Hub as O₂ provider + is extremely pleased with company
	+ service. Pt. declines any other needs for discharge planning. No intervention required. Nsg aware. D. Davenport
04-27	MDI w/ 2 puffs proventil gd. tech. Tol well O2 tx. 5L N.C. — N.C. R. Rose, CPT
04-27	MDI w/ 2 puffs proventil / NSS gd. tech. Tol well. No cough. B.S. ↓, clear. Pt. sitting in chair. O2 tx 5L N.C..
	R. Rose, CPT
04-27	MDI 2 puffs Proventil via spacer. BS ↓'d bases. No cough. HR 68. R 16. O2 on 5LN.C. pre & post tx. E. Blossom, RRT
04-28	MDI w/ 2 puffs proventil /Nss gd. tech. tol well no cough BS clear ↓ ol Pt. sitting in chair O2 tx 5L N.C.
	R. Rose, CPT
04-28	Pt says his chest feels better. i feel this is inflammation. Treatment helping. D. Thompson
04-28	mdi w/ 2 puffs proventil gd. tech. tol well feeling better O₂ Pre & post tx 5L N.C. — N.C. R. Rose, CPT
04-28	MDI w/ 2 puffs proventil gd. tech. Tol well. O₂sat. 5LNC 95%, ↓ 4LNC O₂sat. No cough. B.S. ↓ appear clear.
	Pt. shown how to use O₂ walker. R. Rose, CPT
04-28	MDI 2 puffs Proventil via spacer. BS ↓'d bases. HR 68. R 24. O2 4LNC pre-tx. E. Blossom, RRT
04-29	MDI w/ 2 puffs Proventil. tol Rx well. good technique. NPC O2 on pre & post 4 L NC. H. Figgs, CRTT
4/29	Patient feeling much better. No complaints of chest pain. O2 sat 92÷ on 4 L O2. Discharged to home.

BENSON, Charles	Admission: 04-24-YYYY	DOCTORS ORDERS
Case06	DOB: 12-13-YYYY	
Dr. Thompson	ROOM: 0204	

Date	Time	Physician's signature required for each order. (Please skip one line between dates.)
4-24	1501	1) Admit to Dr. Thompson
		2) Admit to ICCU
		3) Daily Protime
		4) Diltiazem 60 mg q.i.d.
		5) Lasix 40 mg in a.m.
		6) Isosorbide 40 mg
		7) KCI 10 mg in a.m.
		8) Theophylline 200 mg bid
		9) Nitro Patch 0.2 mg daily for 12 hours
		10) Coumadin 4 mg
		11) Albuterol MDI with Rigxair 2 puffs g 4 hours prn for dyspnea and wheezing
		12) Pt. may use own eye drops, right eye
		13) Serum Theophylline level
		14) Mylanta II g 2 hours prn staomch discomfort
		15) Tylenol 4 hrs mild pain
		16) O$_2$ via N.C. 3 L/
		17) Oximetry in 1 hr, g 5 nights
		T.O. Sandra Leary, R.N./D. Thompson, M.D.
		D. Thompson, MD

BENSON, Charles	Admission: 04-24-YYYY	DOCTORS ORDERS
Case06	DOB: 12-13-YYYY	
Dr. Thompson	ROOM: 0204	

Date	Time	Physician's signature required for each order. (Please skip one line between dates.)
04-24		ROUTINE ICU ORDERS
		1. CBC, SR, PT, PTT, SCG II, LYTES, BUN, MAGNESIUM, UA, CPK. Isoenzymes q8h x 24 hrs and
		daily until normal. LDH now and daily x 2 until return to normal range.
		2. EKG STAT and daily x 2 days and with chest pain x one (1).
		3. Oxygen – 3L/min by cannula, PRN. Oximetry PRN.
		4. Chest X-ray.
		5. Diet – Cardiac, clear to regular as tolerated.
		6. MEDICATIONS:
		NTG 0.4mg SL q 5 min x 3 PRN for chest pain.
		Morphine Sulfate 4mg IV q 2 min PRN not to exceed 16mg/hr
		OR Meperidine 50 mg IV q 15 min PRN not to exceed 100mg/4hr for chest pain, dyspnea, extreme restlessness.
		Docusate with Casanthranol BID PRN nausea.
		Acetaminophen 650mg q4h PRN headache.
		7. 500cc D5W at 25CC/HR., if diabetic use Normol R at 25cc/hr.
		8. Bradycardia: Atropine 0.5mg IV q 5 min up to 2mg for symptomatic heart rate. (Pulse less than 50, or less
		than 60 with decreased blood pressure, and/or PVC's).
		9. PVC's: Lidocaine 50mg IV push then start drip of 500ml D5W/Lidocaine 2gm @ 2mg/ml (30cc/hr) for
		greater than six (6) per min or three (3) in a row.
		10. V-Tach: If patient hemodynamically stable Lidocaine 50mg IV push; then start drip of 500 ml
		D5W/Lidocaine 2 gm @ 2 mg/min (30cc/hr.)
		11. V-Tach: If patient becomes unstable, Cardiovert @ 50 watt seconds.
		12. V-Fib: Immediately defibrillate @ 200 watt seconds; if not converted, then
		Immediately defibrillate @ 300 watt seconds; if not converted, then
		Immediately defibrillate @ 360 watt seconds. Give Epinephrine (1:10,000) 1 mg
		IV push, then Lidocaine drip as per V-tach protocol.
		13. Asystole/EMD: Epinephrine (1:10,000) 1mg IV push; if no response, Atropine 1 mg IV push.
		14. Respiratory Arrest: Intubation with Mechanical Ventilation.
		15. Activity: Bedrest with bedside commode if VS stable. *Donald Thompson, MD*
		16. Notify physician for chest pain or arrhythmias requiring treatment. T.O. Sandra Leary, R.N./D. Thompson, M.D.

BENSON, Charles	Admission: 04-24-YYYY	DOCTORS ORDERS
Case06	DOB: 12-13-YYYY	
Dr. Thompson	ROOM: 0204	

Date	Time	Physician's signature required for each order. (Please skip one line between dates.)
04/24	1700	lacrilube eye ung – apply to eyelids @ h.s. daily akwa tears or natural
		tears, drops as needed – may have @ bedside.
		R.A.V. To Dr. Thompson / S. Uollings, RN Donald Thompson, MD
04/24	2220	Increase O$_2$ to 4L min nasal canula
		R.A.V. T.O. Dr. Thompson/S. Uollings, RN Donald Thompson, MD
04-24	0350	ABG in AM
		Increase O$_2$ to 6 LPM – nc
		Consult Dr. Reese to evaluate chest pain in AM
		R.A.V. To Dr. Thompson/R. Underhill Donald Thompson, MD
04-24	0830	Lung Perfusion & Ventilation scan this AM to rule out a PE
		R.A.V. T.O. Dr. Reese/W. Nelson Sandra Reese, M.D.
04-24	0945	Proventil qid Donald Thompson, MD
04-24		Motrin 600 p.o. T.i.D.
		Carafate 1 gm p.o. Q.i.D.
		up in chair
		ABG on RA in AM
		Donald Thompson, MD
4/24	1058	Obtain a.m. blood gas on O2 at 24 min. R.A.V. T.O. Dr. Reese/W. Nelson Sandra Reese, M.D.
04-24		May be out of bed as tolerated Donald Thompson, MD

BENSON, Charles	Admission: 04-24-YYYY	DOCTORS ORDERS
Case06	DOB: 12-13-YYYY	
Dr. Thompson	ROOM: 0204	

Date	Time	Physician's signature required for each order. (Please skip one line between dates.)
4-24	1851	TELEMETRY PROTOCOL
		1. Saline lock, insert and flush every 24 hours and PRN
		2. EKG with chest pain x 1
		3. Oxygen 3 1/min. via nasal cannula PRN for chest pain.
		4. Chest Pain: NTG 0.4mg SL q 5 min x 3.
		5. Bradycardia: Atropine 0.5mg IV q 5 min to total of 2mg for symptomatic heart rate (Pulse less than 50 or 60 with decreased BP and/or PVC's)
		6. PVC's: Lidocaine 50mg IV push
		Start drip 500 cc D5W Lidocaine 2 gm @ 2mg/Min (30 cc/hr) for greater than 6 PVC's per min or 3 PVC's in a row.
		7. V-Tach: (If patient is hemodynamically stable)
		Lidocaine 50mg IV push.
		Start drip 500cc D5W Lidocaine 2 gm @ 2mg/min (30cc/hr)
		(If unstable) Cardiovert @ 50 watt seconds.
		8. V-fib: Immediately defibrillate @ 200 watt seconds, if not converted:
		Immediately defibrillate @ 300 watt seconds, if not converted;
		Immediately defibrillate @ 360 watt seconds, if not converted: Start CPR
		Give Epinephrine (1:10,000) 1 mg IC push
		Give Lidocaine as per V-Tach protocol
		9. Asystole/EMD: Begin CPR
		Epinephrine (1:10,000) 1mg IV push
		Atropine 1 mg IV push if no response with Epinephrine
		10. Respiratory arrest: Intubation with mechanical ventilation.
		11. Notify Physician for chest pain or arrhythmias requiring treatment.
		Donald Thompson, MD

BENSON, Charles	Admission: 04-24-YYYY	DOCTORS ORDERS
Case06	DOB: 12-13-YYYY	
Dr. Thompson	ROOM: 0204	

Date	Time	Physician's signature required for each order. (Please skip one line between dates.)
04-24		1) Transfer to floor on Telemetry. May be up as tolerated.
		2) Heparin iV
		3) O2 via N.C. at 6L/m
		4) Oximetry q shift.
		5) D/C Protimes
		6) Cardizem 60 mg QiD
		7) Lasix 40 mg p.o. tib
		8) isosorbium 40 mg p.o. tib
		9) KCi 10 mg in AM
		10) Theophylline 200 mg bid
		11) Nitro patch
		12) Coumadin 5 mg
		13) Motrin 600 mg tid
		14) Lacrilube - apply to eyelids
		15) Tylenol 2 tabs 14h prn for pain
		16) Resteril 30 mg h.s.
		17) Regular diet
		Donald Thompson, MD
4/24	1950	1500 cal ADA diet. May be up ad lib. Donald Thompson, MD
4/25		↓ o2 to 5 L/min and ok oximetry after 1 hr. Donald Thompson, MD
4/26		D/c telemetry. Donald Thompson, MD

BENSON, Charles	Admission: 04-24-YYYY	DOCTORS ORDERS
Case 06	DOB: 12-13-YYYY	
Dr. Thompson	ROOM: 0204	

Date	Time	Physician's signature required for each order. (Please skip one line between dates.)
04-27	0820	Coumadin 75 mg tid Donald Thompson, MD
04-28	1050	Ambulate ad lib. Donald Thompson, MD
04-29		Discharge home. Donald Thompson, MD

BENSON, Charles   Admission: 04-24-YYYY   LABORATORY DATA
Case06   DOB: 12-13-YYYY
Dr. Thompson   ROOM: 0204

SPECIMEN COLLECTED: 4-24-YYYY   **SPECIMEN RECEIVED:** 4-24-YYYY

TEST	RESULT	FLAG	REFERENCE
URINALYSIS			
DIPSTICK ONLY			
COLOR	CLOUDY YELLOW		
SP GRAVITY	1.025		≤ 1.030
GLUCOSE	110		≤ 125 mg/dl
BILIRUBIN	NEG		≤ 0.8 mg/dl
KETONE	TRACE		≤ 10 mg/dl
BLOOD	0.03		0.06 mg/dl hgb
PH	5.0		5-8.0
PROTEIN	NORMAL		≤ 30 mg/dl
UROBILINOGEN	NORMAL		≤ -1 mg/dl
NITRITES	NEG		NEG
LEUKOCYTE	NEG		≤ 15 WBC/hpf
W.B.C.	5-10		≤ 5/hpf
R.B.C.	RARE		≤ 5/hpf
BACT.	4f		1+(≤ 20/hpf)
URINE PREGNANCY TEST			

End of Report

BENSON, Charles　　Admission: 04-24-YYYY　　　LABORATORY DATA
Case 06　　　　　　DOB: 12-13-YYYY
Dr. Thompson　　　 ROOM: 0204

SPECIMEN COLLECTED:　04-24-YYYY　　　SPECIMEN RECEIVED:　Blood

TEST	RESULT	FLAG	REFERENCE
Sodium	142		136-147 meq/L
Potassium	3.9		3.6-5.0 mmol/L
Chloride	102		99-110 mmol/L
CO2	29		24-32 mg/dl
Glucose	95		70-110 mg/dl
Urea Nitrogen	6	**L**	7-18 mg/dl

End of Report

BENSON, Charles	Admission: 04-24-YYYY		LABORATORY DATA
Case06	DOB: 12-13-YYYY		
Dr. Thompson	ROOM: 0204		

SPECIMEN COLLECTED: 4-24-YYYY **SPECIMEN RECEIVED:** 4-24-YYYY

CBC S DIFF

TEST	RESULT	FLAG	REFERENCE
WBC	7.4		4.5-11.0 thous/UL
RBC	5.02	**L**	5.2-5.4 mill/UL
HGB	15.0		11.7-16.1 g/dl
HCT	45.8		35.0-47.0 %
MCV	91.2		85-99 fL.
MCHC	32.8	**L**	33-37
RDW	15.2	**H**	11.4-14.5
Platelets	165		130-400 thous/UL
MPV	8.4		7.4-10.4
LYMPH %	21.1		20.5-51.1
MONO %	7.8		1.7-9.3
GRAN %	71.1		42.2-75.2
LYMPH x 10^3	1.6		1.2-3.4
MONO x 10^3	.6	**H**	0.11-0.59
GRAN x 10^3	5.3		1.4-6.5
EOS x 10^3	< .7		0.0-0.7
BASO x 10^3	< .2		0.0-0.2
ANISO	SLIGHT		

End of Report

SUNNY VALLEY MEDICAL CENTER ■ 100 MAIN ST, SUNNY VALLEY, NY 14802 ■ (607) 555-1234

BENSON, Charles   Admission: 04-24-YYYY
Case06   DOB: 12-13-YYYY   PULSE OXIMETRY
Dr. Thompson   ROOM: 0204

TIME	SPO$_2$	F1O$_2$	TECHNICIAN
04/24/YYYY			
1530	95%	3L	AS
2000	92%	3L	AS
2300	88%	3L NC	RB
04/24/YYYY			
2335	91%	6L	JJ
2340	94%	6L	LL
2345	95%	6L	WW
04/24/YYYY			
2350	93%	6 LPM	PT
2400	94%	6L	RB
04/25/YYYY			
0715	95%	8L	RCH
0945	93%	6L NC	RCH
1600	95%	6L NC	GER
2100	96%	6L NC	RB

End of Report

BENSON, Charles   Admission: 04-24-YYYY
Case06   DOB: 12-13-YYYY   PULSE OXIMETRY
Dr. Thompson   ROOM: 0204

TIME	SPO$_2$	F1O$_2$	TECHNICIAN
04/26/YYYY			
0730	96%	6L NC	SMC
1520	94%	5L NC	SMC
04/27/YYYY			
1205	93%	5L	SMC
04/28/YYYY			
0715	98%	5L	YE
1530	95%	5L	YE
1615	93%	4L	MM
1630	95%	4L	MM
1640	92%	4L	MM
1650	93%	4L	MM
2310	92%	4L	RB

End of Report

BENSON, Charles   Admission: 04-24-YYYY
Case06   DOB: 12-13-YYYY   RADIOMETRY
Dr. Thompson   ROOM: 0204

SPECIMEN COLLECTED: 04-22-YYYY   SPECIMEN RECEIVED: 04-22-YYYY

TEST	RESULT	REFERENCE
BLOOD GAS VALUES		
pH	7.440	
pCO2	33.4	mmHg
pO2	55.6	mmHg
TEMPERATURE CORRECTED VALUES		
pH	7.440	
pCO2	33.4	mmHg
pO2	55.6	mmHg
ACID BASE STATUS		
HCO3c	22.3	mmol/L
ABEc	-0.4	mmol/L
BLOOD OXIMETRY VALUES		
tHb	17.8	g/dL
O2Hb	89.9	%
COHb	0.6	%
MetHb	0.6	%

End of Report

BENSON, Charles   Admission: 04-24-YYYY

Case06   DOB: 12-13-YYYY

Dr. Thompson   ROOM: 0204

RADIOMETRY

SPECIMEN COLLECTED: 04-23-YYYY   **SPECIMEN RECEIVED:**   04-23-YYYY

TEST	RESULT	REFERENCE
BLOOD GAS VALUES		
pH	7.401	
pCO_2	38.5	mmHg
pO_2	69.8	mmHg
TEMPERATURE CORRECTED VALUES		
pH	7.401	
pCO_2	38.5	mmHg
pO_2	69.8	mmHg
ACID BASE STATUS		
HCO3c	23.4	mmol/L
ABEc	-0.6	mmol/L
BLOOD OXIMETRY VALUES		
tHb	17.4	g/dL
O2Hb	92.7	%
COHb	0.3	%
MetHb	0.8	%

End of Report

SUNNY VALLEY MEDICAL CENTER ■ 100 MAIN ST, SUNNY VALLEY, NY 14802 ■ (607) 555-1234

BENSON, Charles   Admission: 04-24-YYYY   RADIOMETRY
Case06   DOB: 12-13-YYYY
Dr. Thompson   ROOM: 0204

SPECIMEN COLLECTED: 04-24-YYYY   **SPECIMEN RECEIVED:**   04-24-YYYY

TEST	RESULT	REFERENCE
BLOOD GAS VALUES		
pH	7.44	
pCO2	36.0	mmHg
pO2	46.3	mmHg
TEMPERATURE CORRECTED VALUES		
pH	7.44	
pCO2	36.0	mmHg
pO2	46.3	mmHg
ACID BASE STATUS		
HCO3c	24.3	mmol/L
ABEc	1.1	mmol/L
BLOOD OXIMETRY VALUES		
tHb	17.0	g/dL
O2Hb	84.6	%
COHb	0.5	%
MetHb	0.7	%

End of Report

```
BENSON, Charles        Admission: 04-24-YYYY
Case06                 DOB: 12-13-YYYY                 RADIOLOGY REPORT
Dr. Thompson           ROOM: 0204
```

Date Requested: 04-22-YYYY

CHEST: PA and lateral views show that the heart, lungs, thorax and mediastinum are normal.

DD: 04-22-YYYY

DT: 04-22-YYYY

Philip Rogers
_____
Philip Rogers, M.D., Radiologist

BENSON, Charles
Case06
Dr. Thompson

Admission: 04-24-YYYY
DOB: 12-13-YYYY
ROOM: 0204

EKG REPORT

Date of EKG: 04-22-YYYY   Time of EKG: 13:56:20

Rate	66
PR	184
QRSD	60
QT	363
QTC	380
-- Axis --	
P	76
QRS	79
T	71

Normal.

Bella Kaplan
Bella Kaplan, M.D.

BENSON, Charles   Admission: 04-24-YYYY   EKG REPORT
Case06   DOB: 12-13-YYYY
Dr. Thompson   ROOM: 0204

Date of EKG: 04-23-Y Y Y Y   Time of EKG: 13:56:20

Rate	66
PR	184
QRSD	60
QT	363
QTC	380
-- Axis --	
P	76
QRS	79
T	71

Normal.

Bella Kaplan
_____
Bella Kaplan, M.D.

BENSON, Charles   Admission: 04-24-YYYY
Case06   DOB: 12-13-YYYY   EKG REPORT
Dr. Thompson   ROOM: 0204

Date of EKG: 04-24-YYYY   Time of EKG: 13:56:20

Rate   66
PR   184
QRSD   60
QT   363   Normal.
QTC   380
       -- Axis --
P   76
QRS   79
T   71

Bella Kaplan
Bella Kaplan, M.D.

Case 07

SUNNY VALLEY MEDICAL CENTER						INPATIENT FACE SHEET	

SUNNY VALLEY MEDICAL CENTER
100 MAIN ST, SUNNY VALLEY, NY 14802
(607) 555-1234
HOSPITAL #: 000999

INPATIENT FACE SHEET

PATIENT NAME AND ADDRESS			GENDER	RACE	MARITAL STATUS	PATIENT NO.
HOOVER, Holley E.			F	W	Married	Case07

DATE OF BIRTH	MAIDEN NAME	OCCUPATION
01-16-YYYY	Berry	Florist

HOOVER, Holley E.
90 Silver Street
Sunny Valley, NY 14802

ADMISSION DATE	TIME	DISCHARGE DATE	TIME	LENGTH OF STAY	TELEPHONE NUMBER
04-30-YYYY	15:45	05-02-YYYY	10:10	02 DAYS	(607)555-6688

GUARANTOR NAME AND ADDRESS	NEXT OF KIN NAME AND ADDRESS
Hoover, Richard 90 Silver Street Sunny Valley, NY 14802	Hoover, Richard 90 Silver Street Sunny Valley, NY 14802

GUARANTOR TELEPHONE NO.	RELATIONSHIP TO PATIENT	NEXT OF KIN TELEPHONE NUMBER	RELATIONSHIP TO PATIENT
(607)555-6688	Husband	(607)555-6688	Husband

ADMITTING PHYSICIAN	SERVICE	ADMIT TYPE	ROOM NUMBER/BED
Swann MD, Janice	Medical	2	0320/02

ATTENDING PHYSICIAN	ATTENDING PHYSICIAN UPIN	ADMITTING DIAGNOSIS
Swann MD, Janice	100V23	Rule out myocardial infarction

PRIMARY INSURER	POLICY AND GROUP NUMBER	SECONDARY INSURER	POLICY AND GROUP NUMBER
BCBS	332323202 33190	Empire Plan	549087562

DIAGNOSES AND PROCEDURES	ICD-10-CM/PCS
PRINCIPAL DIAGNOSIS	
Reflux esophagitis	K21.0
SECONDARY DIAGNOSES	
Hiatal hernia	K44.9
PRINCIPAL PROCEDURE	
SECONDARY PROCEDURES	
TOTAL CHARGES: $ 1,555.95	

ACTIVITY:	☐ Bedrest	☒ Light	☐ Usual	☐ Unlimited	☐ Other:
DIET:	☒ Regular	☐ Low Cholesterol	☐ Low Salt	☐ ADA	☐ _____ Calorie

FOLLOW-UP: ☐ Call for appointment ☒ Office appointment in _one week_ ☐ Other:

SPECIAL INSTRUCTIONS:

Signature of Attending Physician: J Swann, MD

```
HOOVER, Holley E.        Admission: 04-30-YYYY
Case07                   DOB: 01-16-YYYY
Dr. Swann                ROOM: 0320
```

CONSENT TO ADMISSION

I, _Holley E. Hoover_ hereby consent to admission to the Sunny Valley Medical Center (SVMC), and I further consent to such routine hospital care, diagnostic procedures, and medical treatment that the medical and professional staff of SVMC may deem necessary or advisable. I authorize the use of medical information obtained about me as specified above and the disclosure of such information to my referring physician(s). This form has been fully explained to me, and I understand its contents. I further understand that no guarantees have been made to me as to the results of treatments or examinations done at the SVMC.

Holley E. Hoover _____
Signature of Patient

April 30, YYYY _____
Date

_____
Signature of Parent/Legal Guardian for Minor

_____
Date

_____
Relationship to Minor

Andrea Witteman _____
WITNESS: Sunny Valley Medical Center Staff Member

April 30, YYYY _____
Date

CONSENT TO RELEASE INFORMATION FOR REIMBURSEMENT PURPOSES

In order to permit reimbursement, upon request, the Sunny Valley Medical Center (SVMC) may disclose such treatment information pertaining to my hospitalization to any corporation, organization, or agent thereof, which is, or may be liable under contract to the SVMC or to me, or to any of my family members or other person, for payment of all or part of the SVMC's charges for services rendered to me (e.g., the patient's health insurance carrier). I understand that the purpose of any release of information is to facilitate reimbursement for services rendered. In addition, in the event that my health insurance program includes utilization review of services provided during this admission, I authorize SVMC to release information as is necessary to permit the review. This authorization will expire once the reimbursement for services rendered is complete.

Holley E. Hoover _____
Signature of Patient

April 30, YYYY _____
Date

_____
Signature of Parent/Legal Guardian for Minor

_____
Date

_____
Relationship to Minor

Andrea Witteman _____
WITNESS: Sunny Valley Medical Center Staff Member

April 30, YYYY _____
Date

HOOVER, Holley E.	Admission: 04-30-YYYY	ADVANCE DIRECTIVE
Case 07	DOB: 01-16-YYYY	
Dr. Swann	ROOM: 0320	

Your answers to the following questions will assist your Physician and the Hospital to respect your wishes regarding your medical care. This information will become a part of your medical record.

	YES	NO	PATIENT'S INITIALS
1. Have you been provided with a copy of the information called "Patient Rights Regarding Health Care Decision?"	X		HEH
2. Have you prepared a "Living Will?" If yes, please provide the Hospital with a copy for your medical record.		X	HEH
3. Have you prepared a Durable Power of Attorney for Health Care? If yes, please provide the Hospital with a copy for your medical record.		X	HEH
4. Have you provided this facility with an Advance Directive on a prior admission and is it still in effect? If yes, Admitting Office to contact Medical Records to obtain a copy for the medical record.		X	HEH
5. Do you desire to execute a Living Will/Durable Power of Attorney? If yes, refer to in order: a. Physician b. Social Service c. Volunteer Service		X	HEH

HOSPITAL STAFF DIRECTIONS: Check when each step is completed.

1. ___✓___ Verify the above questions where answered and actions taken where required.

2. ___✓___ If the "Patient Rights" information was provided to someone other than the patient, state reason:

_____

_____   _____
Name of Individual Receiving Information   Relationship to Patient

3. ___✓___ If information was provided in a language other than English, specify language and method.

4. ___✓___ Verify patient was advised on how to obtain additional information on Advance Directives.

5. ___✓___ Verify the Patient/Family Member/Legal Representative was asked to provide the Hospital with a copy of the Advance Directive which will be retained in the medical record.

File this form in the medical record, and give a copy to the patient.

_____
Name of Patient (Name of Individual giving information if different from Patient)

Holley E. Hoover   April 30, YYYY
_____   _____
Signature of Patient   Date

Andrea Witteman   April 30, yyyy
_____   _____
Signature of Hospital Representative   Date

SUNNY VALLEY MEDICAL CENTER ■ 100 MAIN ST, SUNNY VALLEY, NY 14802 ■ (607) 555-1234

HOOVER, Holley E. Admission: 04-30-YYYY	PROGRESS NOTES
Case 07 DOB: 01-16-YYYY	
Dr. Swann ROOM: 0320	

Date	(Please skip one line between dates.)
4/30	CC: 63 year old patient with Chest pain. R/O M.I.
	Plan of Treatment: Rx as needed to R/O M.I.
	Discharge Plan: Home - No services needed J Swann, MD
04/30	MDI 2 puffs each Albuterol/Beclovent. BS harsh. Pulse 68. Resp 20. NPC. Instructed in use of spacer.
	Demonstrated good technique. T. Perry, R.R.T.
05-01	MDI w/ 2 puffs Proventil via spacer - pt. tol well on her own F/B MDI w/ 2 puffs
0800	Vanceril - NPC. BS ↓'d clear. L Seraphin C.P.T.
05/01	MDI 2 puffs each Albuterol/Beclovent via spacer w/ excellent technique. BS ↓ clear.
2035	T. Perry, R.R.T.
05/01	Pt. has no further pain. She feels well but anxious. Results normal so far.
	J Swann, MD
05/02	No pain. Results all normal. Will discharge and see in one week.
	J Swann MD
05-02	MDI w/ 2 puffs Proventil via spacer. F/B MDI w/ 2 puffs Vanceril - pt. tol well on her
0845	her own P 88. RR 20.
	L Seraphin CPT

HOOVER, Holley E.	Admission: 04-30-YYYY	DOCTORS ORDERS
Case07	DOB: 01-16-YYYY	
Dr. Swann	ROOM: 0320	

Date	Time	Physician's signature required for each order. (Please skip one line between dates.)
04/30	1815	1. Heparin lock, insert and flush every shift and PRN
		2. EKG with chest pain.
		3. Oxygen - 3 l /min via nasal cannula PRN for chest pain.
		4. Chest pain: NTG 0.4 mg SL q 5 min. x 3. Call physician if not relieved.
		5. Bradycardia: Atropine 0.5 mg IV q 5 min up to 2mg for symptomatic heart
		rate. (Pulse < 50, or > 60 with decreased BP and/or PVC's).
		6. PVC's: Lidocaine 50mg IV push
		Start drip 500 cc D5/W Lidocaine 2gm @ 2 mg/min (30 cc/hr) for
		> six (6) per min or three (3) in a row.
		7.. V-Tach: (If patient hemodynamically stable);
		Lidocaine 50 mg IV push
		Start drip of 500 cc D5/W Lidocaine 2 gm @ 2 mg/min (30cc/hr.)
		(If unstable) Cardiovert @ 50 watt seconds.
		8. V-Fib: Immediately defibrillate @ 200 watt seconds, if not converted;
		Immediately defibrillate @ 300 watt seconds, if not converted;
		Immediately defibrillate @ 360 watt seconds, if not converted;
		Start CPR
		Give Epinephrine (1:10,000) 1 mg IV push
		Give Lidocaine as per V-tach protocol.
		9. Asystole/EMD: Start CPR
		Epinephrine (1:10,000) 1mg IV push
		Atropine 1mg IV push if no response with Epinephrine
		10. Respiratory Arrest: Intubation with mechanical ventilation
		RAV T.O. Dr. Swann/M. Weathers, R.N.
		J Swann, M.D.
4/30		*MDI w/ reservoir b.i.d. and q4 p.r.n. Albuterol 2 puffs. Beclomethasone Dipropionate*
		200 mcg. Goal of Therapy: Bronchodilation. J. Swann, M.D.

SUNNY VALLEY MEDICAL CENTER ■ 100 MAIN ST, SUNNY VALLEY, NY 14802 ■ (607) 555-1234

HOOVER, Holley E.	Admission: 04-30-YYYY	DOCTORS ORDERS
Case07	DOB: 01-16-YYYY	
Dr. Swann	ROOM: 0320	

Date	Time	Physician's signature required for each order. (Please skip one line between dates.)
4/30		MDI with reservoir b.i.d. Albuterol Sulfate 1 puff q4h p.r.n.
		Beclomethasone Dipropionate 200 mcg b.i.d.
		Goal of Therapy: Bronchodilation. Bronchial Toilet. Relieve Atelectasis. J. Swann, M.D.
04-30	1537	1) Admit to Dr. Swann
		2) Telemetry w/ protocol
		3) Old records
		4) TSH, T4
		5) Oxygen .625 mg po / Daily
		6) Tenoretic - Hold
		7) Depakote 500 mg. po Tid
		8) Vanceril Inhaler 2 puffs Bid
		9) Ventolin Inhaler 1 puff Q4° prn
		10) Zantac 50 mg IV Q8° J. Swann, M.D.
		RAV T.O. Dr. Swann/ C. Love RN
04-30		Resteril 30 mg HS. Tylenol take 2 q 3-4h prn for pain.
		DAT. Telemetr. BRP. J. Swann MD
05/01	1820	Do cardiac profile and EKG now and in AM.
		May take O₂ off and use p.r.n.
		May ambulate as tolerated. RAV T.O. Dr. Swann/ L. Taylor CPN
		J. Swann, M.D.

HOOVER, Holley E.	Admission: 04-30-YYYY	DOCTORS ORDERS
Case07	DOB: 01-16-YYYY	
Dr. Swann	ROOM: 0320	

Date	Time	Physician's signature required for each order. (Please skip one line between dates.)
05/01	2100	Continous oximetry during night tonight 05/01/YYYY. J. Swann, M.D.
		RAV T.O. Dr. Swann/ T. Perry
05/02	0910	D/C IV
		D/C telemetry
		Δ IV Zantac to 150 mg p.o. B.I.D.
		RAV T.O. Dr. Swann/ L. Taylor CPN
05/02	1010	Discharge home.
		J. Swann, MD

HOOVER, Holley E. Admission: 04-30-YYYY LABORATORY DATA
Case07   DOB: 01-16-YYYY
Dr. Swann   ROOM: 0320

SPECIMEN COLLECTED: 04/30/YYYY **SPECIMEN RECEIVED:** 04/30/YYYY

TEST	RESULT	FLAG	REFERENCE
ROUTINE URINALYSIS			
COLOR	STRAW		
SP GRAVITY	1.015		≤ 1.030
GLUCOSE	NEG		≤ 125 mg/dl
BILIRUBIN	NEG		≤ 0.8 mg/dl
KETONE	NEG		≤ 10 mg/dl
BLOOD	NEG		0.06 mg/dl hgb
PH	7.0		5-8
PROTEIN	NEG		≤ 30 mg/dl
UROBILINOGEN	NORMAL		≤ -1 mg/dl
NITRITES	NEG		NEG
LEUKOCYTES	NEG		≤ 15 WBC/hpf
EPITH	4-8		
W.B.C.	RARE		≤ 5/hpf

End of Report

HOOVER, Holley E.   Admission: 04-30-YYYY   LABORATORY DATA
Case07   DOB: 01-16-YYYY
Dr. Swann   ROOM: 0320

SPECIMEN COLLECTED: 4/30/YYYY   **SPECIMEN RECEIVED:**   4/30/YYYY

TEST	RESULT	FLAG	REFERENCE
Glucose	155	**H**	82-115 mg/dl
Creatinine	0.9		0.9-1.4 mg/dl
Sodium	144		136-147 meq/L
Potassium	3.6	**L**	3.7-5.1 meq/L
Chloride	105		98-108 meq/L
Total CO2	29		24-32 meqL
Calcium	9.2		8.8-10.5 mg/dl
WBC	5.0		4.5-10.8 thous/UL
RBC	4.46		4.2-5.4 mill/UL
HGB	13.5		12-16 g/dl
HCT	40.4		37.0-47.0 %
Platelets	288		130-400 thous/UL
PTT	22		< 32 seconds
Protime	12.3		11.0-13.0 seconds

End of Report

HOOVER, Holley E.   Admission: 04-30-YYYY   LABORATORY DATA
Case07   DOB: 01-16-YYYY
Dr. Swann   ROOM: 0320

SPECIMEN COLLECTED: 4/30/YYYY   **SPECIMEN RECEIVED:**   4/30/YYYY

TEST	RESULT	FLAG	REFERENCE
Urea Nitrogen	17		7-18 mg/dl
Alkaline Phosphatase	90		50-136 U/L
SGOT	27		15-37 U/L
Lactic Dehydrogenase	158		100-190 U/L
Phosphorus	2.8		2.5-4.9 mg/dl
Total Bilirubin	0.3		0.0-1.1 mg/dl
Total Protein	6.7		6.4-8.2 g/dl
Albumin	3.4		3.4-5.0 g/dl
Uric Acid	5.7	**H**	2.6-5.6 mg/dl
Cholesterol	193	***	< 200mg/dl

CARDIAC PROFILE & MG PANEL

TEST	RESULT	FLAG	REFERENCE
Creatine Kinase	177		21-215 U/L
CKMB	5.6		0.0-6.0 ng/ml
Relative Index	3.2	**H**	0.0-2.5 U/L
Magnesium	1.8		1.8-2.4 mg/dl

End of Report

HOOVER, Holley E.   Admission: 04-30-YYYY   LABORATORY DATA
Case 07   DOB: 01-16-YYYY
Dr. Swann   ROOM: 0320

SPECIMEN COLLECTED: 05/01/YYYY   **SPECIMEN RECEIVED:** 05/01/YYYY

TEST	RESULT	FLAG	REFERENCE
Creatine Kinase	86		21-215 U/L
CKMB	2.4		0.0-6.0 ng/ml

End of Report

HOOVER, Holley E. Admission: 04-30-YYYY LABORATORY DATA
Case07 DOB: 01-16-YYYY
Dr. Swann ROOM: 0320

SPECIMEN COLLECTED: 05/02YYYY SPECIMEN RECEIVED: 05/02YYYY

TEST	RESULT	FLAG	REFERENCE
Creatine Kinase	69		21-215 U/L
CKMB	1.7		0.0-6.0 ng/ml

End of Report

HOOVER, Holley E.   Admission: 04-30-YYYY   LABORATORY DATA
Case07   DOB: 01-16-YYYY
Dr. Swann   ROOM: 0320

SPECIMEN COLLECTED: 05/03YYYY   **SPECIMEN RECEIVED:** 05/03YYYY

TEST	RESULT	FLAG	REFERENCE
T4	6.3		4.9-10.7 UG/DL
TSH	2.57		0.38-6.15 UIU/ML

End of Report

HOOVER, Holley E.
Case 07
Dr. Swann

Admission: 04-30-YYYY
DOB: 01-16-YYYY
ROOM: 0320

EKG REPORT

Date of EKG   Time of EKG 14:22:13

Rate	81
PR	152
QRSD	72
QT	35
QTC	424
-- Axis --	
P	46
QRS	6
T	-1

04-30-YYYY

Sinus Rhythm Normal

Bella Kaplan, MD

Bella Kaplan, M.D.

Name of Physician

EKG REPORT

HOOVER, Holley E.
Case07
Dr. Swann

Admission: 04-30-YYYY
DOB: 01-16-YYYY
ROOM: 0320
Date of EKG
Time of EKG 17:06:34

Rate	69
PR	153
QRSD	68
QT	383
QTC	410
-- Axis --	
P	4
QRS	1
T	-14

05-01-YYYY
Tw ↓ sl v3-4
st

Minor nonspecific t-wave lowering.
Stable.

Bella Kaplan, MD

Bella Kaplan, M.D.
Name of Physician

HOOVER, Holley E.
Case07
Dr. Swann

Admission: 04-30-YYYY
DOB: 01-16-YYYY
ROOM: 0320

Date of EKG   Time of EKG 8:20:35

EKG REPORT

05-02-YYYY

Rate	66
PR	151
QRSD	65
QT	388
QTC	406
-- Axis --	
P	5
QRS	13
T	0

Normal – twaves back to normal today

Bella Kaplan, MD

Bella Kaplan, M.D.
Name of Physician

Case 08

SUNNY VALLEY MEDICAL CENTER							
100 MAIN ST, SUNNY VALLEY, NY 14802				INPATIENT FACE SHEET			
(607) 555-1234							
HOSPITAL #: 000999							

PATIENT NAME AND ADDRESS			GENDER	RACE	MARITAL STATUS	PATIENT NO.
MASON, Molly P.			F	W	Single	Case08
645 Chicago Lane			DATE OF BIRTH	MAIDEN NAME		OCCUPATION
Sunny Valley, NY 14802			03-01-YYYY			Child

ADMISSION DATE	TIME	DISCHARGE DATE	TIME	LENGTH OF STAY	TELEPHONE NUMBER
04-28-YYYY	23:30	05-02-YYYY	13:00	04 DAYS	(607) 555-8866

GUARANTOR NAME AND ADDRESS	NEXT OF KIN NAME AND ADDRESS
Mason, Irene	Mason, Irene
645 Chicago Lane	645 Chicago Lane
Sunny Valley, NY 14802	Sunny Valley, NY 14802

GUARANTOR TELEPHONE NO.	RELATIONSHIP TO PATIENT	NEXT OF KIN TELEPHONE NUMBER	RELATIONSHIP TO PATIENT
(607) 555-8866	Mother	(607) 555-8866	Mother

ADMITTING PHYSICIAN	SERVICE	ADMIT TYPE	ROOM NUMBER/BED
Ghann, MD Alan	Ped Med	2	0328/02

ATTENDING PHYSICIAN	ATTENDING PHYSICIAN UPIN	ADMITTING DIAGNOSIS
Ghann, MD Alan	100A90	R/O out respiratory syncytial virus

PRIMARY INSURER	POLICY AND GROUP NUMBER	SECONDARY INSURER	POLICY AND GROUP NUMBER
BC/BS of WNY	262723444 44150	Empire Plan	88765431

DIAGNOSES AND PROCEDURES	ICD-10-CM/PCS

PRINCIPAL DIAGNOSIS

Bronchiolitis due to RSV +	J21.0

SECONDARY DIAGNOSES

PRINCIPAL PROCEDURE

SECONDARY PROCEDURES

TOTAL CHARGES: $ 2,605.35

ACTIVITY:	☐ Bedrest	☑ Light	☐ Usual	☐ Unlimited	☐ Other:
DIET:	☑ Regular	☐ Low Cholesterol	☐ Low Salt	☐ ADA	☐ _____ Calorie
FOLLOW-UP:	☐ Call for appointment	☐ Office appointment on ____	☐ Other:		

SPECIAL INSTRUCTIONS: *Call for appt. w/ Dr. Ghann in 4 days; sooner if any problems (555-3456)*

Signature of Attending Physician: *Alan Ghann, MD*

```
MASON, Molly P.        Admission: 04-28-YYYY      CONSENT TO ADMISSION
Case 08                DOB: 03-01-YYYY
Dr. Ghann              ROOM: 0328
```

I, __Molly P. Mason__ hereby consent to admission to the Sunny Valley Medical Center (SVMC), and I further consent to such routine hospital care, diagnostic procedures, and medical treatment that the medical and professional staff of SVMC may deem necessary or advisable. I authorize the use of medical information obtained about me as specified above and the disclosure of such information to my referring physician(s). This form has been fully explained to me, and I understand its contents. I further understand that no guarantees have been made to me as to the results of treatments or examinations done at the SVMC.

Molly P. Mason   _April 28, YYYY_

Signature of Patient   Date

Irene Mason   _April 28, YYYY_

Signature of Parent/Legal Guardian for Minor   Date

Mother

Relationship to Minor

Andrea Witteman   _April 28, YYYY_

WITNESS: Sunny Valley Medical Center Staff Member   Date

CONSENT TO RELEASE INFORMATION FOR REIMBURSEMENT PURPOSES

In order to permit reimbursement, upon request, the Sunny Valley Medical Center (SVMC) may disclose such treatment information pertaining to my hospitalization to any corporation, organization, or agent thereof, which is, or may be liable under contract to the SVMC or to me, or to any of my family members or other person, for payment of all or part of the SVMC's charges for services rendered to me (e.g., the patient's health insurance carrier). I understand that the purpose of any release of information is to facilitate reimbursement for services rendered. In addition, in the event that my health insurance program includes utilization review of services provided during this admission, I authorize SVMC to release information as is necessary to permit the review. This authorization will expire once the reimbursement for services rendered is complete.

Molly P. Mason   _April 28, YYYY_

Signature of Patient   Date

Irene Mason   _April 28, YYYY_

Signature of Parent/Legal Guardian for Minor   Date

Mother

Relationship to Minor

Andrea Witteman   _April 28, YYYY_

WITNESS: Sunny Valley Medical Center Staff Member   Date

MASON, Molly P.	Admission: 04-28-YYYY	ADVANCE DIRECTIVE
Case 08	DOB: 03-01-YYYY	
Dr. Ghann	ROOM: 0328	

Your answers to the following questions will assist your Physician and the Hospital to respect your wishes regarding your medical care. This information will become a part of your medical record.

	YES	NO	PATIENT'S INITIALS
1. Have you been provided with a copy of the information called "Patient Rights Regarding Health Care Decision?"	X		IM
2. Have you prepared a "Living Will?" If yes, please provide the Hospital with a copy for your medical record.		X	IM
3. Have you prepared a Durable Power of Attorney for Health Care? If yes, please provide the Hospital with a copy for your medical record.		X	IM
4. Have you provided this facility with an Advance Directive on a prior admission and is it still in effect? If yes, Admitting Office to contact Medical Records to obtain a copy for the medical record.		X	IM
5. Do you desire to execute a Living Will/Durable Power of Attorney? If yes, refer to in order: a. Physician b. Social Service c. Volunteer Service		X	IM

HOSPITAL STAFF DIRECTIONS: Check when each step is completed.

1. ____✓____ Verify the above questions where answered and actions taken where required.

2. ____✓____ If the "Patient Rights" information was provided to someone other than the patient, state reason:

_____

IRENE MASON	Mother
Name of Individual Receiving Information	Relationship to Patient

3. ____✓____ If information was provided in a language other than English, specify language and method.

4. ____✓____ Verify patient was advised on how to obtain additional information on Advance Directives.

5. ____✓____ Verify the Patient/Family Member/Legal Representative was asked to provide the Hospital with a copy of the Advance Directive which will be retained in the medical record.

File this form in the medical record, and give a copy to the patient.

_____

Name of Patient (Name of Individual giving information if different from Patient)

Irene Mason (Mother)	April 28, YYYY
Signature of Patient	Date
Andrea Witteman	April 28, YYYY
Signature of Hospital Representative	Date

SUNNY VALLEY MEDICAL CENTER ■ 100 MAIN ST, SUNNY VALLEY, NY 14802 ■ (607) 555-1234

MASON, Molly P.	Admission: 04-28-YYYY	HISTORY & PHYSICAL EXAM
Case08	DOB: 03-01-YYYY	
Dr. Ghann	ROOM: 0328	

DATE OF ADMISSION: 04/28/YYYY

CHIEF COMPLAINT, HISTORY OF PRESENT ILLNESS: This six-week-old presented to the office secondary to acute respiratory distress with intercostal retractions, nasal drainage, respiratory distress, difficulty in eating, and rapid respiratory rate. Molly was found to have clinical signs and symptoms of RSV with respiratory decompensation and was recommended admission to the hospital for the same.

PAST MEDICAL HISTORY: Was born of an uncomplicated birth. She had been healthy up until this date. No pre-existing medical problems. No surgeries.

PAST SUGICAL HISTORY: Negative.

HABITS: None.

ALLERGIES: None.

MEDICATIONS: None.

SOCIAL HISTORY: Noncontributory.

FAMILY HISTORY: Noncontributory.

REVIEW OF SYSTEMS: As noted in PMH and CC above.

VITAL SIGNS: TPR's were 98.9, birth weight was 6 lbs. 1 oz., pulse 160, respirations 40, actual weight was 11 lbs. 4 oz. Height was 21 ¼".

HEENT: Head was normocephalic. Ears were clear. She had a serious rhinitis, thick, with posterior pharynx noninjected.

NECK: Noncontributory.

LUNGS: Ausculted with diffuse wheezes and rhonchi with intercostal retraction. Rapid respiratory rate at the time of admission to the office was up to 50-60.

CARDIAC: Noncontributory.

ABDOMEN: Soft without organomegaly or masses.

EXTERNAL GENITALIA: Normal.

RECTAL: Externally was normal.

EXTREMITIES: Revealed good pedal pulses. No ulcerations, cyanosis, clubbing or edema.

NEUROLOGIC: Intact with no neurologic abnormalities.

LABS: RSV testing was positive by EIA testing. She had 9.4 white count on admission with 14.7 hgb, 429 platelets, 18 segs, 70 lymphs, 10 monos, 2 eos. O2 sats on room air were between 96 and 98.

IMPRESSION: 1) RSV with associated bronchiolitis and bronchospasms.

PLAN: Patient is to be admitted to the hospital with croup tent. CPT therapy. See orders.

DD: 04-30-YYYY

DT: 04-30-YYYY

Alan Ghann, MD

Alan Ghann, MD

MASON, Molly P.	Admission: 04-28-YYYY	PROGRESS NOTES
Case 08	DOB: 03-01-YYYY	
Dr. Ghann	ROOM: 0328	

Date	(Please skip one line between dates.)
04-29 0025	Hhn 0.25 ml Proventil NSS via blow-by w/ pt. held by grandmother; HR 148-150 R 32
	O2 Sat R/A 98%. BS ↓'d. Harsh cough w/ I-E squeaks, squaks. Pt out of tent.
	Tent analyzed @ 37 % w/ tent windowed. E. Blossom, CRTT
04-29 0730	HHN w/ 0.25 ml Proventil / N.S.S. tx given blow by while pt.slept in tent. Pt tolerated tx well.
	B.S. ↓'d bases - no cough O₂ Sat 100% in O₂ tent. D. Davenport, CRTT
04-29 1130	Hhn w/ 0.25 ml Proventil + normal saline. Tol. Rx well. BS↓ clear. NPC In tent pre + post.
	R. Rose, CPT
04-29 1530	Rx as above. No changes
	R. Rose, CPT
04-29 1800	↓ Wheezing and responding to CPT therapy. Lungs difuse ronchi. Wheeze and vitals good. RSV - responding to tx.
	Alan Ghann, MD
04-29 2005	Hhn w/ 0.25 ml Proventil / N.S.S. tx given blow by. HR 149, RR 40. Pt cried through entire tx. Pt was in
	tent pre- and post. E. Blossom, CRTT
04-30 0750	Hh neb Rx w/ 025 ml Proventil + NSS given - P 130 - RR 40 BS harsh w/ wheezes in
	tent. Sleeping. SPo2 - 99% in tent - tol well. L. Seraphin CPT
04-30	~~Slow improvement of croup s&s. Only 3 hrs of cough jag last. Slept 7-7 last evening to a.m.~~
	~~Afebrile. Cough less harsh and throat ↓ soreness. Lungs clear. Cardiac RRR. Ab soft.~~
	~~Imp~~ Error. Note written in wrong patient's chart. M. Harris, M.D.

MASON, Molly P.	Admission: 04-28-YYYY
Case08	DOB: 03-01-YYYY
Dr. Ghann	ROOM: 0328

PROGRESS NOTES

Date	(Please skip one line between dates.)
04-30	No evidence of wheeze today. Green → white nasal drainage. Afebrile.
	Lungs clear. Cardiac RRR. O₂ SAT ↓ last evening.
	Imp: RSV, resolving. Bronchitis.
	Plans as per orders.
	Alan Ghann, MD
04-30	Referral received for hand held nebulizer at home - contact w/ mother -
1600	She chooses Hub as DME provider - Mother chooses to go to Hub & pick up
	HHN this noon. Hub's notified. Nursing aware.
	E. Kravitz, RN
04-30	HH neb. Rx w/ 0.25 ml Proventil + NSS - P 120 - RR 28. BS wheezes - pt. cried
1130	for Rx in tent pre & post Rx. L Seraphin CPT
04-30	HH neb. Rx given by mom w/ 0.25 ml Proventil + NSS - BS harsh - pt. tol. well - Mom
1520	understood med & Rx. SPO2 - 99% in tent. L Seraphin CPT
04-30	HHN w/ 0.2 ml Albuterol & NSS via blow-by. Slept thru tx. BS harsh. Pulse 150. Resp 30.
1945	E. Blossom, RRT
04-30	O2 SAT ↓ out of tent. Pt. has loose cough, no active wheezing, and is afebrile. Eats well.
	Imp: RSV resolving. Plan: Home HHN. O2 SAT good
	Alan Ghann, MD
05-01	HH neb. Rx w/ 0.25 ml Proventil + NSS given - P 164 - RR 44. BS harsh. Pt. in tent, sleeping.
0745	For Rx - SPO2 - 96-97% - tent 32% - harsh cough. L Seraphin CPT

MASON, Molly P. Case08 Dr. Ghann	Admission: 04-28-YYYY DOB: 03-01-YYYY ROOM: 0328	PROGRESS NOTES
Date	(Please skip one line between dates.)	
05-01 1115	Hh neb. Rx w/ 025 ml Proventil + NSS given - P 163 - RR 48. BS harsh. Pt. out of tent for Rx - SPo2 - 98% on RA - pt. cried for Rx - given by dad.	
		L. Seraphin CPT
05-01 1520	Hh neb. Rx w/ 025 ml Proventil + NSS given - P 162 - RR 28. BS clearing w/ harsh NPC - out of tent for Rx - SPo2 - 97-98% on RA - Rx given by Grandma. Tol. Well.	
		L. Seraphin CPT
05-01 1930	HHN w/ 0.25 ml Albuterol & NSS via blow-by. BS harsh. O2 SAT 93% RA Pulse 160. Resp 40.	
		E. Blossom, RRT
05-02	S: Feeding well. Virtually no residual wheeze or cough.	
	O: Afebrile. VSS. SATS maintaining outside tent > 92%.	
	Chest - good air on vent, no retractions - wheeze or stridor.	
	COR: RRR	
	ABD: soft	
	EXTR: ⊖ cyanosis.	
	A/P. RSV +. Bronchiolitis, resolving.	
	D/C to home w/ hhn and steroids. See instructions.	
		Alan Ghann, MD
05-02 0720	Hh neb. Rx w/ 025 ml Proventil + NSS given - P 180 - RR 48 BS harsh w/ wheezes SPo2 - 98% - RA - pt. tol Rx well.	
		L. Seraphin CPT
05-02 1100	Rx same as above BS wheezes P 120 RR 40 pt. out of tent. tol. well.	
		L. Seraphin CPT

MASON, Molly P.	Admission: 04-28-YYYY	DOCTORS ORDERS
Case08	DOB: 03-01-YYYY	
Dr. Ghann	ROOM: 0328	

Date	Time	Physician's signature required for each order. (Please skip one line between dates.)
04-28		Hand Held Nebulizer (Spontaneous Aerosol) q.i.d. and q4° p.r.n.
		Nebulizer and IPPB Medications: Albuterol Sulfate (Proventil) 0.5% 0.25 ml, Normal Saline 3 ml
		Croupette, low O2 30-50%
		O2 SAT q shift
		Bronchodilation
		Alan Ghann, MD
04-28	2330	Admit to Service Dr. Ghann.
		Dx: RSV - Bronchiolitis
		Chest x-ray - R/O pneumonia
		CBC
		UA
		O2 Croup Tent
		Tylenol 0.4 ml infant dropper q 4° prn temp
		RSV - nasal aspirator for titre
		Old chart to floor
		Diet
		Similac formula
		Pedialyte
		Alan Ghann, MD
04-29	0330	Contact isolation.
		R.A.V. T.O. Dr. Ghann/M. Smith, RN
		Alan Ghann, MD

MASON, Molly P. Case08 Dr. Ghann	Admission: 04-28-YYYY DOB: 03-01-YYYY ROOM: 0328	DOCTORS ORDERS

Date	Time	Physician's signature required for each order. (Please skip one line between dates.)
04-30	0855	For home HHN
		Begin Decadron 1/2 tsp, t.i.d. x 2 days, then b.i.d.
		Alan Ghann, MD
05-02	1300	D/C to home if home nebulizer & parental instruction in use of HHN is arranged.
		Label Decadron Elixir for home
		1/2 tsp 2x day for 2 days then
		1/2 tsp 1x day for 2 days then stop
		R.A.V. T.O. Dr. Ghann/ G. Goebel, RN
		Alan Ghann, MD

MASON, Molly P.   Admission: 04-28-YYYY
Case08   DOB: 03-01-YYYY   LABORATORY DATA
Dr. Ghann   ROOM: 0328

SPECIMEN COLLECTED: 04/30/YYYY   SPECIMEN RECEIVED: 04/30/YYYY

TEST	RESULT	FLAG	REFERENCE
ROUTINE URINALYSIS			
COLOR	STRAW		
SP GRAVITY	1.001		≤ 1.030
GLUCOSE	NEG		NEG
BILIRUBIN	NEG		≤ 0.8 mg/dl
KETONE	NEG		≤ 10 mg/dl
BLOOD	NEG		0.06 mg/dl hgb
PH	8.0		5-8.0
PROTEIN	NEG		≤ 30 mg/dl
UROBILINOGEN	NORMAL		≤ -1 mg/dl
NITRITE	NEG		NEG
LEUKOCYTES	NEG		≤ 15 WBC/hpf
EPITH	5-8		/hpf
W.B.C.	0-3		≤ 5/hpf

End of Report

MASON, Molly P.   Admission: 04-28-YYYY
Case08   DOB: 03-01-YYYY   LABORATORY DATA
Dr. Ghann   ROOM: 0328

SPECIMEN COLLECTED: 04/30/YYYY   SPECIMEN RECEIVED: 04/30/YYYY

TEST	RESULT	FLAG	REFERENCE
CBC			
RBC	4.93		4.2-5.4 mill/UL
WBC	9.4		4.5-10.8 thous/UL
HGB	14.7		12-16 g/dl
HCT	43.6		37.0-47.0 %
Platelets	429		130-400 thous/UL
Total CO2	29.8		24-32 meqL
SEGS	18		
LYMPH	70		
MONO	10		
EOS	2		
BASO			

End of Report

SUNNY VALLEY MEDICAL CENTER ■ 100 MAIN ST, SUNNY VALLEY, NY 14802 ■ (607) 555-1234

MASON, Molly P.   Admission: 04-28-YYYY
Case08   DOB: 03-01-YYYY
Dr. Ghann   ROOM: 0328

LABORATORY DATA

SPECIMEN COLLECTED: 04/29/YYYY   **DATE DONE:** 04/29/YYYY

TEST	**RESULT**	**FLAG**	**REFERENCE**

RSV - Nasal Aspirate for Titre

POS by EIA Testing

End of Report

MASON, Molly P.   Admission: 04-28-YYYY

Case08   DOB: 03-01-YYYY

Dr. Ghann   ROOM: 0328

PULSE OXIMETRY

TIME	SPO2	F102	TECH
04/28 2235	98%	R/A	RB
2400	Tent analyzed	@	36.7
04/29 0730	100%	O2 tent	GM
2005	84%	R/A	PT
2350	91%	O2 tent	PT
04/30 0750	99%	35.5 tent	DS
1625	99%	tent	DS
1930	98%	R/A out of tent	HK
05/01 0155	96%	O2 tent	GB
0745	96%	32% tent	DS
0830	96%	R/A	DS
1520	97%	R/A	DS
2030	93%	R/A x 1 hr	LT
2245	96%	R/A tent	LT
05/02 0355	98%	R/A	GB
0720	98%	R/A	DS

End of Report

SUNNY VALLEY MEDICAL CENTER ■ 100 MAIN ST, SUNNY VALLEY, NY 14802 ■ (607) 555-1234

```
MASON, Molly P.          Admission: 04-28-YYYY        RADIOLOGY REPORT
Case08                   DOB: 03-01-YYYY
Dr. Ghann                ROOM: 0328
```

Initial Diagnosis/History:

Date Requested:

Transport: ☑ Wheelchair ☐ Stretcher ☐ O$_2$ ☐ IV
              ☑ IP ☐ OP ☐ ER ☐ PRE OP ☐ OR/RR   ☐ Portable

CHEST: PA and lateral views reveals the heart and mediastinum to be normal. The lung fields are clear and the bony thorax is normal.

CONCLUSION: Normal chest.

DD: 04-29-YYYY

DT: 04-29-YYYY

Philip Rogers
_____
Philip Rogers, M.D., Radiologist

Case 09

SUNNY VALLEY MEDICAL CENTER 100 MAIN ST, SUNNY VALLEY, NY 14802 (607) 555-1234 HOSPITAL #: 000999				INPATIENT FACE SHEET			

PATIENT NAME AND ADDRESS				GENDER	RACE	MARITAL STATUS	PATIENT NO.
LUCK, Deborah L. 2399 Route 244 Sunny Valley Station, NY 14802				F	W	M	Case09
				DATE OF BIRTH	MAIDEN NAME		OCCUPATION
				11-21-YYYY	Steinbeck		Teacher

ADMISSION DATE	TIME	DISCHARGE DATE	TIME	LENGTH OF STAY	TELEPHONE NUMBER
05-01-YYYY	11:30	05-02-YYYY	11:50	01 DAYS	(607) 555-0909

GUARANTOR NAME AND ADDRESS		NEXT OF KIN NAME AND ADDRESS	
LUCK, David 2399 Route 244 Sunny Valley Station, NY 14802		LUCK, David 2399 Route 244 Sunny Valley Station, NY 14802	
GUARANTOR TELEPHONE NO.	RELATIONSHIP TO PATIENT	NEXT OF KIN TELEPHONE NUMBER	RELATIONSHIP TO PATIENT
(607) 555-0909	Husband	(607) 555-0909	Husband

ADMITTING PHYSICIAN	SERVICE	ADMIT TYPE	ROOM NUMBER/BED
Ghann, MD Alan	Medical	2	0374/01

ATTENDING PHYSICIAN	ATTENDING PHYSICIAN UPIN	ADMITTING DIAGNOSIS	
Ghann, MD Alan	100A90	Asthma	

PRIMARY INSURER	POLICY AND GROUP NUMBER	SECONDARY INSURER	POLICY AND GROUP NUMBER
Empire Plan	556705250		

DIAGNOSES AND PROCEDURES	ICD-10-CM/PCS
PRINCIPAL DIAGNOSIS Severe RAD	J45.901
SECONDARY DIAGNOSES w/ metabolic acidosis	E87.2
PRINCIPAL PROCEDURE	
SECONDARY PROCEDURES TOTAL CHARGES: $ 1,955.95	

ACTIVITY:	☐ Bedrest	☐ Light	☐ Usual	☐ Unlimited	☐ Other:
DIET:	☐ Regular	☐ Low Cholesterol	☐ Low Salt	☐ ADA	☐ _____ Calorie
FOLLOW-UP:	☐ Call for appointment	☐ Office appointment on _____		☐ Other:	

SPECIAL INSTRUCTIONS:

Signature of Attending Physician: *Alan Ghann. MD*

LUCK, Deborah L.
Case 09
Dr. Ghann

Admission: 05-01-YYYY
DOB: 11-21-YYYY
ROOM: 0374

CONSENT TO ADMISSION

I, *Deborah L. Luck* hereby consent to admission to the Sunny Valley Medical Center (SVMC), and I further consent to such routine hospital care, diagnostic procedures, and medical treatment that the medical and professional staff of SVMC may deem necessary or advisable. I authorize the use of medical information obtained about me as specified above and the disclosure of such information to my referring physician(s). This form has been fully explained to me, and I understand its contents. I further understand that no guarantees have been made to me as to the results of treatments or examinations done at the SVMC.

Deborah L. Luck

May 1, YYYY

Signature of Patient

Date

Signature of Parent/Legal Guardian for Minor

Date

Relationship to Minor

Andrea Witteman

May 1, YYYY

WITNESS: Sunny Valley Medical Center Staff Member

Date

CONSENT TO RELEASE INFORMATION FOR REIMBURSEMENT PURPOSES

In order to permit reimbursement, upon request, the Sunny Valley Medical Center (SVMC) may disclose such treatment information pertaining to my hospitalization to any corporation, organization or agent thereof, which is, or may be liable under contract to the SVMC or to me, or to any of my family members or other person, for payment of all or part of the SVMC's charges for services rendered to me (e.g., the patient's health insurance carrier). I understand that the purpose of any release of information is to facilitate reimbursement for services rendered. In addition, in the event that my health insurance program includes utilization review of services provided during this admission, I authorize SVMC to release information as is necessary to permit the review. This authorization will expire once the reimbursement for services rendered is complete.

Deborah L. Luck

May 1, YYYY

Signature of Patient

Date

Signature of Parent/Legal Guardian for Minor

Date

Relationship to Minor

Andrea Witteman

May 1, YYYY

WITNESS: Sunny Valley Medical Center Staff Member

Date

LUCK, Deborah L.	Admission: 05-01-YYYY	ADVANCE DIRECTIVE
Case 09	DOB: 11-21-YYYY	
Dr. Ghann	ROOM: 0374	

Your answers to the following questions will assist your Physician and the Hospital to respect your wishes regarding your medical care. This information will become a part of your medical record.

	YES	NO	PATIENT'S INITIALS
1. Have you been provided with a copy of the information called "Patient Rights Regarding Health Care Decision?"	X		DLL
2. Have you prepared a "Living Will?" If yes, please provide the Hospital with a copy for your medical record.		X	DLL
3. Have you prepared a Durable Power of Attorney for Health Care? If yes, please provide the Hospital with a copy for your medical record.		X	DLL
4. Have you provided this facility with an Advance Directive on a prior admission and is it still in effect? If yes, Admitting Office to contact Medical Records to obtain a copy for the medical record.		X	DLL
5. Do you desire to execute a Living Will/Durable Power of Attorney? If yes, refer to in order: a. Physician b. Social Service c. Volunteer Service		X	DLL

HOSPITAL STAFF DIRECTIONS: Check when each step is completed.

1. ___✓___ Verify the above questions where answered and actions taken where required.

2. ___✓___ If the "Patient Rights" information was provided to someone other than the patient, state reason:

_____

_____   _____
Name of Individual Receiving Information   Relationship to Patient

3. ___✓___ If information was provided in a language other than English, specify language and method.

4. ___✓___ Verify patient was advised on how to obtain additional information on Advance Directives.

5. ___✓___ Verify the Patient/Family Member/Legal Representative was asked to provide the Hospital with a copy of the Advance Directive which will be retained in the medical record.

File this form in the medical record, and give a copy to the patient.

_____
Name of Patient (Name of Individual giving information if different from Patient)

Deborah L. Luck   *May 1, YYYY*
_____   _____
Signature of Patient   Date

Andrea Witteman   *May 1, YYYY*
_____   _____
Signature of Hospital Representative   Date

SUNNY VALLEY MEDICAL CENTER ■ 100 MAIN ST, SUNNY VALLEY, NY 14802 ■ (607) 555-1234

LUCK, Deborah L.	Admission: 05-01-YYYY	HISTORY & PHYSICAL EXAM
Case09	DOB: 11-21-YYYY	
Dr. Ghann	ROOM: 0374	PAGE 1 OF 2

Mrs. Luck is a 37-year-old white female with past medical history significant for severe reactive airways disease who presents to the Emergency Room in respiratory distress. CHIEF COMPLAINT: Difficulty breathing progressive over the past two days.

HPI: Patient was in her usual state of health until approximately two days ago when she developed worsening of her asthma. She did not seek medical attention at that time and her symptoms progressed over the point where last night she was having difficulty sleeping. She was sitting on the edge of her bed most of the night in moderate respiratory distress. She presented to the ER this morning for evaluation and was found to be in moderately severe respiratory distress with impaired oxygenation. She is unable to give a meaningful history at this point because she is so dyspneic she cannot talk. However, she states she has not had fevers or chest pain. She has had a slight cough and she is not sure if this is due to bronchitis, infectious process or if this was due to her dyspnea. She has had a scant amount of sputum production over the past 12 hrs.

PAST HISTORY: Reactive airways disease as mentioned in the HPI. She has had one previous hospital admission. Status post C-section times two. Tonsillectomy, adenoidectany. Cholecystectany. Appendectomy. Right shoulder surgery. Bilateral tubal ligation.

MEDICATIONS: Proventil MDI p.rn. Azrnacort 2 puffs bi.d. Prednisone courses are required from time to time. She is currently taking Advil for a toothache. ALLERGIES: Codeine, Penicillin

FAMILY HISTORY: Her father is alive with coronary artery disease post MI. Her mother is alive with diabetes mellitus, CAD, cerebrovascular disease. She has two female siblings who are alive and well with no identified health problems. There is no identified history of reative airways disease or extrinsic asthma.

SOCIAL HISTORY: She lives with her husband and two children in Sunny Valley Station, NY. Her children are ages 13 and 15. Habits include nonsmoking, minimal alcohol use. No excessive caffeine use. She denies excessive over the counter drug use.

ROS: LMP three weeks ago. She denies swallowing difficulties, chest pain, change in bowel habits. She has had no urinary symptoms of dysuria, frequency or urgency. She has had no joint pain, weight loss, weight gain, temperature intolerance. She performs breast self exam and has noted no new breast lesions. The remainder of the ROS is noncontributory except as mentioned in the HPI.

VITAL SIGNS: Upon presentation to the Emergency Room blood pressure was 180/120. Later repeated was 160/100. Temperature was 97.8 orally, pulse 140, respirations 40 initially. Slowed to 24 after a nebulizer treatment.

GENERAL: The patient is in moderate respiratory distress sitting on the hospital cart, alert and oriented and answers questions although she is severely dyspneic.

HEENT: Head atraumatic, normocephalic. TM's are grey bilaterally. PERRL at 2 mm. diameter. Sclera anicteric. Pharynx is moist with no lesions noted. NECK: Supple. There is no adenopathy.

CHEST: Reveals very poor air movement and marked expiratory wheezing throughout her entire lung field. There are no areas of decreased breath sounds. There are no crackles or rhonchi. HEART: Tachycardic, regular with no murmurs.

ABDOMEN: Soft, obese, nontender. No organomegaly.

BREASTS: Without masses, retractions, dimpling. There is no adenopathy.

PELVIC/RECTAL: Deferred due to patient discomfort. Will be performed during her hospital course.

Continued on next page.

LUCK, Deborah L.	Admission: 05-01-YYYY	HISTORY & PHYSICAL EXAM
Case 09	DOB: 11-21-YYYY	
Dr. Ghann	ROOM: 0374	PAGE 2 OF 2

EXTREMITIES: Without edema, cyanosis. They are warm to touch and well perfused. Good distal pulses are appreciated.

NEUROLOGIC: Is nonfocal. She is alert and oriented. Has no motor or sensory deficits. Cranial nerves 2-12 are grossly intact.

LAB DATA: White count 21,300, hgb. 14.8, platelets 369, segs 87, bands 4, lymphs 7. SCG II is pending. Initial blood gas on 15 liters nonrebreather face mask revealed pH of 7.286, PCO2 of 43.8, PO2 90.4, 94.6 saturated. Chest X-ray is pending at the time of this dictation.

IMPRESSION/PLAN: 37-year-old white female with known reactive airways disease with an acute exacerbation probably due to an infectious process. Her white count is markedly elevated with a left shift, however she was given Epinephrine subcutaneously by Dr. Smith in the Emergency Room and this could have conceivably caused demargination of her white blood cells. She is however, breathing more comfortably on a 50% face mask at this time with oxygen saturations in the mid 90's. She is less tachypneic and she is breathing more comfortably. She is mentating well. We will load with IV Aminophyllin at 6 per kilo, ideal body weight, and follow with an infusion. Will check Theophylline level later tonight to be certain that we are avoiding toxicity. Frequent hand held nebulizer treatments, IV steroids. The rest of the regimen can be discerned from the admission orders.

DD: 05-01-YYYY

DT: 05-03-YYYY

_____

Alan Ghann, MD

Date	(Please skip one line between dates.)
LUCK, Deborah L. Case09 Dr. Ghann	Admission: 05-01-YYYY DOB: 11-21-YYYY ROOM: 0374 PROGRESS NOTES

Date	
05-01	Chief Complaint: Respiratory distress.
	Diagnosis: Severe RAD w/ metabolic acidosis.
	Plan of Treatment: IV steroids, HHN txs, IV Aminophylline, O2 sats.
05-01	3 pm Pt. seen improved. No distress. Alan Ghann, MD
05-01	Late entry
1400	Tx given Hhn w/ 0.5 ml Proventil/nss via mask w/pt. tolerating well. BS↓ w/ I + exp. Wheeze.
	P 130. R 28. No cough. O2 on a 50% Venti. R. Rose, CPT
05-01	Tx given as above. BS↓ w/ harsh exp. Wheeze. P 130. R 32. NPC. O2 on a 50% Venti.
1530	R. Rose, CPT
05-01	Tx given as above. BS↓ w/ faint I + exp. Wheeze. P 120. R 32. Harsh NPC. O2 on a 50% Venti mask.
1610	R. Rose, CPT
05-01	HHN 0.5 ml Albuterol/nss. HR 121. RR 20. BS diminished w/ occasional exp. Wheeze. Sa O2 _ 98% on 3L.
1900	E. Blossom, RRT
05-01	HHN 0.5 ml Albuterol/nss. HR 120. RR 24. BS - occasional rhonchi. No wheezes. Sa O2 _ 95% on 35% - ↓ to 30% VM,
2230	E. Blossom, RRT
05-02	HHN as above. HR 96. RR 20. BS - occasional exp. Wheeze. Tight NPC O2 on 28%. Sa O2 on 30% VM. 95.
0150	E. Blossom, RRT
05-02	HHN tx given w/ .5 ml Albuterol/nss via mask. BS scattered exp. wheeze loose nec HR 112, RR 20.
0450	P 130. R 28. No cough. SA O2 94% on 28%. O2 on @ 28% venti mask. Δ to 2L nasal cannula. R. Rose, CPT

LUCK, Deborah L.	Admission: 05-01-YYYY	PROGRESS NOTES
Case09	DOB: 11-21-YYYY	
Dr. Ghann	ROOM: 0374	

Date	(Please skip one line between dates.)
05-02	Rx given HHN w/ 0.5 ml Proventil/nss via mask w/ pt. tol well. BS↓ w/ exp. wheeze. P 110. R 20.
0800	Harsh NPC O2 on a 2L N/C. R. Rose, CPT
05-02	S: Breathing much better. Adament about discharge today.
	O: Afebrile. VSS. O2 sats on 2L = 95%.
	CHEST- good air intake. No wheeze.
	COR - RRR. No murmur.
	ABD - soft.
	A: Severe RAD, prompt resolution. Patient insists on discharge today.
	P. Taper IV meds to p.o. Check sats. Possible disch. later.
	Alan Ghann, MD
05-02	Tx given as above. BS↓ clear. NPC.
1110	P 120. R 20. O2 was ↓ to 1L N/C.
	R. Rose, CPT

LUCK, Deborah L. Case09 Dr. Ghann		Admission: 05-01-YYYY DOB: 11-21-YYYY ROOM: 0374	DOCTORS ORDERS

Date	Time	Physician's signature required for each order. (Please skip one line between dates.)
05-01		Admit: Ghann MD
		Dx: Severe Asthma w/ resp distress
		Vs Q2 x 24° then Q4°
		Allerg. PCN Ⓢ Codeine
		Diet - regular
		IVF- D5 NS @ 125 cc/hr.
		O2 15 L NRBFM - wean to face mask if SATS > 92%.
		STUDIES: sputum C Ⓢ S if not obtained in ED
		Lytes in AM UA w/ c Ⓢ s
		MEDS: Albuterol HHN 0.5 cc om 2cc NS Q3° Ⓢ Q1° PRN
		Solumedrol 125 mg IV Q6° ATC
		Ancef 1 gm IV Q8 pending sputum results
		Aminophylin 40 mg/hr IV Pharmacist to determine solu Ⓢ rate
		Tylenol 650 mg po Q4° PRN
		Theophyline level @ 27:00 - call if < 10 or > 20.
		O2 SATS - continuous x 8 hrs - alarms @ 92%, then Q treatment
		Thank you
		Alan Ghann. MD
5/1	1515	↓ IVF to 75 cc/hr while Aminophylline is infusing. SCG II results to chart please.
		Alan Ghann. MD

LUCK, Deborah L.	Admission: 05-01-YYYY	DOCTORS ORDERS
Case09	DOB: 11-21-YYYY	
Dr. Ghann	ROOM: 0374	

Date	Time	Physician's signature required for each order. (Please skip one line between dates.)
05-02		D/C Aminophyline
		D/C IV Solumedrol
		Start Prednisone 20mg po tid
		D/C Ancef
		Start Ceclor 250mg po tid
		Δ HHN to QID and Q 4° PRN
		D/C IV
		Possible D/C later today
		Alan Ghann, MD
05-02		Wean O2 to off if SATS > 92%.
		Please have pt ambulate off O2. Check O2 sats with ambulatory at 2:00 p.m.
		If sats > 92% please discharge to home.
		Thanks
		Alan Ghann, MD

LUCK, Deborah L.   Admission: 05-01-YYYY
Case09   DOB: 11-21-YYYY   LABORATORY DATA
Dr. Ghann   ROOM: 0374

SPECIMEN COLLECTED: 05-01-YYYY   **SPECIMEN RECEIVED:** 05-01-YYYY

TEST	RESULT	FLAG	REFERENCE
SCG2, LYTES, BUN PANEL			
Glucose	162		70-110 mg/dl
Creatinine	0.8		0.6-1.0 mg/dl
Sodium	143		136-147 MEQ/L
Potassium	4.9		3.7-5.1 MEQ/L
Chloride	104		98-108 MEQ/L
TOTAL CO2	24		24-32 MEQ/L
Calcium	9.9		8.8-10.5 mg/dl
WBC	21.3	**H**	4.5-11.0 thous/UL
RBC	5.21		5.2-5.4 mill/UL
HGB	14.8		11.7-16.1 g/dl
HCT	45.2		35.0-47.0 %
MCV	86.8		85-99 fL.
MCH	32.7		32-37
Platelets	369		140-400 thous/UL

End of Report

LUCK, Deborah L.   Admission: 05-01-YYYY
Case09   DOB: 11-21-YYYY   LABORATORY DATA
Dr. Ghann   ROOM: 0374

SPECIMEN COLLECTED: 05-01-YYYY   SPECIMEN RECEIVED: 05-01-YYYY

TEST	RESULT	FLAG	REFERENCE
URINALYSIS			
DIPSTICK ONLY			
COLOR	CLOUDY YELLOW		
SP GRAVITY	1.025		≤ 1.030
GLUCOSE	110		≤ 125 mg/dl
BILIRUBIN	NEG		≤ 0.8 mg/dl
KETONE	TRACE		≤ 10 mg/dl
BLOOD	11	**H**	0.06 mg/dl hgb
PH	5.0		5-8.0
PROTEIN	TRACE		≤ 30 mg/dl
UROBILINOGEN	NORMAL		≤ -1 mg/dl
NITRITES	POS		NEG
LEUKOCYTE	NEG		≤ 15 WBC/hpf
EPITH	5-10		
W.B.C.	5-10		≤ 5/hpf
R.B.C.	RARE		≤ 5/hpf
BACT.	4f		1+(≤ 20/hpf)

End of Report

LUCK, Deborah L.   Admission: 05-01-YYYY
Case09   DOB: 11-21-YYYY   LABORATORY DATA
Dr. Ghann   ROOM: 0374

SPECIMEN COLLECTED: 05-01-YYYY   **SPECIMEN RECEIVED:** 05-01-YYYY

TEST	RESULT	FLAG	REFERENCE
Urea Nitrogen	8		7-18 mg/dl
Alkaline Phosphatase	176	**H**	50-136 U/L
GLUCOSE	162	**H**	70-110 mg/dl
SGOT	19		15-37 U/L
Lactic Dehydrogenase	182		100-190 U/L
Phosphorus	2.7		2.5-4.9 mg/dl
Total Bilirubin	0.3		0.0-1.1 mg/dl
Total Protein	7.5		6.4-8.2 g/dl
Albumin	4.2		3.4-5.0 g/dl
Uric Acid	3.0		2.6-5.6 mg/dl
Cholesterol	186		≤ 200mg/dl

End of Report

LUCK, Deborah L.   Admission: 05-01-YYYY
Case09   DOB: 11-21-YYYY   LABORATORY DATA
Dr. Ghann   ROOM: 0374

SPECIMEN COLLECTED: 05-02-YYYY   **SPECIMEN RECEIVED:** 05-02-YYYY

TEST	RESULT	FLAG	REFERENCE
ELECTROLYTES PANEL			
Sodium	139		136-147 MEQ/L
Potassium	3.9		3.7-5.1 MEQ/L
Chloride	106		98-108 MEQ/L
TOTAL CO2	20		24-32 MEQ/L

End of Report

LUCK, Deborah L.   Admission: 05-01-YYYY
Case09   DOB: 11-21-YYYY   LABORATORY DATA
Dr. Ghann   ROOM: 0374

SPECIMEN COLLECTED: 05-01-YYYY   **SPECIMEN RECEIVED:** 05-01-YYYY

Theophylline Level

TEST	RESULT	FLAG	REFERENCE
Theophylline	9.3	**L**	10.0-20.0 UG/ML

End of Report

LUCK, Deborah L.   Admission: 05-01-YYYY
Case09   DOB: 11-21-YYYY   LABORATORY DATA
Dr. Ghann   ROOM: 0374

SPECIMEN COLLECTED: 05-01-YYYY   **SPECIMEN RECEIVED:**   05-01-YYYY

TEST: Urine Culture

2+ gram negative rod

1. cc ≥ 100,000

E. coli

End of Report

LUCK, Deborah L.   Admission: 05-01-YYYY
Case09   DOB: 11-21-YYYY   RADIOMETRY
Dr. Ghann   ROOM: 0374

SPECIMEN COLLECTED: 05-01-YYYY   **SPECIMEN RECEIVED:** 05-01-YYYY

TEST	RESULT
BLOOD GAS VALUES	
pH	7.286
pCO_2	43.8 mmHg
pO_2	90.4 mmHG
TEMPERATURE CORRECTED VALUES	
pH(98.6°)	7.286
pCO_2(98.6°)	43.8 mmHg
pO_2(98.6°)	90.4 mmHg
ACID BASE STATUS	
HCO_3c	20.2 mmol/L
ABEc	-5.9 mmol/L
BLOOD OXIMETRY VALUES	
tHb	14.4 g/dL
O_2Hb	94.6%
COHb	0.2%
MetHb	0.8%

End of Report

Case 10

| SUNNY VALLEY MEDICAL CENTER
100 MAIN ST, SUNNY VALLEY, NY 14802
(607) 555-1234
HOSPITAL #: 000999 | | | | INPATIENT FACE SHEET | | | |

PATIENT NAME AND ADDRESS				GENDER	RACE	MARITAL STATUS	PATIENT NO.
PAULSON, Paula P. 49 Hillbottom Way Sunny Valley, NY 14802				F	W	M	Case10
				DATE OF BIRTH	MAIDEN NAME		OCCUPATION
				01-20-YYYY	King		Waitress

ADMISSION DATE	TIME	DISCHARGE DATE	TIME	LENGTH OF STAY	TELEPHONE NUMBER	
04-26-YYYY	16:00	05-01-YYYY	09:30	05 DAYS	(607) 555-2836	

GUARANTOR NAME AND ADDRESS		NEXT OF KIN NAME AND ADDRESS	
PAULSON, Patrick 49 Hillbottom Way Sunny Valley, NY 14802		PAULSON, Patrick 49 Hillbottom Way Sunny Valley, NY 14802	

GUARANTOR TELEPHONE NO.	RELATIONSHIP TO PATIENT	NEXT OF KIN TELEPHONE NUMBER	RELATIONSHIP TO PATIENT
(607) 555-2836	Husband	(607) 555-2836	Husband

ADMITTING PHYSICIAN	SERVICE	ADMIT TYPE	ROOM NUMBER/BED
Thompson MD, Donald	Medical	2	0367/01

ATTENDING PHYSICIAN	ATTENDING PHYSICIAN UPIN	ADMITTING DIAGNOSIS	
Thompson MD, Donald	100B01	Congestive Heart Failure	

PRIMARY INSURER	POLICY AND GROUP NUMBER	SECONDARY INSURER	POLICY AND GROUP NUMBER
BCBS	432763201 77690	Empire Plan	5739057512

DIAGNOSES AND PROCEDURES	ICD-10-CM/PCS
PRINCIPAL DIAGNOSIS	
Acute Bronchitis	J20.8
SECONDARY DIAGNOSES	
Chronic obstructive pulmonary disease	J44.9
Restrictive Lung Disease	J98.4
Congestive heart failure	I50.9
PRINCIPAL PROCEDURE	
SECONDARY PROCEDURES	
TOTAL CHARGES: $ 7,236.95	

ACTIVITY:	☐ Bedrest	☑ Light	☐ Usual	☐ Unlimited	☐ Other:

DIET:	☐ Regular	☐ Low Cholesterol	☐ Low Salt	☐ ADA	☐ _____ Calorie

FOLLOW-UP: ☑ Call for appointment ☑ Office appointment in 2 wks Other:

SPECIAL INSTRUCTIONS: Go to Pulmonary lab for blood test 1 hr before appt.

Signature of Attending Physician: Donald Thompson, MD

PAULSON, Paula P.   Admission: 04-26-YYYY
Case 10   DOB: 01-20-YYYY
Dr. Thompson   ROOM: 0367

CONSENT TO ADMISSION

I, _Paula P. Paulson_ hereby consent to admission to the Sunny Valley Medical Center (SVMC), and I further consent to such routine hospital care, diagnostic procedures, and medical treatment that the medical and professional staff of SVMC may deem necessary or advisable. I authorize the use of medical information obtained about me as specified above and the disclosure of such information to my referring physician(s). This form has been fully explained to me, and I understand its contents. I further understand that no guarantees have been made to me as to the results of treatments or examinations done at the SVMC.

Paula P. Paulson | _April 26, YYYY_
Signature of Patient | Date

_____ | _____
Signature of Parent/Legal Guardian for Minor | Date

_____
Relationship to Minor

Andrea Witteman | _April 26, YYYY_
WITNESS: Sunny Valley Medical Center Staff Member | Date

CONSENT TO RELEASE INFORMATION FOR REIMBURSEMENT PURPOSES

In order to permit reimbursement, upon request, the Sunny Valley Medical Center (SVMC) may disclose such treatment information pertaining to my hospitalization to any corporation, organization, or agent thereof, which is, or may be liable under contract to the SVMC or to me, or to any of my family members or other person, for payment of all or part of the SVMC's charges for services rendered to me (e.g., the patient's health insurance carrier). I understand that the purpose of any release of information is to facilitate reimbursement for services rendered. In addition, in the event that my health insurance program includes utilization review of services provided during this admission, I authorize SVMC to release information as is necessary to permit the review. This authorization will expire once the reimbursement for services rendered is complete.

Paula P. Paulson | _April 26, YYYY_
Signature of Patient | Date

_____ | _____
Signature of Parent/Legal Guardian for Minor | Date

_____
Relationship to Minor

Andrea Witteman | _April 26, YYYY_
WITNESS: Sunny Valley Medical Center Staff Member | Date

PAULSON, Paula P.	Admission: 04-26-YYYY		ADVANCE DIRECTIVE
Case 10	DOB: 01-20-YYYY		
Dr. Thompson	ROOM: 0367		

Your answers to the following questions will assist your Physician and the Hospital to respect your wishes regarding your medical care. This information will become a part of your medical record.

	YES	NO	PATIENT'S INITIALS
1. Have you been provided with a copy of the information called "Patient Rights Regarding Health Care Decision?"	X		*PP*
2. Have you prepared a "Living Will?" If yes, please provide the Hospital with a copy for your medical record.		X	*PP*
3. Have you prepared a Durable Power of Attorney for Health Care? If yes, please provide the Hospital with a copy for your medical record.		X	*PP*
4. Have you provided this facility with an Advance Directive on a prior admission and is it still in effect? If yes, Admitting Office to contact Medical Records to obtain a copy for the medical record.		X	*PP*
5. Do you desire to execute a Living Will/Durable Power of Attorney? If yes, refer to in order: a. Physician b. Social Service c. Volunteer Service		X	*PP*

HOSPITAL STAFF DIRECTIONS: Check when each step is completed.

1. ___✓___ Verify the above questions where answered and actions taken where required.

2. ___✓___ If the "Patient Rights" information was provided to someone other than the patient, state reason:

_____

_____   _____
Name of Individual Receiving Information   Relationship to Patient

3. ___✓___ If information was provided in a language other than English, specify language and method.

4. ___✓___ Verify patient was advised on how to obtain additional information on Advance Directives.

5. ___✓___ Verify the Patient/Family Member/Legal Representative was asked to provide the Hospital with a copy of the Advance Directive which will be retained in the medical record.

File this form in the medical record, and give a copy to the patient.

_____
Name of Patient (Name of Individual giving information if different from Patient)

Paula P. Paulson   *April 26, YYYY*

_____   _____
Signature of Patient   Date

Andrea Witteman   *April 26, YYYY*

_____   _____
Signature of Hospital Representative   Date

SUNNY VALLEY MEDICAL CENTER ■ 100 MAIN ST, SUNNY VALLEY, NY 14802 ■ (607) 555-1234

PAULSON, Paula P. Case10 Dr. Thompson	Admission: 04-26-YYYY DOB: 01-20-YYYY ROOM: 0367	PROGRESS NOTES

Date	(Please skip one line between dates.)
4-26	Chief Complaint: 53 year old with Shortness of breath.
	Diagnosis: CHF
	Plan of Treatment: See orders.
04-26	Hhn w/ 0.25 ml Proventil / N.S.S. tx given Pt. tol. tx well P 92 + R 16
1820	B.S. clear RC w/ green sputum O₂ off pt. pre tx on pot at 3 l n.C.
	D. Davenport, CPT
04-26	Tx given as above. B.S. rhonchi + wheezes — pt. tol. tx well dry N.P.C.
2200	O₂ on 3 l n.c. pre + post tx.
	D. Davenport, CPT
04-27	Pt. is less short of breath today. Weight ↓ 6 lbs. But still has a lot of rales
	at bases Continue same treatment.
	Donald Thompson, MD
04-27	Hh neb. Rx w/ 25 ml Proventil + NSS P 72 – RR 24 BS rales + exp wheezes LNPC
0715	SAT 90% on 3 l – pt. tol rx well L. Seraphin CPT
04-27	Hh neb. Rx w/ 25 ml Proventil + NSS P 72 – RR 24 BS rales + wheezes NPC
1140	O2 3 l n/c pre + post Respirdyne done.
	L. Seraphin CPT
04-27	Hh neb. Rx w/ 25 ml Proventil + NSS P 72 – RR 20 BS ↓ d NPC O2 on 3 l pt. tol rx
1520	Well w/ fine rales bases.
	L. Seraphin CPT

PAULSON, Paula P.	Admission: 04-26-YYYY	PROGRESS NOTES
Case10	DOB: 01-20-YYYY	
Dr. Thompson	ROOM: 0367	

Date	(Please skip one line between dates.)
04-27	HHN 25mg Proventil & NSS **BS** ↓ ↓'d **L** ↓'d **R** rales ½ up bilat. LNPC; HR 80; R 20 O2 el NC
1940	E. Blossom, CPT
04-28	Hhn rx w/ 05 ml Albuterol/nss **BS** ↓ w/ rales bilaterally in bases. **NPC** at this time.
0710	P 88 RR 20 stable O2 on 3l nc pre & post rx
	L. Seraphin CPT
04-28	Pt. sleeping well with no orthopnea or PND. Rales diminished in bases.
	Donald Thompson, MD
04-28	Hhn rx w/ 05 ml Albuterol/nss **BS** rales in bases bilaterally. **NPC**
1100	O2 on 3l nc
	L. Seraphin CPT
04-28	Rx as above. **BS** rales bilaterally in bases. **NPC** O2 on 3l nc
1500	L. Seraphin CPT
04-28	HHN 25mg Proventil & NSS **BS** ↓'d **L** ↓'d **R** rales ½ up bilat. LNPC; HR 78; R 20 O2 3l nc pre & post
1900	E. Blossom, CPT
04-29	Hhn w/ 0.25 ml Proventil / N.S.S. tx given Pt. tol. tx well P 86 + R 16
0710	B.S. clear w/ few scattered rales P.C. w/ clear sputum O2 3l nc pre + post tx
	D. Davenport, CPT
04-29	Pt. is steadily improving with breather, few rales at bases yet, will ↑ Act.
	Home tomorrow if stable. Donald Thompson, MD

PAULSON, Paula P.		Admission: 04-26-YYYY
Case10		DOB: 01-20-YYYY
Dr. Thompson		ROOM: 0367

DOCTORS ORDERS

Date	Time	Physician's signature required for each order. (Please skip one line between dates.)
04-26	1630	ABG and CXR done as OP copy for chart
		O2 3L via NC
		Saline lock
		Lasix 40 mgm IV now then bid
		CBC, BUN, lytes, seg #11. Check iso today and a.m.
		Urinalysis, HIV
		Sputum C & S
		HHN w/ Proventil 2.5 mgm qid
		NAS diet
		Lanoxin 0.25 gm po now and BT then daily
		Capaten 12.5 mgm now and BT then q 12 hrs 8 am – 8 pm
		R.A.V. To Dr. Thompson/T. Perry
04-26		T4 & TSH D Thompson, MD
04-27	1025	BUN & lytes in A.M. D Thompson, MD
04-28		O2 SAT in AM. on Room air
		Ceftin 250 p.o. D Thompson, MD
04-29	0150	Tylenol 650 mg PO Q4° prn pain or fever
		R...A.V. To Dr.Thompson/F. Hill D Thompson, MD
04-30	1100	Cancel O2 sat for today. Chest X-ray in a.m.. Weigh daily.
		ABG room air. Lanoxin level, BUN, Digoxin level. Lasix 40 po bid.
		D Thompson MD

PAULSON, Paula P.	Admission: 04-26-YYYY	DOCTORS ORDERS
Case10	DOB: 01-20-YYYY	
Dr. Thompson	ROOM: 0367	

Date	Time	Physician's signature required for each order. (Please skip one line between dates.)
04-29	1620	Oximetry on RA; if above 90% leave O2 off.
		R.A.V. To Dr. Thompson/T. Perry D Thompson, MD
04-29	1620	Please do a VQ scan & PFT (before & after) today
		R.A.V. To Dr. Thompson/C. Moore D Thompson, MD
04-30	0955	Do diffusion capacity with PFT
		R.A.V. T.O. Dr. Thompson D Thompson, MD
04-30	1410	Instruct pt. on NAS diet
		R.A.V. T.O. Dr. Thompson/T. Perry D Thompson, MD
05-01		Discharge home.
		D Thompson MD

PAULSON, Paula P.   Admission: 04-26-YYYY
Case10   DOB: 01-20-YYYY   LABORATORY DATA
Dr. Thompson   ROOM: 0367

SPECIMEN COLLECTED: 04-27-YYYY   SPECIMEN RECEIVED: 04-27-YYYY

BLOOD PROFILE

TEST	RESULT	FLAG	REFERENCE
HIV	**Neg**		

End of Report

PAULSON, Paula P.   Admission: 04-26-YYYY
Case10   DOB: 01-20-YYYY   LABORATORY DATA
Dr. Thompson   ROOM: 0367

SPECIMEN COLLECTED: 04-26-YYYY   **SPECIMEN RECEIVED:** 04-26-YYYY

CBC c̄ DIFF

TEST	RESULT	FLAG	REFERENCE
WBC	7.4		4.5-11.0 thous/UL
RBC	5.02	**L**	5.2-5.4 mill/UL
HGB	15.0		11.7-16.1 g/dl
HCT	45.8		35.0-47.0 %
MCV	91.2		85-99 fL.
MCHC	32.8	**L**	33-37
RDW	15.2	**H**	11.4-14.5
Platelets	165		130-400 thous/UL
MPV	8.4		7.4-10.4
LYMPH %	21.1		20.5-51.1
MONO %	7.8		1.7-9.3
GRAN %	71.1		42.2-75.2
LYMPH x 10^3	1.6		1.2-3.4
MONO x 10^3	.6	**H**	0.11-0.59
GRAN x 10^3	5.3		1.4-6.5
EOS x 10^3	< .7		0.0-0.7
BASO x 10^3	< .2		0.0-0.2
ANISO	SLIGHT		

End of Report

PAULSON, Paula P.   Admission: 04-26-YYYY
Case10   DOB: 01-20-YYYY   LABORATORY DATA
Dr. Thompson   ROOM: 0367

SPECIMEN COLLECTED: 04-26-YYYY   SPECIMEN RECEIVED: 04-26-YYYY

URINALYSIS – DIPSTICK ONLY

TEST	RESULT	FLAG	REFERENCE
COLOR	YELLOW		
SP GRAVITY	1.020		≤ 1.030
GLUCOSE	NEG		≤ 125 mg/dl
BILIRUBIN	NEG		≤ 0.8 mg/dl
KETONE	NEG		≤ 10 mg/dl
BLOOD	NEG		0.06 mg/dl hgb
PH	5.5		5-8.0
PROTEIN	NEGATIVE		≤ 30 mg/dl
UROBILINOGEN	NORMAL		≤ -1 mg/dl
NITRITES	NEG		NEG
LEUKOCYTE	NEG		≤ 15 WBC/hpf
EPITH	10-15		/lpf
W.B.C.	1-2		≤ 5/hpf
R.B.C.	1-2		≤ 5/hpf
BACT.	RARE		1+(≤ 20/hpf)

End of Report

PAULSON, Paula P.   Admission: 04-26-YYYY
Case10   DOB: 01-20-YYYY   LABORATORY DATA
Dr. Thompson   ROOM: 0367

SPECIMEN COLLECTED: 04-26-YYYY   SPECIMEN RECEIVED: 04-26-YYYY

UNIT WORKUP PANEL

TEST	RESULT	FLAG	REFERENCE
Sodium	145		136-147 MEQ/L
Potassium	5.1		3.7-5.1 MEQ/L
Chloride	103		98-108 MEQ/L
TOTAL CO2	38	**H**	24-32 MEQ/L
Urea Nitrogen	14		7-18 mg/dl
Creatine Kinase	43		21-215 U/L
Lactic Dehydrogenase	150		100-190 U/L
Alkaline Phosphatase	120		50-136 U/L
GLUCOSE	86		70-110 mg/dl
SGOT	24		15-37 U/L
Creatinine	0.9		0.6-1.0 mg/dl
Calcium	9.3		8.8-10.5 mg/dl
Phosphorus	4.3		2.5-4.9 mg/dl
Total Bilirubin	0.5		0.0-1.1 mg/dl
Total Protein	7.0		6.4-8.2 g/dl
Albumin	3.2	**L**	3.4-5.0 g/dl
Uric Acid	9.3	**H**	2.6-5.6 mg/dl ·
Cholesterol	157		≤ 200mg/dl
CKMD	1.5		0.0-6.0 ng/ml

End of Report

PAULSON, Paula P.   Admission: 04-26-YYYY
Case10   DOB: 01-20-YYYY   LABORATORY DATA
Dr. Thompson   ROOM: 0367

SPECIMEN COLLECTED: 04-27-YYYY   **SPECIMEN RECEIVED:** 04-27-YYYY

CARDIAC PROFILE

TEST	RESULT	FLAG	REFERENCE
Creatine Kinase	35		21-215 U/L
CKMD	0.7		0.0-6.0 ng/ml

End of Report

PAULSON, Paula P. Admission: 04-26-YYYY
Case10 DOB: 01-20-YYYY LABORATORY DATA
Dr. Thompson ROOM: 0367

SPECIMEN COLLECTED: 04-28-YYYY SPECIMEN RECEIVED: 04-28-YYYY

TEST	RESULT	FLAG	REFERENCE
ELECTROLYTES PANEL			
Sodium	141		136-147 MEQ/L
Potassium	4.5		3.7-5.1 MEQ/L
Chloride	94	**L**	98-108 MEQ/L
Total CO_2	35	**H**	24-32 MEQ/L
UREA NITROGEN	16		7-18 MG/DL
THYROID PANEL			
T4	5.2		4.9-10.7 UG/DL
TSH	1.28		0.38-6.15 UIU/ML

End of Report

PAULSON, Paula P.   Admission: 04-26-YYYY
Case10   DOB: 01-20-YYYY   LABORATORY DATA
Dr. Thompson   ROOM: 0367

SPECIMEN COLLECTED: 04-30-YYYY   **SPECIMEN RECEIVED:** 04-30-YYYY

TEST	RESULT	FLAG	REFERENCE
ELECTROLYTES	PANEL		
Sodium	140		136-147 MEQ/L
Potassium	5.2	**H**	3.7-5.1 MEQ/L
Chloride	92	**L**	98-108 MEQ/L
Total CO_2	34	**H**	24-32 MEQ/L
UREA NITROGEN	25	**H**	7-18 MG/DL
DIGOXIN	1.6		0.5-2.0 NG/ML
DIGOXIN NOTE	REF.INT=RX LEVEL AT PEAK TISSUE LEVEL > 8 HRS POST ORAL DOSE. OTHER FACTORS MAY AFFECT LEVEL AND ACTIVITY.		

End of Report

PAULSON, Paula P.   Admission: 04-26-YYYY
Case10   DOB: 01-20-YYYY   RADIOMETRY
Dr. Thompson   ROOM: 0367

SPECIMEN COLLECTED: 04-26-YYYY   **SPECIMEN RECEIVED:**   04-26-YYYY

TEST	RESULT	REFERENCE
BLOOD GAS VALUES		
pH	7.340	
pCO2	62.1	mmHg
pO2	44.5	mmHg
TEMPERATURE CORRECTED VALUES		
pH(98.6°)	7.340	
pCO2(98.6°)	62.1	mmHg
pO2(98.6°)	44.5	mmHg
ACID BASE STATUS		
HCO3c	32.6	mmol/L
ABEc	5.3	mmol/L
BLOOD OXIMETRY VALUES		
tHb	14.5	g/dL
O2Hb	78.3	%
COHb	1.0	%
MetHb	0.7	%

End of Report

PAULSON, Paula P.   Admission: 04-26-YYYY
Case10   DOB: 01-20-YYYY   RADIOMETRY
Dr. Thompson   ROOM: 0367

SPECIMEN COLLECTED: 04-30-YYYY   SPECIMEN RECEIVED: 04-30-YYYY

TEST	RESULT	REFERENCE
BLOOD GAS VALUES		
pH	7.385	
pCO2	67.7	mmHg
pO2	40.3	mmHg
TEMPERATURE CORRECTED VALUES		
pH(98.6°)	7.385	
pCO2(98.6°)	67.7	mmHg
pO2(98.6°)	40.3	mmHg
ACID BASE STATUS		
HCO3c	39.6	mmol/L
ABEc	11.2	mmol/L
BLOOD OXIMETRY VALUES		
tHb	16.3	g/dL
O2Hb	74.8	%
COHb	0.7	%
MetHb	0.7	%

End of Report

PAULSON, Paula P.	Admission: 04-26-YYYY	RADIOLOGY REPORT
Case10	DOB: 01-20-YYYY	
Dr. Thompson	ROOM: 0367	

Initial Diagnosis/History: CHF

Date Requested: 04-26-YYYY

Transport: ☑ Wheelchair   ☐ Stretcher   ☑ O$_2$ ☐ IV

         ☐ IP   ☑ OP   ☐ ER   ☐ PRE OP   ☐ OR/RR   ☐ Portable

Technical Data: PA and left Lat CXR T2 ↑. TBA. Shortness of breath.

CHEST: PA and lateral view show that the heart appears slightly enlarged compared to our study of 06-09-YYYY. The central pulmonary arteries are prominent and there is a tiny right pleural effusion. The left diaphragm is elevated with some overlying fibrosis but this is unchanged from previously.

CONCLUSION: Findings compatible with mild congestive heart failure.

DD: 04-26-YYYY

DT: 04-26-YYYY

Philip Rogers

Philip Rogers, M.D., Radiologist

PAULSON, Paula P.   Admission: 04-26-YYYY   NUCLEAR MEDICINE
Case10   DOB: 01-20-YYYY
Dr. Thompson   ROOM: 0367

Reason for Nuclear Scan: Ventilation Perfusion Scan. Determine the reason for poor oxygenation.

Date Requested: 04-30-YYYY

Transport: ☑ Wheelchair   ☐ Stretcher   ☑ O$_2$ ☐ IV

☑ IP   ☐ OP   ☐ ER   ☐ PRE OP   ☐ OR/RR   ☐ Portable

VENTILATION PERFUSION LUNG SCAN: Following inhalation of technetium aerosol and intravenous injection as the MAA films were made of AP, PA and both lateral projections. The activity throughout both lungs is quite patchy which appears to be due to chronic lung disease or residual change from the patient's heart failure. I do not see any segmental perfusion defects or areas of mismatch to suggest an embolus.

CONCLUSION: No evidence of a pulmonary embolus.

DD: 04-30-YYYY

DT: 04-30-YYYY

Philip Rogers

Philip Rogers, M.D., Radiologist

PAULSON, Paula P.   Admission: 04-26-YYYY   RADIOLOGY REPORT
Case10   DOB: 01-20-YYYY
Dr. Thompson   ROOM: 0367

Initial Diagnosis/History: CHF.

Date Requested: 04-30-YYYY

Transport: ☑ Wheelchair   ☐ Stretcher   ☑ O$_2$ ☐ IV

       ☑ IP   ☐ OP   ☐ ER   ☐ PRE OP   ☐ OR/RR   ☐ Portable

CHEST: PA and lateral views show that the interstitial markings are less prominent on today's film than they were in the previous study of 04-26. Other than this, there hasn't really been a significant change. There is no evidence of pneumonia and I certainly would not say that the patient has any congestive heart failure on the current study. There is abnormal elevation of the left diaphragm which is probably due to paralysis or eventration. The overall cardiac size has not increased.

CONCLUSION: Probable resolution of the mild CHF since 04-26.

DD: 04-30-YYYY

DT: : 04-30-YYYY

Philip Rogers
_____
Philip Rogers, M.D., Radiologist

Appendix II

Electronic Health Record Activities

The following is a series of lab activities that allows the student to explore the use of an electronic health record (EHR). These labs are designed to be used with EHR Go™, the all-new version of Neehr Perfect®. EHR Go is an educational EHR developed give students practical experience with using an electronic record system.

LAB 1   EHR Orientation

This lab needs to be completed as a prerequisite for the remaining labs.

LAB 2   The Power of the EHR

This lab needs to be completed following Lab 1.

LAB 3   Health Information Terminology

This lab introduces terms used in health care, the medical office, and in the EHR Go system. It is suggested that this lab be used with Chapter 1 of *Essentials of Health Information Management,* fourth edition.

LAB 4   EHR Documentation Standards

In this activity the student will be presented with generally accepted professional standards of documentation, the use of abbreviations in medical records, and the application of medical terminology. It is suggested that this lab be used with Chapter 4 of *Essentials of Health Information Management*, fourth edition.

LAB 5   Retrieval of Data

This activity involves data retrieval within the EHR focusing on finding key information from a patient's chart. It is suggested that this lab be used with Chapter 6 of *Essentials of Health Information Management*, fourth edition.

LAB 6   Introduction to Chart Deficiencies

In this lab the student will review the data in the patient chart in detail and, by using critical thinking skills, list what is present, deficient, incorrect, or incomplete in the patient chart. It is suggested that this lab be used with Chapter 8 of *Essentials of Health Information Management*, fourth edition.

LAB 7   Introduction to Privacy and Security

This lab introduces the basic meaning and application of privacy, security, and confidentiality in the EHR as related to patient's health information. It is suggested that this lab be used with Chapter 9 of *Essentials of Health Information Management*, fourth edition.

LAB 8   Release of Information

This lab introduces concepts and activities that relate to the release of information function. It is suggested that this lab be used with Chapter 9 of *Essentials of Health Information Management*, fourth edition.

LAB 1   EHR Orientation

OVERVIEW

This activity is an introductory level exercise intended to provide basic navigation skills, patient data review, and opportunities to perform data entry in an electronic health record system.

LEARNING OBJECTIVES

1. **Demonstrate** the technical skills necessary to access an EHR system.
2. **Locate** and **evaluate** patient data and details.
3. **Navigate** essential information of a patient's electronic medical chart.
4. **Complete** documentation.
5. **Submit** a progress report of completed work.

ASSIGNMENT LINK

https://web21.ehrgo.com/rd/?courseActivityId=63

LAB 2   The Power of the EHR

OVERVIEW

This activity focuses on how the electronic health record system can be used to improve health care outcomes.

LEARNING OBJECTIVES

1. **Identify** the differences between coded and non-coded data entry.
2. **Identify** the differences between structured and unstructured data entry.
3. **Evaluate** the clinical implications of structured versus unstructured data entry in the EHR.
4. **Relate** the use of coded data to meeting the objectives of the Meaningful Use effort for implementation of electronic health records.
5. **Apply** current knowledge of electronic health records and appropriate, accurate documentation.

ASSIGNMENT LINK

https://web21.ehrgo.com/rd/?courseActivityId=1826

LAB 3   Health Information Terminology

OVERVIEW

This activity introduces terms used in health care, the medical office, and in the EHR Go system.

LEARNING OBJECTIVE

1. **Apply** health care legal terminology.

ASSIGNMENT LINK

https://web21.ehrgo.com/rd/?courseActivityId=10305

LAB 4   EHR Documentation Standards

OVERVIEW

In this activity, the student will be presented with generally accepted professional standards of documentation, the use of abbreviations in medical records, and the application of medical terminology.

LEARNING OBJECTIVES

1. **Identify** acceptable health care terminology.
2. **Identify** the roles and responsibilities of various providers and disciplines, to support documentation requirements.
3. **Interpret** patient's medical information as it's seen in the electronic health record.
4. **Apply** current knowledge of electronic health records and appropriate, accurate documentation.

ASSIGNMENT LINK

https://web21.ehrgo.com/rd/?courseActivityId=171

LAB 5   Retrieval of Data

OVERVIEW

In this activity, students will locate key information from a patient's chart to support the application of national safety standards.

LEARNING OBJECTIVES

1. **Collect** and **maintain** health data.
2. **Demonstrate** documentation in the health record that is complete and accurate.
3. **Apply** data entry skills.

ASSIGNMENT LINK

https://web21.ehrgo.com/rd/?courseActivityId=10497

LAB 6   Introduction to Chart Deficiencies

OVERVIEW

The student will review data in the patient chart and identify what is present, deficient, incorrect, or incomplete.

LEARNING OBJECTIVES

1. **Analyze** the documentation in the health record to ensure it supports the diagnosis and reflects the patient's progress, clinical findings, and discharge status.
2. **Verify** the documentation in the health record is timely, complete, and accurate.
3. **Identify** a complete health record according to organizational policies, external regulations, and standards.
4. **Develop** appropriate physician queries to resolve data and coding discrepancies.

ASSIGNMENT LINK

https://web21.ehrgo.com/rd/?courseActivityId=4740

LAB 7   Introduction to Privacy and Security

OVERVIEW

This activity introduces the student to the basic laws and rules involving privacy, security, confidentiality, and cybersecurity with electronic health records.

LEARNING OBJECTIVES

1. **Differentiate** between privacy, security, and confidentiality related to the electronic health record.
2. **Discuss** how electronic health records affect privacy and security.
3. **Recognize** threats to security as it relates to the internet, cybersecurity, and mobile devices.
4. **Identify** when a patient's health information may be shared without written consent.
5. **Discuss** the implications and complications of violating HIPAA.
6. **Apply** current knowledge of electronic health records.

ASSIGNMENT LINK

https://web21.ehrgo.com/rd/?courseActivityId=187

LAB 8   Release of Information

OVERVIEW

The student will review a patient's chart and apply the legal background provided within the activity to analyze and apply established principles of HIPPA and release of information.

LEARNING OBJECTIVES

1. **Apply** health care legal terminology.
2. **Identify** the use of legal documents.
3. **Apply** legal concepts and principles to the practice of HIM.
4. **Apply** policies and procedures surrounding issues of access and disclosure of protected health information.
5. **Apply** confidentiality, privacy, and security measures and policies and procedures for internal and external use and exchange to protect electronic health information.
6. **Analyze** policies and procedures to ensure organizational compliance with regulations and standards.
7. **Adhere** to the legal and regulatory requirements related to health information management.

ASSIGNMENT LINK

https://web21.ehrgo.com/rd/?courseActivityId=10318